NOLO *Your Legal Companion*

"In Nolo you can trust." —THE NEW YORK TIMES

Whether you have a simple question or a complex problem, turn to us at:

NOLO.COM

Your all-in-one legal resource

Need quick information about wills, patents, adoptions, starting a business—or anything else that's affected by the law? **Nolo.com** is packed with free articles, legal updates, resources and a complete catalog of our books and software.

NOLO NOW

Make your legal documents online

Creating a legal document has never been easier or more cost-effective! Featuring Nolo's Online Will, as well as online forms for LLC formation, incorporation, divorce, name change—and many more! Check it out at **http://nolonow.nolo.com**.

NOLO'S LAWYER DIRECTORY

Meet your new attorney

If you want advice from a qualified attorney, turn to Nolo's Lawyer Directory—the only directory that lets you see hundreds of in-depth attorney profiles so you can pick the one that's right for you. Find it at **http://lawyers.nolo.com**.

ALWAYS UP TO DATE

Sign up for NOLO'S LEGAL UPDATER

Old law is bad law. We'll email you when we publish an updated edition of this book—sign up for this free service at nolo.com/legalupdater.

Find the latest updates at NOLO.COM

Recognizing that the law can change even before you use this book, we post legal updates during the life of this edition at **nolo.com/updates**.

Is this edition the newest? ASK US!

To make sure that this is the most recent edition available, just give us a call at **800-728-3555**.

(Please note that we cannot offer legal advice.)

Please note

We believe accurate, plain-English legal information should help you solve many of your own legal problems. But this text is not a substitute for personalized advice from a knowledgeable lawyer. If you want the help of a trained professional—and we'll always point out situations in which we think that's a good idea— consult an attorney licensed to practice in your state.

2nd edition

Wow!
I'm in Business
A Crash Course in
Business Basics

by Richard Stim and Lisa Guerin

SECOND EDITION	JULY 2008
Editor	LISA GUERIN
Cover & Book Design	SUSAN PUTNEY
Proofreading	SUSAN CARLSON GREENE
Index	SONGBIRD INDEXING
Printing	DELTA PRINTING SOLUTIONS, INC.

Stim, Richard

    Wow! I'm in Business : a crash course in business basics / by Richard Stim and Lisa Guerin. -- 2nd ed.

      p. cm.

    Rev. ed. of: Whoops! I'm in business. 1st ed. 2005.

    Includes index.

    ISBN-13: 978-1-4133-0215-8 (pbk.)

    ISBN-10: 1-4133-0215-7 (pbk.)

    1. New business enterprises. 2. Success in business. 3. Home-based businesses. I. Guerin, Lisa, 1964-   II. Stim, Richard. Whoops! I'm in business. III. Title.

HD62.5.S753 2008

658.1'1--dc22

          2008001607

Acknowledgments

Thanks to Mary Randolph for great editing, to Susan Putney for great book and cover design, and to ARS (for CEO-ing).

Table of Contents

Your Business Companion 1

1 Is This the Right Business for You? 3

Do You Love What You Do? 4

Are You Good at It? 7

Is There a Market Demand? 8

If It's Not the Right Business 10

2 Managing Your Money 11

Record Keeping and Bookkeeping 12

Accounting Method 14

What Is Cash Flow and Why Is It Essential? 16

What Accounting Principles Do You Need To Know? 19

What Is Forecasting? 22

What Are Ratios and Why Do They Matter? 25

Separate Business and Personal 27

3 Should You Incorporate or Form an LLC? 29

What Are You? Sole Proprietorship or Partnership? 30

What's the Difference? LLC vs. Corporation 33

How to Convert to an LLC or a Corporation 38

An Interview With LLC and Corporations Expert Anthony Mancuso 41

4 **Insurance** 47
Basic Coverage 49
Consider a Package Deal 54
What You Need If You Have Employees 54
Getting Group Insurance Through an Association 56
Tips for Saving Money on Insurance 58

5 **Raising Money for Your Business** 65
What's the Difference? Equity vs. Debt Financing 66
Borrowing With Credit Cards 68
Signature Loans 69
Bank Loans 70
What Motivates a Bank to Lend Money? 71
SBA Loans 73
State Lending Assistance 74
Borrowing From Family and Friends 75
Social Lending Networks 75
Angel Investing 76
What People With Money Want to Know About Your Business 80
Venture Capital 82
Selling Stock to the Public 82

6 **Do You Need a Business Plan?** 83
How to Create a Business Plan in 24 Hours 84
The Elements of a Business Plan 93

7 **Getting Paid** 97
Invoiced Accounts 98
Checks 100
Credit Cards 100
Collections 102

8   Hiring Help 107

What's the Difference? Employee vs. Independent Contractor 109

Should You Hire an IC or an Employee? 113

Finding the Right Person 116

Legal and Paperwork Requirements: ICs 119

Legal and Paperwork Requirements: Employees 120

9   Working With or Bringing in Family Members 125

What's the Difference? Family Business vs. Nonfamily 126

A Few Pointers for Family Businesses 127

Avoiding Problems If You Ever Divorce 129

Incorporate the Family Business 132

10   Who's Afraid of Contracts? 135

Check 'Em Out 137

Oral Agreements: Legal But … 138

Using Form Agreements 138

Find the Bias 139

Drafting and Formatting Your Agreement 140

Who Signs the Agreement? 142

Common Contract Provisions 142

Boilerplate 145

Dispute Resolution 147

When You Have to Review a Contract 149

Maintaining Paperwork 150

Do You Have a Fear of Negotiating Contracts? 151

11   Protecting Business Ideas 153

Four Steps to Protect Your Ideas 154

What Ideas Have You Got? 156

Ensuring Rights: Registration and Other Measures 158

Chasing People Who Rip Off Your Ideas 162

Licensing or Selling Your Rights 163

What If You Copy Somebody Else's Ideas? 163

Ideas Your Employees or Contractors Come Up With 165

Two Companies That Made Money From Great Ideas 166

12   Using Names and Trademarks 167

What's the Difference? Legal Name vs. Trademark 168

Choosing or Changing a Name 168

Perform a Simple "Knockout" Search 170

Federally Registering a Trademark 170

Staying Out of Trouble 174

13   Licenses, Permits, and Other Paperwork 179

Basic Registration Requirements 180

Register Your Fictitious Business Name 183

If You Sell Goods, Get a Seller's Permit 184

Permits and Licenses for Specialized Fields 186

14   Marketing Basics 187

What's the Difference? Marketing vs. Advertising 190

Ten Marketing Tips 190

Your Marketing Toolbox 196

Do You Need a Marketing Plan? 204

15   Shipping and Returns 207

What's the Difference? Drop Shipping vs. Traditional Shipping 208

Shipping and Delays 209

Returns and Refunds 210

16 Working From Home 213

Best Businesses to Run From Home 215

Self-Assessment: Should I Keep Working at Home? 216

Tips for Maximum Home Office Efficiency 224

17 Leasing Space 229

What's the Difference? Commercial vs. Residential 230

What to Ask When You Look at the Space 232

When You Talk About the Rent 233

Things to Consider When You Negotiate Your Lease 234

Subleasing 236

Interview with Attorney Janet Portman 237

18 Taking Your Business Online 243

How to Get a Site Up Tomorrow 244

Driving Traffic to Your Site 249

19 Should You Quit Your Day Job? 255

Go Part-Time, Flextime, or Telecommute 256

Three Reasons to Keep Your Day Job 259

How Do You Know When to Quit Your Day Job? 259

20 Hobby or Business: How It Affects Taxes 263

What's the Difference? Hobby vs. Business 264

How the IRS Judges Your Business 264

Use Depreciation to Show a Profit 265

Proving a Profit Motive 266

If You're Audited 268

Classic Hobby Loss Abuse 269

21 Paying Your Taxes 271

Audit Flags: Who's More Likely to Get Audited? 272

How Businesses Are Taxed 273

What Taxes Your Business Will Have to Pay 275

Paying Estimated Taxes 276

Preparing Your Taxes 279

Keeping Records for the IRS 282

22 Tax Deductions 285

What's a Tax Deduction Worth? 286

Tax Deduction Basics 290

Deducting Home Office Expenses 292

Qualifying for the Home Office Deduction 292

What You Can Deduct 295

Deducting Long-Term Assets 297

Section 179 298

Depreciation 299

Deducting Vehicle Expenses 300

Deducting Travel Expenses 301

Deducting Meals and Entertainment 303

An Interview with Attorney Stephen Fishman 304

Index 309

Your Business Companion

If you never took a business course, never mastered spreadsheets, and never read *Who Moved My Cheese?*, then this book is for you. If your hobby has grown into a small-scale enterprise, or your idea—installing ergonomic office equipment or selling fabrics made in Singapore—has become more popular than you expected, this book is also for you. In other words, this book is for people who "fell" into business.

Are there really that many people who stumble into business this way? Well, there's a woman who started making wedding favors for friends and soon got calls from strangers who'd seen her products and wanted to buy them. And there's someone who began helping an Alzheimer's patient and quickly found her services in demand and well paid. And there's a man, unable to find a quality yo-yo, who began creating them himself and soon received orders from around the world.

And then there's me.

I love audiobooks and have experience in sound recording—and I fell into business myself when I somehow talked my way into producing an audiobook for a large publisher. Caught up in the entrepreneurial euphoria of landing a big contract, I forgot for a moment that I already had a full-time job as an editor and a small legal practice on the side.

A few days after signing the contract, the magnitude of my task hit me—I had to produce four audio disks consisting of about 60 separate segments read by six different narrators along with about 70 musical cues. My mood went from an incredibly unfounded confidence—the type often exhibited by reality show contestants right before they are kicked off the island—to teeth-clenching wide-awake-at-3-a.m. despair.

Surely, other small business owners had found themselves in the same position as me. There must be plenty of advice on how to manage small business anxiety. I looked through the resources I'd gathered and skimmed a few of the business books I had purchased. No help. Nothing spoke directly to the overwhelming angst of people who fell into business. We "accidental businesspeople" need more than the stories and fables found in popular business books like the *E-Myth Revisited*. What we need—besides a daily neck massage and a renewable prescription for Zoloft—is some reassurance that this confusing state of affairs is both normal and temporary.

And that became my mission for this book. I wanted to provide the type of practical guidance that I was not finding in other start-up guides—the reassurance and guidance that I hoped would reduce my own small-business anxiety.

Following some of my own advice, one of the first things I did was get some help writing this book. Working with coauthor Lisa Guerin helped me benefit from her experience counseling small business owners. She made the book more concise, organized, and practical.

Looking back, I think we succeeded in our mission. That's not to say that you can read this book and stop worrying about your business. But the material in this book should, at a minimum, help you separate those things worth worrying about from those that aren't. You may be surprised at how much you don't need to freak out about.

—Rich Stim

Is This the Right Business for You?

Do You Love What You Do? 4

Are You Good at It? 7

Is There a Market Demand? 8

    Primary Research 8

    Secondary Research 9

If It's Not the Right Business 10

We wrote this book for the same reason you bought it: We want your business to succeed.

But what is success? How do you measure it? We believe that success in business consists of three things: profits, personal satisfaction, and longevity. Profits, obviously, are essential. But studies have shown that a profit motive, by itself, is not enough to sustain a business. If you want to be one of the 20% of small businesses that make it to their fifth birthday, you're going to need more.

One thing is certain: You're unlikely to achieve profits, personal satisfaction, and longevity if you're in the wrong business.

How do you know whether you've made the right choice? You'll have to honestly answer questions such as: Do you like what you do? Are you good at it? Is there a demand for what you're selling?

If you're unsure, this chapter can help you decide.

One other note: Some business owners mistakenly believe that perseverance will overcome all obstacles and eventually lead to success. Perseverance is essential for success, but there's a difference between perseverance and obstinacy. As Henry Ward Beecher said, "One comes from a strong will; and the other from a strong won't." To proceed when you're in the wrong business puts you and your family at financial risk.

Do You Love What You Do?

Odds are good that you love (or at least like) what you do in your business. For example, if you buy and sell troll dolls, play music, craft furniture, or give massages, you probably have more passion for it than you do for your day job (if you have one), and you probably get more satisfaction and happiness from it as well. That's likely why you started it in the first place.

It may seem touchy-feely, but your love for your business is probably a crucial factor in determining whether you will succeed. Small business can be all-consuming, and it often alternates between crisis and boredom. Only your love for your business and its core products or services will carry you through.

A Profit Motive Is Not Enough

One thing is clear: If your primary reason for choosing your business is big profits, you're probably headed for a problem.

Back in the 1980s, business guru Michael Phillips analyzed a group of 650 San Francisco Bay Area businesses informally linked as the Briarpatch Network. These businesses included the full gamut of product and service providers and were linked by a loose set of principles—for example, to operate openly, honestly, and in a manner that was dedicated to serving customers and the community.

What was remarkable about Briarpatch businesses was that their failure rate within the first three years of start-up was less than 10%. When surveyed, the owners gave several reasons why they pursued their businesses. They said they loved their type of business, they had the appropriate skills, they liked serving the community, they wanted to be their own boss, and they wanted to earn enough to support their lifestyle. Big profit was never among the primary reasons for starting a business. Most of the Briarpatch business owners were content to earn a reasonable salary and to own the business.

When Phillips surveyed non-Briarpatch business owners, profit was always one of the top three reasons for starting a business. The failure rate for these other small businesses during their first three years: 80%.

Phillips concluded that having profit as your primary motivator is likely to lead to problems, especially because small businesses seldom lead to great wealth, and business owners motivated primarily by greed quickly become disenchanted. A profit motive also often leads to poor decision making. For example, a business owner seeking strong profits may cut features of the business attractive to consumers solely on the basis of the bottom line.

We're not saying that a profit motive is irrelevant. Obviously, business couldn't exist if revenues did not exceed expenses. But when making a lot of money is the main goal of your business, you will have a hard time sustaining it.

If you have fallen out of love with your business, there are ways to rekindle the feeling. *How to Run a Thriving Business*, by Ralph Warner (Nolo) offers several suggestions for maintaining and increasing your interest. Here are some of them:

Delegate administrative activities. If some activities—for example, bookkeeping, documentation, or contracts—obstruct your enjoyment of business, say "Hell, no" and delegate them to others. (Control freaks, this means you.) Sometimes family members can be helpful in picking up the slack, but beware; there are issues when bringing in a spouse, sibling, child, or parent. (See Chapter 9 for more on family businesses.)

Develop new business approaches. Is there a way to modify your products or services so that you find yourself re-interested in the business? Can you prune out products or services that don't excite you and keep only those that do? Implementing changes—even as mundane as changing the appearance of your company website—can often stimulate interest for you and for your customers.

Invest your business with a sense of purpose. It's a lot easier to stave off boredom if your business has a sense of purpose. You don't have to save the whales, but adding an altruistic element to your enterprise can keep you interested—for example, a barbershop that decides to educate men about legitimate remedies to reverse baldness, or a coffee shop that offers fair trade blends, or a business—like Newman's Own food products—that contributes a portion of profits to charities.

Age Matters

When trying to determine whether you're in the right business, age makes a difference. "The owner of every startup wants to have some enjoyment," says Chicago-based business coach Jeff Williams, "but this desire is particularly acute for people over 50. They don't want to give up everything to drive the business. They often don't want to move or to have to travel a lot." Williams believes that for the over-50 entrepreneur, the business must integrate with daily life and with family, and it must provide a sense of satisfaction or meaning, more so than for a younger business owner.

Are You Good at It?

There's a British reality television show called "Ramsay's Kitchen Nightmares," in which chef Gordon Ramsay visits unsuccessful restaurants and attempts to turn them around. The near-universal problem that Ramsay encounters is that a restaurant owner or chef is passionate about food but lacks the skills, experience, and talent to run a restaurant kitchen.

It's not enough to love what you do; you also need to be good at it. According to happiness researcher (yes, there are experts on happiness) Dr. Ed Diener of the University of Illinois, work is most satisfying when our ability and our ambition are closely matched. Contradictions are what make people miserable. Someone who desperately wants to become a concert pianist or pro volleyball player but lacks the talent to compete at this rarified level is going to be heartbroken.

There's a big problem, though, when it comes to assessing our skills. It's difficult to provide an honesty check. Nobody wants to admit that they lack the talent or skills to produce goods or services competitively.

So how do you honestly assess whether you're good at what you do? One way is to consider whether—if you were hiring someone to run your business—you would hire yourself. You might ask yourself some of these questions.

What's your experience and track record? If you were in an interview for this position, what in your resume could convince someone to give you the job? What's your training? Do you have experience in this industry or business? Have you successfully run a similar business before? How is your current business performing? How is your performance compared to local competitors? What about national competitors? If, for example, you maintain an eBay store, does it perform as well or better than competitors? If you haven't competed within this industry, do you have other life or business experiences that qualify you to run this business?

Are you good with people? Commerce requires an ability to deal with people, whether they're vendors, employees, or customers. If you're a musician who's not good at dealing with fans or record companies, or if you're a chef who can't inspire and direct suppliers or your kitchen crew, then you're lacking an essential skill needed in your business.

Have you gotten positive feedback? How have customers or clients responded to your business? Do customers love your chocolate cakes, automotive detailing, or dog shampoos? Does your Amazon store get consistently good ratings? Do customers comment on your affinity for the business?

Is There a Market Demand?

Business guru Peter Drucker says that businesses exist to create customers. If you can't create customers, your business will end. If you're already generating revenue with a solid, consistent customer base, you have market demand. But if you're unsure whether market demand exists (or whether current demand will continue), you'll need to do some market research.

What's market research? It's a collection of facts about your industry, your customers, your area, and your business. It's referred to as primary research when it's gathered for a particular purpose—for example, you survey local residents. Secondary research is information that's already been gathered about a business or industry.

Primary Research

It's not difficult to do primary research, and it can be very informative. You need to find people—customers, focus groups, or a random sample of folks at a shopping center—and ask them questions that will help you determine whether there is a market for your services or products. These surveys can also be conducted over the Internet, by phone, or by mail. Choosing the right questions requires some skill. For example, should you use open-ended questions that the person completes or closed-ended questions that provide choices?

If you're attempting to do primary marketing research, we suggest reading *The Market Research Toolbox*, by Edward F. McQuarrie (Sage Publications), or Jim Nelens' *Research to Riches: The Secret Rules of Successful Marketing* (Longstreet Press). McQuarrie's book discusses the basics of setting up focus groups, surveys, and customer questionnaires. Nelens's book focuses on how to choose a market research firm and how to judge the accuracy of research.

If you are selling a new product, you can assess potential demand by conducting a marketability study. For $500 or less, you can submit your product for a marketing evaluation at many university marketing departments—for example, at the University of Wisconsin's Innovation Service Center (http://academics.uww.edu/business/innovate).

Secondary Research

Secondary research requires digging through Internet data or searching at your local library. You're looking for demographics in your area, trends within your industry, and economic forecasts. When you're done, you should be able to answer questions such as "Should I open a Balinese restaurant in San Diego?" or "Is there a national market for my line of vegan desserts?"

Common sources for secondary research are:

- **Trade associations.** Check the *Encyclopedia of Associations*, available at many libraries, or use an Internet search engine to find the group representing businesses within your industry.

- **Trade publications.** Check for magazines or newsletters published for your industry. For help, look in *Newsletters in Print* or *The Gale Directory of Publications and Broadcast Media*, or use an Internet search engine.

- **Government websites.** Tons of free information is available, for example, at the websites of the U.S. Department of Commerce (www.commerce.gov) or the U.S. Census Bureau (www.census.gov).

- **Business directories.** Check for information about your competition online in business directories such as Big Yellow (www.bigyellow.com) or look in print form, for example, at your local chamber of commerce.

INTERNET LINK

You can find links for all the resources in this book at www.nolo .com/wowbusiness.

If you're prepared to spend hundreds or thousands of dollars on research, companies on the Internet such as Informars.com (www.informars.com) can provide customized market research.

If It's Not the Right Business

If you've decided you're not in the right business, you've got three options: continue and hope for the best, close it, or sell it. If you choose to continue, we recommend that you consider ways to increase your interest and skills in the business. You may want to consult a business coach or mentor.

If you can get out of the business before it goes under (which it surely will if you're not good at it), you can live to start a new business. Many business owners pull the plug on various enterprises until they find the right match. At the same time, just because you're not particularly good at your business now doesn't mean that you won't someday achieve competency. There's a saying that business owners are paid in two coins: money and experience. What you'll need to decide at this point is whether you can afford to educate yourself while running your business.

Can Money Buy Happiness?

Still obsessed with that profit motive? Here's something to consider: Data indicates that after basic needs are met, money seems to have little effect on a person's perception of happiness. For example, lottery winners receive a huge happiness spike after winning but soon return to previous happiness levels, according to studies. A survey of America's corporate CEOs revealed they were a little happier than average folks, but hardly enough to justify the effort they put into getting and spending. And despite the fact that America's gross domestic product and income have risen 450% in the past 50 years, life satisfaction has stayed essentially stable. In short, don't expect a happiness infusion when the profits start rolling in.

Managing Your Money

Record Keeping and Bookkeeping 12

Accounting Method 14

What Is Cash Flow and Why Is It Essential? 16

    Common Causes of Cash Flow Problems 16

    Business That Are Prone to Cash Flow Problems 17

    The Three Keys to Managing Cash Flow 18

What Accounting Principles Do You Need To Know? 19

    Assets and Liabilities 19

    Looking at a Balance Sheet 20

    Equity and Debt 20

    Accounts Receivable and Accounts Payable 21

    Income Statements 21

    Cash Flow Statements 22

What Is Forecasting? 22

    The Break-Even Analysis 23

    The Profit and Loss Forecast 24

    Cash Flow Projection 24

What Are Ratios and Why Do They Matter? 25

    Current Ratio 25

    Quick Ratio (Also Known as "Acid-Test Ratio") 26

    Debt-to-Worth Ratio (Also Known as "Debt-to-Equity" Ratio) 26

    Current Debt to Net Worth 26

    Profit Margin 27

Separate Business and Personal 27

You don't need a degree in economics to run a small business. Richard Branson, Walt Disney, Coco Chanel, Henry Ford, and Milton Hershey created business empires without earning a high school diploma. But even without a formal education, these entrepreneurs still learned some basic financial principles and took care of bookkeeping and accounting chores. You can do the same without much hassle or number-crunching skills.

Record Keeping and Bookkeeping

Bookkeeping—at least in terms of the IRS requirements—doesn't require that you hire an accountant or use bookkeeping software. As long as you can accurately state your income and expenses on your tax forms (and you've got the records necessary to prove that you're correct), you've satisfied the IRS.

But if you have employees, carry an inventory, have a large number of customers, or incur lots of expenses, you will need to institute standardized bookkeeping procedures, either on paper, or on a computer. Keeping good records will make your business more profitable by helping you:

- identify every tax deduction you're entitled to take
- recognize problems early (such as disappearing inventory, increased costs for products or equipment, or customers who aren't paying on time), before they have a chance to bring down your business
- maintain your cash flow at acceptable levels
- figure out whether it's time to raise (or lower) your prices
- put together the financial reports you need to get loans and investment, and
- prepare your tax returns quickly and accurately.

If you're an accounting illiterate and you've been dreading having to finally deal with business bookkeeping, don't worry. Even if you hid in the back of the algebra class, there are simple accounting solutions available to you. Here's how to proceed.

I don't want to deal with numbers (except to periodically review financial information). Solution: Hire someone. If you're weak with numbers, too busy, or just don't want to think about it, hire a bookkeeper or an accountant to handle your numbers. Go over your financials on a regular basis (monthly or quarterly) with your bookkeeper. By the way, accounting costs are tax deductible.

I want to handle some of it and use an accountant for other tasks. Solution: Buy *QuickBooks*, the software accounting program from Intuit. *QuickBooks* is popular—so popular that it controls 87% of the accounting software market—and most bookkeepers and accountants are familiar with it. We'd recommend not installing the software yourself but instead have someone else install it—for example your bookkeeper, accountant or a qualified *QuickBooks* expert—so that you end up with the proper reports and charts customized for your accounts.

I want to handle all of it. If you want to do it all, we'd recommend *QuickBooks* or a customized software accounting solution created for your business. Since you will also be preparing your own taxes, we recommend *TurboTax* which works seamlessly with *QuickBooks*. If you're new to business finances, we'd also recommend reviewing a few of the resources listed below.

INTERNET LINK

You can find links for all the resources in this book at www.nolo .com/wowbusiness.

Accounting and Bookkeeping

What's the difference between accounting and bookkeeping? Accounting is the process of managing and forecasting a business's finances. An accountant advises a business and prepares financial reports. Bookkeeping is part of the accounting program; it refers only to the recording and maintenance of your financial records. A bookkeeper inputs information and keeps your accounts up to date.

Accounting and Bookkeeping Resources

Because we advise small business owners to use *QuickBooks* accounting software, we don't cover how to keep accounting ledgers on paper. However, there are lots of good books and websites that explain how to keep your books on paper or on a computer spreadsheet. Some of our favorites are:

- *Accounting and Finance for Small Business Made Easy*, by Robert Low (Entrepreneur Press). Low demystifies accounting mumbo jumbo.
- *Accounting for Dummies*, by John A. Tracy (Wiley). Tracy creates easy-to-grasp explanations of business financing principles.
- IRS Publication 583, *Starting a Business and Keeping Records*, free at www.irs.gov. This is a handy guide to basic bookkeeping.
- *Minding Her Own Business: The Self-Employed Woman's Guide to Taxes and Recordkeeping*, by Jan Zobel (Sphinx). This book provides detailed examples (and it's not just for women).
- *QuickBooks for Dummies*, by Stephen L. Nelson (Wiley). This is an excellent companion for first-time *QuickBooks* users.
- The "Business Owner's Toolkit" (www.toolkit.cch.com), a site that offers plenty of helpful free information. Click "Managing Your Business Finances" for a crash course in basic accounting principles.
- *The Accounting Game: Basic Accounting Fresh From the Lemonade Stand*, by Darrell Mullis and Judith Orloff (Sourcebooks). This is a fun, simplified explanation of accounting for beginners.
- *The Complete Idiot's Guide to Accounting*, by Lita Epstein and Shelly Moore (Alpha). This book offers good detail on keeping basic and complex financial records.

Accounting Method

The IRS doesn't require all businesses to use a prescribed accounting method, but it does require businesses to use a system that accurately reflects their income and expenses.

The two common ways to account for your income and expenses are the cash method and the accrual method (and some businesses use a hybrid). What do most small business owners prefer? According to a 2006 survey, 41% use the cash method, 17% used accrual, 13% used a hybrid, and a surprising 28% did not know what system they used (attributed to the fact that these owners did not have a "hands-on approach" to record keeping).

The cash method. Using the cash method, you record income when you actually receive it and expenses when you actually pay them. For example, if you complete a project in December 2008 but don't get paid until March 2009, you record the income in March 2009. Similarly, if you buy a digital camera for your business on credit, you record the expense not when you charge the camera and take it home, but when you pay the bill. (The IRS won't let you manipulate your income by, for example, not cashing a client's check until the next year; you must report income when it becomes available to you, not when you actually decide to deal with it.)

The accrual method. Under the accrual method, you record income as you earn it and expenses as you incur them. For example, if you complete a project in December 2008, that's when you record the income you expect to receive from the project, no matter when the client actually gets around to paying you. (If the client never puts the check in the mail, you can eventually deduct the money as a bad debt.) And if you charge some furniture, you record the expense on the day of purchase, not when you pay the bill.

Which method is better? The cash method is much easier to use; most of us deal with our personal finances this way, so it's a system we're familiar with. It also gives you a clear picture of your actual cash on hand at any point in time. The accrual method can't tell you how much cash you've got, but it provides a more accurate picture of your business's overall financial health, particularly if your clients or customers are pretty good about paying their bills. It will show money that you've obligated yourself to pay, so you'll know that you can't count on using that money for other purposes. It will also show money you can look forward to receiving (again, if your customers pay you as promised).

As long as you make less than $1 million a year, you may choose which-ever method seems right for your business. (If you've made more than $1 million in any of the last three tax years and your business carries an inventory, you might have to use the accrual method.) For more information, check out IRS Publications 334, *Tax Guide for Small Business*, and 538, *Accounting Periods and Methods*, both available at www.irs.gov.

What Is Cash Flow and Why Is It Essential?

You've probably heard people complain about cash flow and maybe wondered what exactly that means. Simply put, the money that comes in and goes out of your business is your cash flow. Business cash flow is really no different from personal cash flow. For example, when you're in a furniture store trying to decide whether to spend a portion of your paycheck on a new sofa, that's a cash flow decision. If you use the money on the sofa, you may not have enough to pay for your new hubcaps or that dinner out in a fancy restaurant.

Proper cash flow management is the key to profitability and to survivability—allowing you, for example, to pay employees and your rent even when a major customer goes belly up. Think of cash flow as your business's lifeblood. If it is interrupted—and this is true even for highly profitable ventures—it can lead to a business's cardiac arrest.

Common Causes of Cash Flow Problems

The common reasons that businesses have cash flow problems are:

Accounts receivables are late. Accounts receivable is money owed to your business. When people are not paying you in a timely manner, you'll always be short of cash. Are you reluctant to approach your customers? We discuss how to deal with collections in Chapter 7.

Inventory is turning slowly. Inventory is cash transformed into products. So when you're holding lots of unsold inventory, you're really preventing access to cash. In addition, inventory costs create a financial burden. That's why it's often best to sell inventory at break-even prices (or even incur a loss) rather than have it take up space without generating revenue.

Expenses are not controlled. It may be axiomatic, but your failure to control costs can be a major factor for cash flow problems. Always look for ways to lower expenses. Throughout this book we provide tips on lowering fixed expenses (such as insurance and rent) and variable expenses (such as marketing, staff expenses, and professional fees). You'll be surprised: Even the leanest business can shed a few pounds.

The business was started with insufficient funds. Undercapitalization is a leading cause of negative cash flow. Should you borrow more than you believe is necessary? We discuss funding in Chapter 5.

Bills are paid before they're due. When possible, we recommend paying your bills early, but usually there are more benefits to waiting—for example, 30 days—and then paying the bill. However, in terms of holding on to your cash, it's even better to get longer terms for paying back your suppliers.

Business That Are Prone to Cash Flow Problems

Certain businesses, by their nature, may have more cash flow challenges. Some examples include:

A business that relies on one customer for all its income. Whether by choice or because of circumstance, some businesses must place all their eggs in one customer's basket. If you find yourself growing quickly with one customer, you may be tempted to terminate smaller accounts. Keep in mind that loyal smaller accounts give a business a constant, reliable source of income even if it is dwarfed by large orders from one customer.

A seasonal business. When it comes to seasonal income, it's not so much a matter of getting paid on time—you already know with some certainty when you'll be paid—it's how to deal with the lack of income throughout the rest of the year. Obviously, you can't just close your store for nine months of the year—that would create some seriously nonproductive real estate. The solution is to ramp up staff and inventory in a timely manner and avoid carrying large expenses during the rest of the year.

A business that relies on an insurer for payments. What could be worse than waiting 120 days for payment from an insurer? How about if your invoice is also reduced by one-third? In order to stay open, a business that relies on insurance income needs to carefully manage billings and, if possible, to add noninsured billings into the income mix. Many such businesses use third-party claims processors—companies that will bill and collect insurance payments on your behalf. That frees you from some administrative tasks and sometimes makes the collection process less cumbersome. But a third-party agent doesn't relieve you from monitoring claims for timeliness and accuracy.

A business that relies on sales of one product. Would you like to diversify your income sources? Diversification comes in many colors. Are any of them right for your business? When handled properly, product diversification can reduce financial risk and improve cash flow—for example, Toys 'R' Us began selling diapers in order to attract customers during slow selling seasons. But an unsuccessful diversification can drain cash and divert a business from its mission. The key with product diversification is making sure the new products are central and complementary to the existing business.

The Three Keys to Managing Cash Flow

The three tasks (or strategies) for managing cash flow are:

Be prepared. You can never completely avoid cash flow problems—unpredictable and catastrophic events can overtake any small business owner. But smart financial strategies—for example, not relying on a single customer, maintaining a revolving line of credit, and having staffing flexibility—can prepare you for economic downturns, faltering suppliers, and sudden growth spurts.

Know your funding options. Are you borrowing money because of a temporary negative cash flow or because of a fundamental problem with your business? If you don't know the difference, you could find yourself shoveling your way out of a mountain of debt. We provide more information in Chapter 5.

Always know your numbers. A reliable bookkeeping system can prevent (and predict) many financial problems.

What Accounting Principles Do You Need To Know?

There's no escaping it. You will have to grasp a few basic accounting terms in order to manage your business efficiently (and, if necessary, to borrow money). Here are the basics.

Assets and Liabilities

Assets and liabilities are the yin and yang of your business. Assets are your "pluses," the things your business owns and is owed—for example, cash, real estate, inventory, accounts due, other property (like patents or trademarks), and prepaid expenses (costs that are paid in advance, such as taxes and insurance). Long-term assets, such as buildings, equipment, or property, that are not expected to be converted to cash, are known as fixed assets.

Liabilities are your "minuses," the business obligations or things that are owed—for example, tax payments, repayments to investors, or money owed to banks. Also included in the liabilities column—though it's not actually a liability—is owners' equity (the amount invested by the owners of the business).

How do assets and liabilities apply to your business? Assets and liabilities figure into several financial reports, but are most prominent on the balance sheet—a snapshot of your business at a given time. A balance sheet is commonly required when you seek funding or loans. It also gives you a snapshot of your business at any particular moment—think of it as taking your business's blood pressure. If you use a software accounting program, generating a balance sheet is just a matter of a few mouse clicks. (For example, in *QuickBooks*, you click "Reports, Accountant & Taxes," and then "Trial Balance.") A balance sheet adds up the assets and liabilities in two separate columns. As the name implies, the columns must balance—that is, they should equal each other. An example of a balance sheet is provided, below.

Looking at a Balance Sheet

A balance sheet is a snapshot in the life of your business—just one financial moment preserved. It's one of several financial report cards that a business prepares. Sometimes it's referred to as a "Statement of Financial Condition." Below is a simple example of a balance sheet prepared for a surfboard rental service:

SURFBOARD RENTAL SHOP BALANCE SHEET			
ASSETS		**LIABILITIES**	
$2,000	Money owed by customer (accounts receivable)	$10,000	Accounts payable (loan from parents)
$8,000	Inventory (40 surfboards)	$2,000	Equity (investment by owner)
$1,000	Fixed assets (surfboard racks and store fixtures)	$1,000	Equity (investment by uncle)
$500	Prepaid expense (insurance payment)		
$500	Cash		
$12,000	TOTAL ASSETS	$12,000	TOTAL LIABILITIES

Equity and Debt

Outside of sales revenue, the two common ways that cash comes into a business are equity and debt—investments and loans. Equity is the money or property invested and retained in the business by the owners (sometimes referred to as "owner's equity"). If you don't properly track and account for all equity, you will have tax problems and angry investors.

Debt—the loans, lines of credit, and any other borrowing you've done—refers to money that must be repaid, usually with interest, over a fixed period of time. If you don't properly manage a debt, the lender will foreclose on the loan, sometimes leading to a business bankruptcy.

Accounts Receivable and Accounts Payable

Accounts receivable are the amounts you are owed from sales of your products or services. Some retail businesses, since they receive payment immediately, have little or no accounts receivable. Accounts payable are amounts you owe to vendors and suppliers, as well as any other short-term bills—for example, payments for inventory, supplies, or other goods or services. Loans and similar interest-bearing debts are not included in accounts payable.

Monitoring receivables and payables is a key element in cash flow management. As a general rule, your cash flow is always weakened the longer you must wait for your accounts receivable to get paid. Conversely, you'll always have less cash on hand if you pay bills (accounts payable) before they are due.

Income Statements

In order to avoid the mistake of looking at a payment and guessing at your profit, you should use an income statement. An income statement provides a line by line breakdown of revenue and the various sums that are subtracted from the revenue to determine profit. (*QuickBooks* will generate similar statements of profitability. For example, to see how much profit you've earned from a particular item in your inventory, go to the "Reports" menu, click "Jobs, Time & Mileage," and then click "Item Profitability.")

The top line in an income statement is the total sales revenue (or "gross income"). That's followed by the sales costs—the direct costs involved in producing the items that are sold (also known as cost of goods sold, CGS, or COGS). For example, if you are a book publisher, these costs might be the costs of paper and printing, or the costs to pay a writer to create the book. When you deduct the cost of goods from total sales revenue, you get the "gross profit."

The next lines are a series of operating expenses—for example, expenses associated with running your company, known as the general and administration costs (or G&A), and expenses associated with sales, marketing, and product development. When you subtract these operating expenses from your gross profit, you get your "operating income."

A company next subtracts interest on debt and arrives at an amount referred to as its "income before taxes." After taxes are subtracted, the income statement shows "net income from continuing operations," and finally, after subtracting all its expenses listed above and any one-time losses (for example, a legal judgment) from its total sales revenue, the final number is considered the "net income."

Cash Flow Statements

Some call it a cash flow statement, some call it a statement of cash flows, and some just call it a cash statement, but no matter what it's called, the purpose is the same: to report your cash on hand and enable you to forecast your cash in the future. But is a cash flow statement really as helpful as it sounds?

A cash flow statement summarizes all the cash coming in and going out of a business during a specific period by analyzing cash in three classes: operations (sales and operating expenses), financing activities (loans and equity), and investing activities (ownership of real estate, securities and nonoperating assets).

The challenge with cash flow statements is they sometimes become too cumbersome to decipher. That's why the cash flow statement, along with other monthly statements should be the subject of a periodic review by you and your bookkeeper or accountant. That way, you can efficiently get a pulse on the movement of cash, accounts receivable, and checking account balances.

What Is Forecasting?

Financial forecasting helps you predict the cost of your products or services, the amount of sales revenue, and profit you can anticipate. If your business is not already off the ground, financial forecasting will predict how much you'll have to invest or borrow.

Obviously, financial forecasting depends on your type of business—that is, whether you are a retail business, service business, manufacturing or wholesale business, or a project development business (such as real estate rehabilitation, in which you work on one house at a time).

Forecasting is always easier if you've been in business for a little while, because you have months (or years) of actual revenue and expenses upon which to base your forecasts. If you haven't got any history, this section can help you get started.

First, don't be intimidated. Financial forecasting is not so bad. It's a matter of making educated guesses as to how much money you will take in and how much you will spend—and then using these estimates to calculate how and when your business will be profitable. The numbers you use are not written in stone. You can alter them to create "what if" scenarios. We've listed some of the financial projections you may want to make, below.

The Break-Even Analysis

This analysis tells you how much revenue you'll need each week or month to break even. To calculate it, you need to make two estimates:

- **Fixed costs.** Also known as overhead, these costs usually include rent, insurance, and other regular, set expenses. (Loan repayments and the costs you pay for any goods you will resell are not fixed costs.)

- **Gross profit percentage.** Start with your gross profit—what's left after you deduct the direct costs for each sale. For example, if you paid $150 for a bicycle and sold it for $250, your gross profit is $100. In order to determine your gross profit percentage, you divide your profit by the selling price—in this case, 40% ($100 ÷ 250).

To calculate your break-even amount, divide your monthly overhead expenses by your profit percentage (as a decimal). For example, if your bicycle shop has fixed monthly costs of $4,000 and your profit percentage is 40%, then you need sales revenue of $10,000 a month to break even ($4,000 ÷ 0.40). As a practical matter, if you were selling bicycles at $250 a bicycle, you would need to sell 40 bikes a month to break even. If this amount is below your anticipated sales revenue, then you're facing a loss—and you'll need to lower expenses or increase sales to break even.

The Profit and Loss Forecast

In your profit and loss forecast, you refine the sales and expense estimates that you used for your break-even analysis, into a formal, month-by-month projection of your business's profit for one or two years of operation. It's basically a spreadsheet that details your expected expenses and revenue on a month-by-month basis. For example, you plug in estimates of monthly revenue and of phone service, depreciation, shipping, and other expenses. An example of a profit and loss forecast is provided in Chapter 6.

QuickBooks can prepare a profit and loss report. To create one, go to the "Reports" menu, click "Company & Financial," and then click "Profit & Loss Standard." To compare your profits and losses to what you budgeted in *QuickBooks*, go to the "Reports" menu, choose "Budgets & Forecasts," and then click "Profit & Loss Budget Performance."

Cash Flow Projection

Earlier, we described a cash flow statement—a look at the movement of cash during a specific period. The cash flow projection attempts to predict your cash flow needs. For example, the cash flow projection for the first few months of a business may be negative. In order to survive, you may need to borrow money during that period. Cash flow projections are useful for every business, but they're particularly helpful if you have not yet opened. An example of a cash flow forecast is provided in Chapter 6.

To make your cash flow projection, you'll have to prepare a spending plan, setting out items your business needs to buy and expenses you will need to pay. You then feed these numbers, along with information from your profit and loss forecast, into a spreadsheet. You'll need to determine and add in details such as whether you will be making credit sales and how much time is granted—for example, you grant 90 days to pay a bill (net 90) on your invoices. That helps determine when you can expect payments. *QuickBooks* can project your cash flows. To create a projection, click "Company," then "Planning & Budgeting," then "Cash Flow Projector," and follow the wizard.

What Are Ratios and Why Do They Matter?

The challenge you have when looking at your various reports and forecasts is that these numbers don't tell you how you are doing in relation to other businesses or within your industry. For example, is it healthy or unhealthy if your nail salon's total debt equals your total assets? Since companies come in different shapes and sizes, the best way to make comparisons is by using ratios—comparisons of different elements from your balance sheet.

Ratios are commonly expressed as a percentage (usually x divided by y), or simply as "x:y." At the end of each accounting period, you should review and calculate certain ratios.

Since ratios differ within industries, you need to locate the ratios for your type of business. This may require an SIC code (Standard Industrial Classification). To find out the SIC for your industry, go to the SIC section of the Department of Labor website (www.osha.gov/pls/imis/sicsearch.html). Once you know the SIC, you can plug that into one of the many business ratio sources on the web, or review the *Annual Statement Studies* produced annually by Risk Management Associates (RMA). There also several business ratio calculators available on the Internet—plug in your raw data and the calculator produces your ratio. Many experts recommend using one or more of these benchmark ratios listed below.

Current Ratio

This measures how well your business can pay off short-term debts (or, as it is sometimes referred to, the size of your "buffer" or "cushion"). It's determined by dividing current assets by current liabilities. For example, if your current assets total $100,000 and your current liabilities total $50,000, the current ratio is expressed as a healthy 2 (or 2:1). If you paid off $40,000 of the current liabilities leaving $60,000 in current assets and $10,000 in current liabilities, your current ratio would improve to 6 (or 6:1). If on the other hand, you had $50,000 in assets and $100,000 in debt, you would have a risky ratio of 0.5 (or 1:2).

Quick Ratio (Also Known as "Acid-Test Ratio")

Like your current ratio, the quick ratio measures your company's ability to pay outstanding liabilities. The difference is that it looks at the amount of cash (or assets that can be quickly converted to cash) as a means of paying off the liabilities. For that reason, you determine the quick ratio by subtracting inventory from current assets, then dividing the result by current liabilities. (You subtract the inventory because that cannot be quickly converted to cash.) Therefore, if you had current assets of $100,000, current liabilities of $50,000, and inventory of $50,000, the quick ratio is expressed as a good 1 (or 1:1).

Debt-to-Worth Ratio (Also Known as "Debt-to-Equity" Ratio)

This is a measurement of your total debt (including accounts payable, long-term debt, and other loans) divided by your net worth (assets minus liabilities). This ratio measures a company's ability to handle losses while paying off existing debts. The lower your debt-to-worth ratio, the less risk for your business (and for a lender). For example, if your business's total debt is $50,000 and your net worth is $50,000, your debt-to-worth ratio is 1 or 1:1. If that ratio were to rise dramatically—for example, if your debt rose to $100,000 making the ratio 2 (or 2:1)—it's a signal that your company should hold off on incurring more debt, such as purchasing additional inventory or assets.

Current Debt to Net Worth

Ideally, your company's debts should not exceed the amount invested into it. This ratio (also referred to as debt-to-equity) measures risk to current or future creditors—the higher the ratio, the greater the risk. (A ratio above 60%, for example, is usually a sign of trouble.) This ratio is calculated by dividing the total liabilities by the total equity in the company.

Profit Margin

Another ratio which you may be familiar with is your profit margin. This is the calculation that matters the most to many business owners because it makes clear how much of each dollar in sales ultimately becomes profit. It's a percentage calculated by dividing net income for any period by the net sales from that period. That is, it tells you how much of your profit is being eaten by your expenses. For example, if your appliance store netted $100,000 on sales of $1 million during the last twelve months, your profit margin is 10%.

Separate Business and Personal

One of the first things you should do is get your business money out of your personal accounts. A lot of businesspeople pay their business expenses with a personal check or credit card and deposit business income into their household checking account, along with a spouse's salary, tax refunds, client reimbursements, inheritances, lottery winnings, and heaven knows what else. As long as you keep very careful records, this may work for a while, but it can create unnecessary problems. (Take note: One downside of using a personal credit card to pay bills is that your business does not acquire any "creditworthiness" from the use of a personal card.)

If you do business under a name other than your own legal name, you might not be able to deposit checks made out to your business in your personal account. If you have a joint account with anyone other than a co-owner in your business, that person could be dragged into a business audit. He or she will also have access to all of your business funds, which could be a problem if, for example, you have to pay a large bill for your business on the same day that your joint account holder decides to make a major purchase for your household. And you'll have a much harder time figuring your business deductions for interest, banking fees, and so on, because you'll have to separate out the costs attributable to personal purchases.

Even if you have to pay a bit extra to open more accounts, it will simplify your bookkeeping life greatly to have separate business accounts. At the very least, open a business checking account. And if you can't find a no-fee business credit card, simply use one of your personal credit cards just for business—that way, you'll have no trouble calculating your interest deduction. ●

Should You Incorporate or Form an LLC?

What Are You? Sole Proprietorship or Partnership? 30

    Sole Proprietorship 31

    Partnership...32

What's the Difference? LLC vs. Corporation 33

    How Are LLCs and Corporations Taxed? 34

How to Convert to an LLC or a Corporation..38

An Interview With LLC and Corporations Expert Anthony Mancuso.....41

Has a friend or relative suggested that you form a limited liability company (LLC) or corporation? It may sound too fancy for your business to become a corporation, but your advisers may be on the right track. LLCs and corporations can shield your personal assets—your house and savings, for example—from many business debts and court judgments.

On the other hand, 18 million small businesses in the U.S. have not chosen to incorporate or form an LLC. One reason is that insurance is often a better form of protection. If your business simply isn't going to run up many debts or run many risks—for example, your eBay business sells used DVDs—you probably don't need personal liability protection.

Finally, there's the cost. Forming an LLC or a corporation usually costs from $500 to $2,000 depending on who does it and in which state it's being formed. In many states there are annual fees (sometimes over $1,000 a year) for maintaining an LLC or a corporation.

So, if you're not that concerned with liability, or you believe that insurance can cover any liability, or you're just not that interested in paying the fees or dealing with the additional formalities, maybe an LLC or a corporation is not the right choice for your business. If you're one of the businesses that doesn't need the protection of a corporation or an LLC, you can skip this chapter. But if you are concerned about these issues, or if you'd like to learn more about business forms, such as sole proprietorships, partnerships, LLCs, and corporations, read on.

What Are You? Sole Proprietorship or Partnership?

If you're already in business, we'll assume that you're either a sole proprietorship (operating as one-person business) or a general partnership (an informal group of owners). Below we've charted the basics of these types of businesses. Later in the chapter, we've charted their limited liability cousins—LLCs and corporations. As you'll see, what differentiates these business forms are taxation, liability, and formalities (the requirements and costs for forming and maintaining the entity).

Sole Proprietorship

If you're operating by yourself (or maybe with your spouse) and haven't incorporated or formed an LLC, you're a sole proprietorship. A sole proprietorship is the least expensive and easiest way to operate a business.

SOLE PROPRIETORSHIPS AT A GLANCE	
TAXATION	A sole proprietorship is a pass-through entity. Your profits (and losses) pass through the business entity, and you pay taxes on any profits on your individual return at your individual tax rate. You report this business income on IRS Schedule C, *Profit and Loss From Business (Sole Proprietorship)*, which you file with your 1040 individual federal tax return.
LIABILITY	As a sole proprietor, you're personally liable for all business debts and legal claims. Liability insurance may pay for some of your legal claims.
FORMALITIES	A sole proprietorship is created automatically when you go into business. There is no fee to create one and no paperwork

Can a Husband and Wife Be a Sole Proprietorship?

If spouses co-own and run a business in a community property state (Arizona, California, Idaho, Nevada, New Mexico, Texas, Washington, and Wisconsin), they can operate as a sole proprietorship and report their business income as part of their joint tax return or they can operate as a partnership and file a K-1 partnership return. If spouses co-own and run a business in a non-community property state, they must operate as a partnership and file a K-1 partnership return.

In all states, if one spouse owns the business and the other works for it, the business is a sole proprietorship, and the owner will have to declare the spouse as an employee or independent contractor. If the spouse occasionally volunteers to help the business without pay, you won't have to declare the spouse as an employee or independent contractor. For more on spouse-owned (and other family) businesses, see Chapter 9.

Partnership

If you're operating with others and haven't incorporated or formed an LLC, then you're a general partnership. (Limited partnerships are discussed below.)

GENERAL PARTNERSHIPS AT A GLANCE	
TAXATION	A general partnership is a pass-through tax entity. The profits (and losses) pass through the business entity to the partners, who pay taxes on any profits on their individual returns at their individual tax rates. Even though a partnership does not pay its own taxes, it must file an "informational" tax return, IRS Schedule K-1 (Form 1065). In addition, the partnership must give each partner a filled-in copy of this form showing the proportionate share of profits or losses that each partner reports on an individual 1040 tax return. A partner pays taxes on his or her entire share of profits, even if the partnership chooses to reinvest the profits in the business, rather than distributing them to the partners.
LIABILITY	Each partner is personally liable for business debts and legal claims. The partnership should have liability insurance that will cover most claims. What's more, a creditor of the partnership can go after any general partner for the entire debt, regardless of that partner's ownership interest. Any partner may bind the entire partnership (in other words, the partners) to a contract or business deal.
FORMALITIES	You don't have to pay any fees or prepare any paperwork to form a general partnership; you can start it with a handshake. It makes far more sense, however, to prepare a partnership agreement. (See "Partnerships: Get It in Writing," below.) You may want to hire an accountant to manage the annual tax returns and documents.

Partnerships: Get It in Writing

If you're going into business with someone as partners, you should write a partnership agreement. Without an agreement, the one-size-fits-all rules of each state's general partnership laws will apply to your partnership. These provisions usually say that profits and losses of the business should be divided equally among the partners (or according to the partner's capital contributions in some states), and they impose a long list of other rules. You'll undoubtedly prefer to make your own rules. Your agreement should cover issues such as division of profits and losses, partnership draws (payments in lieu of salary), and the procedure for selling a partnership interest back to the partnership or to an outsider. *The Partnership Book*, by Denis Clifford and Ralph Warner (Nolo), explains how to form a partnership and create a partnership agreement. If you're not comfortable preparing your own agreement, an attorney should be able to prepare one for between $500 and $1,000.

What's the Difference? LLC vs. Corporation

The LLC combines the best feature of corporations (limiting the owners' personal liability) without any changes in tax reporting (you file the same tax documents as sole proprietorships and partnerships). An LLC can be formed by one or more people. LLCs have largely replaced corporations as the favorite choice among small business owners and are discussed in more detail later in this chapter.

Corporations are the most formal of the business entities. Owners hold shares (becoming shareholders) and elect a board of directors that directs management. If you incorporate your small business, you become an employee but still run it. Corporations are distinguished for tax purposes, as "C" corporations or "S" corporations. A C corporation is a regular for-profit corporation taxed under normal corporate income tax rules. (When we use the term "corporation" in this book, we always mean a C corporation.) In contrast, S corporations are taxed like partnerships—their income is passed on to the owners.

Running a corporation is more time-consuming and requires more formality than other entities. State laws usually require that, at the least, a president (CEO) and a secretary be appointed and, in many states, a treasurer as well. In practice, however, a small corporation's shareholders act as both its board of directors and its officers.

How Are LLCs and Corporations Taxed?

Most start-up business owners prefer LLCs because reporting and paying individual income taxes is easier than the corporate alternative. If you switch from sole proprietor or general partnership to an LLC, there won't be any changes in how you do your income tax reporting. That's because, like sole proprietorships and partnerships, most LLCs are pass-through entities. Pass-through taxation means that you report the money you earned from your business on your individual tax return and pay tax at individual income tax rates.

A corporation is not a pass-through entity; it's taxed as a separate entity, at a corporate tax rate. When the corporate profits are passed to the owners, they are taxed again on individual returns.

As a business develops and income increases, however, some owners prefer corporate taxation. One reason is that the owners of a corporation can split business income between themselves and their business so that some business profits are taxed at the lower corporate tax rate. This allows corporate owners to pay lower overall taxes on business profits. For example, earnings kept in the corporation are taxed at initial corporate income tax rates of 15% and 25%. Because these rates are usually lower than the marginal individual income tax rates of the owners, the owners will face a lower overall tax burden.

Although corporations have more complex tax rules than other entities, they are a better choice for businesses seeking investment. Small corporations can also offer employees fringe benefits, such as fully deductible group life and disability insurance, enhanced retirement plans, stock options, and other incentive plans. The owner/employees of corporations are not taxed on their individual tax returns for these benefits.

LLCS AND CORPORATIONS AT A GLANCE	
LLC	**CORPORATION**
TAXATION		

	LLC	**CORPORATION**
TAXATION	An LLC is taxed like a partnership—or, for a one-owner LLC, as a sole proprietorship. LLC income, loss, credits, and deductions are reported on the individual income tax returns of the LLC owners. The LLC itself does not pay income tax.	A corporation is a legal entity separate from its shareholders. The corporation files its own tax return (IRS Form 1120) and pays its own income taxes on the profits kept in the company.
LIABILITY	The owner/members of an LLC are not personally liable for business debts and other liabilities. However, owners are liable for debts that they personally guaranteed and tax debts.	The owners (shareholders) of a corporation are not personally liable for the business liabilities. However, as with LLCs, owners are liable for debts that are personally guaranteed, tax debts, and claims resulting from owners' negligence.
FORMALITIES	To start an LLC, you must file articles of organization with the state business filing office. You and the other owners should also prepare an operating agreement to spell out how the LLC will be owned, how profits and losses will be divided, how departing or deceased members will be bought out, and other essential ownership issues.	To form a corporation, you pay corporate filing fees and prepare and file formal organizational papers, usually called articles of incorporation, with a state agency (in most states, the secretary or department of state). Directors must hold annual meetings and keep minutes, prepare formal documentation (in the form of resolutions or written consents to corporate actions) of important decisions made during the life of the corporation, and keep a paper trail of all legal and financial dealings between the corporation and its shareholders. The board of directors must appoint officers to supervise daily corporate business.

FEDERAL TAX RATES ON TAXABLE CORPORATE INCOME	
ANNUAL REVENUE	CORPORATE TAX RATE
$0 to $50,000	15%
$50,001 to $75,000	25%
$75,001 to $100,000	34%
$100,001 to $335,000	39%
$335,001 to $10,000,000	34%
$10,000,001 to $15,000,000	35%
$15,000,001 to $18,333,333	38%
Over $18,333,333	35%

Those Pesky California LLC Fees

Both corporations and LLCs may be subject to state fees—and in some states, these fees may be a major turn-off. For example, all California LLCs must pay a minimum annual $800 LLC tax each year. They must pay an additional yearly fee depending on the LLC's annual gross receipts. If your LLC is one of those that must include the cost of its goods as part of its total receipts, you may be in for a shock. For example, imagine you paid $300,000 for materials you needed to complete a project. Your client repaid you for the materials but has not yet made any other payments under the contract. You would have to include the $300,000 as gross receipts and have to pay an additional LLC fee of $900 (in addition to the regular $800 annual LLC tax), even though you have not received any profits under the contract.

DON'T

Don't assume that forming an LLC or corporation will always shield all of your personal assets. Even if you operate as a corporation or an LLC, a creditor can still go after your personal assets if:

- **You personally guarantee a loan or lease.** Most lenders and landlords condition small business loans and leases upon the business owner's personal guarantee. The only way you could escape these debts is for the business and each owner seeking protection to file for bankruptcy.
- **You owe federal or state taxes.** If your business fails to pay income, payroll, or other taxes, the IRS or the state tax agency can try to recover the unpaid taxes personally from you or the other directors, officers, and owners of your LLC or corporation.
- **You act negligently.** If you run a business subject to potential negligence claims—for example, an establishment open to the public, or a manufacturer of consumer products—you can be personally liable for the damage. In these cases, buying insurance will usually do you more good than will forming a corporation or an LLC.
- **You fail to abide by corporate rules.** If you don't take corporate responsibilities seriously—for example, you mix corporate and personal funds and don't keep records of meetings and shareholders—a judge may strip away the asset protection feature of the corporation or LLC. It's called "piercing the veil."

What Good Is Stock?

A corporation sells stock to raise money to invest in the business. This system is unique in the world of business entities and leads to a few special benefits. For example, stock can be divided into classes, each with different rights to vote, receive dividends, participate in management, and receive cash if the business is liquidated. Stock can also fund employee stock option or bonus plans. It can be used to fund a buyout of another business. It can be exchanged or converted into the shares of another corporation if two companies merge.

How to Convert to an LLC or a Corporation

When Steve Wozniak and Steve Jobs brought their first Apple 1 computer to the Homebrew Computer Club in Palo Alto, California, in 1976, few people took them—or their computer—seriously. Once the two partners started taking orders, however, their low-cost ($666.66) microcomputer system slowly began to sell. Within nine months, Jobs and Wozniak filed incorporation documents and on January 3, 1977, converted their partnership to a corporation.

Their migration from partnership to corporation was typical of many successful business entities in the 1970s and 80s. Today, many successful partnerships decide to form LLCs rather than corporations, to help the owners avoid personal legal liability for business debts and claims while maintaining their pass-through tax status.

As a sole proprietor or partnership, you can convert to an LLC in most states with a modest amount of paperwork and fees, and with no change to your income tax treatment and filing requirements. Here are three ways you can handle the conversion:

- **Do it yourself.** You can learn more about incorporation or LLC formation procedures and fees for your state by visiting your state's business filing office website—usually the secretary of state's. (Start by finding your state's home page at www.statelocalgov.net, then look for links to business resources.) You can also get step-by-step instructions on forming an LLC in *Form Your Limited Liability Company*, or forming a corporation in *Incorporate Your Business: A Legal Guide to Forming a Corporation in Your State*, both by Anthony Mancuso (Nolo).

- **Hire an incorporation service.** Companies such as Nolo (www.nolo .com), and the Company Corporation (www.incorporate.com) will incorporate your business or form an LLC on your behalf, usually for $200 to $300 in addition to the regular filing fees. To locate one of these services, type "incorporation service" into your Internet search engine.

- **Hire an attorney.** An attorney can help form a corporation or an LLC, usually for a fixed fee between $500 and $1,000 (plus filing fees).

INTERNET LINK

You can find links for all the resources in this book at www.nolo.com/wowbusiness.

If you're a sole proprietor, you can convert your one-person business to a corporation or an LLC or bring additional owners into the business when converting. You don't need to be a resident of the state where you form your LLC, or even of the United States, for that matter.

If you are a partnership, you and your partners must agree to terminate the partnership and convert to a corporation or an LLC. You may have to complete additional paperwork to legally terminate your partnership when you convert it to an LLC—for example, publish a notice of dissolution in a newspaper. Check with your secretary of state.

Finally, before you decide to convert to another entity, you should seek the advice of a tax consultant about the possible tax consequences, as well as having your new corporation or LLC assume the debts of your prior partnership.

DON'T

Don't forget about payroll taxes. For payroll tax purposes, an LLC owner who receives a share of the profits is not considered an employee. However, if the owner receives a salary—that is, guaranteed payments from the business regardless of how much it earns—you are an employee, and the LLC must withhold and pay income and other payroll taxes on the salary payout.

Limited Partnerships and S Corporations

Two types of business entities that have faded from favor in the last few decades are limited partnerships and S corporations.

A **limited partnership** has two types of partners: general partners who manage the business and limited partners—typically investors—who contribute capital to the business, but are not involved in day-to-day management. (One type of limited partnership—the family limited partnership—is discussed in Chapter 9.) Only the limited partners are granted limited liability protection. General partners are personally liable for business debts and claims. The limited partnership is taxed like a general partnership, with all partners individually reporting and paying taxes on their share of the profits each year. To create a limited partnership, you must pay an initial fee and file papers with the state—usually a certificate of limited partnership. With the introduction of the LLC—which offers liability protection to all owners—the limited partnership has lost favor with small business owners.

S corporations still exist, but like limited partnerships, they have, for the most part, been replaced by LLCs. The S corporation's shareholders receive the same basic pass-through tax treatment afforded sole proprietorships, partnerships, and LLC owners. S corporation shareholders have limited personal liability for the debts and other liabilities of the corporation. To form an S corporation, you must first form a regular C corporation, then convert it to an S corporation by filing an S corporation tax election with the IRS. Generally, an S corporation may have no more than 75 shareholders, all of whom must be U.S. citizens or residents or be certain types of trusts or estates.

An Interview With LLC and Corporations Expert Anthony Mancuso

The following is an interview with attorney Anthony Mancuso, who's a recognized expert on business formations and the author of such best-selling titles as *Incorporate Your Business*, *Form Your Own Limited Liability Company*, and *How To Form A Nonprofit Corporation* (Nolo).

QUESTION: Tony, when people find out that you've written all these books on business formation and corporations and LLCs, is there one common question that you're often asked?

ANTHONY MANCUSO: People usually ask a very general question—"What is the best form of business?"—when they hear that I write books for Nolo. I usually tell them the best form is no form at all until you have a reason to think about. If you're worried about lawsuits, if you're going into business with someone else and want to make sure you have an agreement in place that covers some of the contingencies, then it might be time to start thinking about it.

Typically, once people worry about limited liability issues or take a look at insurance costs and worry about uninsured risks and those types of things, that's when they may think about forming an LLC, a limited liability company. When they want to raise capital, or find that they're making a little too much money and getting taxed on everything, then they may think of forming a corporation to shelter some money in their corporation. But generally, that's my answer: Wait until there's a need and it becomes important; more than a theoretical question.

QUESTION: Is the LLC always the best choice for the owner of a start-up business seeking to limit personal liability?

ANTHONY MANCUSO: It generally is, and people that haven't heard the news about LLCs often think of S corporations, but really, the LLC has replaced the S corporation. [The LLC] lets you form a legal entity that insulates you from liability for business—that's claims against your business—and at the same time, it keeps your current tax status. So if you're a sole proprietor and you form a one-person LLC, you'll continue to be taxed as a sole proprietor. If you're a partnership and you convert to an LLC, you'll continue to have your business taxed as a partnership, so you don't change your tax status.

And another important part of it is if you're ever thinking of having your business own real estate, it can be a very, very big mistake to form a corporation, because you'll get hit with double tax on the appreciation of any real estate owned by the business. That's not true of an LLC.

QUESTION: If you're trying to form an LLC or a corporation by yourself—that is, without the aid of an attorney—are there one or two things that you really need to watch out for?

ANTHONY MANCUSO: The first thing is to really stay focused on forming an LLC in your own state. If you go on the web and you take a look at a number of the books, you may see a lot of talk and titles about forming a Delaware LLC or a Nevada LLC, or forming out of state where the taxes are lower. That doesn't do you much good. In fact, it just creates more problems. You want to stay in your home state because that's where you'll be taxed, ultimately. It won't matter if you form a Delaware corporation and you make your money in California—California is going to want to tax you anyway. So you won't save anything. In fact, you'll be setting yourself up for double costs if you do that.

So, stay within your own state. I would suggest if you know someone who's experienced with business taxes and law, it's always a good idea to have a consultation with them for an hour, just to make sure about your decision to form an LLC and the tax consequences. Because LLCs, if they're co-owned, they're taxed as partnerships, and partnership taxation is quite complicated, and there's a number of elections to think about ahead of time. So it's really a good idea, particularly from a tax perspective, to go over your decision to form an LLC with a tax person who really knows partnership taxation.

QUESTION: There's a lot of advice available for people who want to form an LLC or a corporation, but you don't see much discussion about what it takes to shut down one of these entities. How hard is it to dissolve an LLC or a corporation?

ANTHONY MANCUSO: Well, fortunately, most secretaries of state have online forms to do it. It's usually just a one-step process. At least, legally it's a one-step process. You'll file a dissolution form in most cases, with the state, and it'll dissolve it. It's a little more involved from a tax perspective because you have to get a tax clearance, usually, as well from your state tax agency, and that's simple enough. Some states, though, it's not quite as simple. In California, for instance, that has its own tax forms—it doesn't follow the federal tax forms, and you'll have to file a special tax form with the Franchise Tax Board. But you'll also need a tax clearance.

QUESTION: Income shifting seems very complex. Is there an easy way to describe what that is?

ANTHONY MANCUSO: Try to not think of it as income shifting, because it's all your money and it continues to be your money. But if you form a corporation, you can split your income between yourself and your corporation. And the way to think about it is if you start making more money than you actually put in your pocket, if you have an unincorporated business form, what happens is, since we have a progressive tax rate structure, the more money you make, the higher your tax rate is. That's your marginal tax rate—that is, the amount of tax you pay on each new dollar earned in your business.

So, since that can go up to 35%, some people feel that their marginal tax rate is a little high because they're really not seeing that money. That money is being kept in their business. So, if you incorporate, you can keep some of your money in the lower corporate 15% and 25% tax bracket.

So, if it's really kept in your business anyway, you can save some money. I wouldn't suggest incorporating just for this reason, although some people who are desperate to save every possible tax dollar do talk about it this way. I tend not to. It's just one of a number of factors in the decision to incorporate, but it can help save you a little money so that maybe money kept in a corporation is taxed at 25%. If it were taxed to you, if you had an LLC or a partnership or a sole proprietorship, it might get taxed at a 10% higher rate, at 35%.

So, you can save some money if it's being kept in your business, because corporate tax rates start lower than most business owners' marginal tax rates. So, instead of paying 35%, keep it in your corporation—you could pay 15% or 25% of that money.

QUESTION: If you register your business in one state, what does it mean for you to have to qualify in another?

ANTHONY MANCUSO: Qualifying means you have to file papers, very similar to incorporation papers or LLC articles of organization. It's basically having a formal legal presence in another state. If you have only incidental contacts in another state—you sell through mail order, over the Web, or you have a physical presence in another state—you generally don't have to qualify and you shouldn't worry too much about it. But, if you start having a real presence there, if you hire people who are there, who are telecommuting and they're on your payroll but they live somewhere else, you can maintain inventory in another state, if you travel there a lot and talk to people a lot, if you just really start becoming more physically present in another state, then it's time to think about qualifying. Basically, it's a similar process to incorporating or filing articles for an LLC in another state. You have to pay a qualification fee, and you have to appoint a registered agent in that state.

The downside of not doing it when you're required is that you won't be able to sue other people in another state if you have to – if you have contracts in another state, you won't be able to enforce them. And generally, to use the courts in another state, you'll have to qualify and pay any back penalties for not qualifying.

So, it's just neater all around, once you're physically present in another state, to just go ahead and file those papers and pay the initial fee. They're not terribly high and it just makes you fully legal in the other state you're working in.

QUESTION: Tony, you hear lawyers talking about "piercing the corporate veil"—what is it, and how often does it happen?

ANTHONY MANCUSO: Yeah, it's a really bad mixed metaphor, but it generally means that the owners of a corporation or of an LLC can be held personally liable for the debts of the business or claims made against it. So, someone can sue your LLC or corporation, and if they can convince a court to pierce the corporate veil, they can go after your personal assets. And, of course, the main reason for forming an LLC or a corporation is to insulate yourself from those types of personal liabilities, and in fact, they've defeated your incorporation or your LLC formation, and that's something you don't want to see happen.

It's very, very rare and that's the main thing to keep in mind. It only happens in cases where someone has committed a fairly serious fraud against someone else, and a court determines that the only fair way to resolve a dispute is to hold someone personally liable.

QUESTION: Tony, you often read that the District of Columbia and Massachusetts are the only two states that require at least two members to form an LLC. But that's not true anymore, is it?

ANTHONY MANCUSO: Up until recently they did require. They were the last two holdout states that required two members to form an LLC. And now, there's a carryover from the old tax rules that no longer applies.

QUESTION: Of all your books, which is the one that's probably best for the business owner who doesn't know which business entity or which business form to adopt?

ANTHONY MANCUSO: The one that I've done that I like, that goes into a little more depth than the typical business form comparison book is *LLC or Corporation?* (Nolo). It digs beneath the surface a little bit more than the average business comparison book and talks about the tax and legal ramifications of forming an LLC or a corporation and converting from one to the other.

Those converging areas are very important, because during the life cycle of a business, it's not enough to form the right entity, you also have to consider, when you're forming a business, how it can migrate to another form, and your initial choice will determine that.

So, if you choose the wrong one to start with, you often can't move to the next proper choice as your business evolves.

QUESTION: Do people really need to worry about personal liability if they have sufficient business insurance?

ANTHONY MANCUSO: If you feel comfortable with your current level of coverage, given the type of business you're in, then you don't really need to worry too much about your business form, at least for legal liability reasons. You may want to form a particular type of business for tax purposes. But the main reason to form an LLC or a corporation, for legal purposes, is to limit your liability. If you have adequate insurance, by the way, you're in the minority, but if you do, then maybe you don't have to think about it, and you can just go about your life and your business without worrying about this. But, for most people, that's not true.

If you're dealing with the public, if you have people come on your premises, or if you're doing any kind of contract type of business with others, it's just true these days that disputes often end up in court or have the potential to—it helps business owners sleep better at night to have this type of automatic liability insurance, this kind of automatic insurance they obtain by incorporating or forming an LLC. ●

Insurance

Basic Coverage...49

    Property Insurance...49

    Liability Insurance..50

    Car Insurance 51

    Business Interruption Coverage...51

    Key Person Insurance...53

Consider a Package Deal..54

What You Need If You Have Employees 54

Getting Group Insurance Through an Association.............................56

Tips for Saving Money on Insurance...58

When you're just getting started in business, money is usually tight—and you're probably reluctant to spend what little you have insuring against disasters that will probably never strike. On the other hand, it's foolish to do business without some basic insurance coverage. If something goes wrong, you could lose all of the time and money you've invested in your business. What's more, you may be required to have some types of insurance by law or by those you do business with (lenders, landlords, and others).

The trick is to get only the coverage you really need—and to pay as little as possible for it. This chapter explains the basic types of coverage available and offers tips for finding the right policies at the right price.

Before we begin our discussion of insurance, let's review a few key terms:

KEY INSURANCE TERMS	
POLICY	Your policy is the written document or contract between you and the insurance company.
PREMIUM	The premium is the periodic payment you pay to the insurance company for the benefits provided under the policy.
RIDER	A rider is a special provision attached to a policy that either expands or restricts the policy.
CLAIM	A claim is your notification to an insurance company that you believe a payment is due to you under the terms of the policy.
COMMISSION	This is a fee or percentage of the premium you pay to an insurance broker or agent.
DEDUCTIBLE	The deductible is the amount of out-of-pocket expenses that you must pay before the insurance payment begins. For example, if your deductible for business equipment loss is $1,000 per year and you suffer $1,000 in damages in one year, there will be no payment under the policy.
ENDORSEMENT	An endorsement is paperwork that is added to your policy and that reflects any changes or clarifications in the policy.
EXCLUSIONS	Exclusions are things your insurance policy will not cover.
UNDERWRITER	This is the person or company that evaluates your business and determines what insurance you may qualify for.

> ### Insurance Benefit Programs For You and Your Employees
>
> This chapter doesn't cover insurance that you might want to provide for your employees (or yourself) as a fringe benefit, such as health insurance, life insurance, or long-term disability coverage. If you're interested in these types of insurance, a good place to start looking is the National Association for the Self-Employed (www.nase.org).

Basic Coverage

No matter what kind of business you have, you'll want to insure it against common hazards. Virtually every business needs some form of property insurance and liability insurance, and many need auto insurance as well. Here's a brief description of some common insurance protections.

Property Insurance

Business property insurance compensates you for damage or loss of your property—both the physical space where you work (your home office, for example) and the equipment and other furnishings of your business. If you rent commercial space, your lease may require you to carry a specified amount of property insurance.

A "named peril" policy protects against only the types of damage listed in the policy—typically, fire, lightning, vehicles, vandalism, storms, smoke, and sprinkler leaks. A "special form" policy offers broader coverage, commonly against all but a few excluded risks (often including earthquakes), and is more expensive. A good insurance professional can help you decide which choice makes more sense for your business. (Choosing and working with an insurance pro is covered below.)

If yours is a home business, you can probably take care of your property insurance needs through an inexpensive endorsement to your homeowners' policy, particularly if you don't have much pricey business equipment. But don't assume that your homeowners' policy will cover business losses— most offer very limited coverage (if any) for business property (see below).

When you're buying property insurance, you'll have a choice between an actual cash value policy, which pays you whatever your damaged property is actually worth on the day it is damaged, or a replacement cost policy, which pays to replace your property at current prices. A replacement cost policy is always more expensive, but it's worth the extra money. Business equipment, such as computers, fax machines, copiers, and so on, lose their value quickly. And if you're like most new business owners, you're probably using some equipment that's already out of date. If you suffer a loss, you'll need to replace this equipment and get back to work—not to go out to a fancy lunch on the $100 your insurance company thinks your old computer was worth.

Liability Insurance

Liability insurance covers damage to other people or their property for which you are legally responsible. This includes, for example, injuries to a customer who trips on your son's skateboard on the way to your home office; damage caused by your products (called products liability coverage); and harm caused by your errors in providing professional services (called professional liability coverage). Liability insurance policies typically pay the injured person's medical bills and other out-of-pocket losses, any amount you are ordered to pay in a lawsuit for a covered claim, and often the cost of defending you in such a lawsuit.

If you have a home business and are seldom visited there by clients or customers, you may be able to get a relatively inexpensive liability endorsement to your homeowners' policy.

DON'T

Don't treat your business status as a corporation or an LLC as a substitute for insurance. Incorporating or forming an LLC will limit your personal liability for business debts, but it won't do anything to protect your business from loss. If you're like most budding entrepreneurs, you've probably poured a good portion of your personal assets into your business, and you certainly don't want to lose that investment.

Car Insurance

If you have a car, you probably already have insurance that covers your personal use. However, your personal insurance policy may not cover business use of your car. If it doesn't, you'll want to get business coverage to protect against lawsuits for damage you cause to others or their vehicles while using your car for business.

If you don't do much business driving—and particularly if you don't often have business passengers, such as clients or customers—then you can probably get coverage simply by informing your insurance company of your planned business use (and paying a slightly higher premium). Many insurance companies simply factor in occasional business use of a vehicle, along with commuting miles, driver experience, and many other factors, in setting your insurance premium. If you use a commercial vehicle (such as a van or delivery truck) or put most of the miles on your car while doing business, you will probably have to get a separate business vehicle insurance policy.

Business Interruption Coverage

A business interruption policy replaces the income you won't be able to earn if you must close, rebuild, or relocate your business due to a covered event, such as a fire or storm. These policies typically provide both money to replace your lost profits, based on your business's earnings history (as shown by its financial records), and money to pay the operating expenses you still have to pay even though you can't do business (like rent and overhead). Business interruption policies are not typically sold as stand-alone products; instead, they're added to property insurance policies or sold as part of a business insurance package (see below).

Unless you have little to no overhead costs, you shouldn't do business without interruption coverage. According to Mike Mansel, a certified insurance counselor in California, this type of policy is "absolutely critical to a business's survival—easily the most important coverage for a business to have." If you don't have business interruption coverage, your chances of going back into business after having to close are very slim.

When you're shopping for this type of insurance (or any other, for that matter), always check the exclusions and coverage. For example, some policies may provide an "extended period of indemnity," which kicks in after you reopen, to cover your continuing losses until you are fully back on your feet. If your customers don't immediately flock back to your new location, your policy will pay for the business you're still not getting during this transition period.

You might also want to look for coverage for the loss of business income from "dependent properties"—companies whose losses affect your business. Mike Mansel gives the example of a small boutique in a mall that depends on a flagship store for its business. "If that large store, which brings a lot of customers to the area, burns down, all of the smaller stores are going to suffer." Similarly, if your products will spend any time on someone else's premises where they could be damaged or lost, this type of coverage will pay for losses you suffer as a result.

Event Insurance: Worth the Price of Admission?

It's possible to buy insurance to cover a one-time event—for example, a large sales convention or demonstration. You might think that you could save money by going light on your general business insurance and insuring these events separately, but that's not the case. Because the primary insurance companies don't write these policies, you'll have to shop in what insurance pros call "the wholesale market"—and you'll pay for the privilege. Because most general liability policies cover events anyway, you're almost always better off skipping event insurance and putting your premium dollars towards more pressing coverage needs.

Key Person Insurance

Once known as key man insurance, this is a life insurance policy on the indispensable person(s) in a business. The policy is paid for by the business, and proceeds are payable to it, in case of the key person's death. This type of policy protects a business against the devastation a business can suffer if a crucial person—generally a partner or founder—dies; it provides money to keep paying the bills while you figure out what to do.

For a partnership or other business that relies heavily on the efforts of more than one person, key person insurance can be a lifesaver. For example, if one partner is an introverted type who invents and engineers products, while the other partner raises capital, sells products, and generally represents the business to the public, both partners are essential to the company's success. If either dies, the other could use the proceeds of a key person policy to stay afloat while searching for another partner or coming up with some new business strategies.

And when you're trying to borrow or raise significant amounts of money, lenders or investors may require you to get key person coverage on one or two crucial players in your business.

If you run your business alone and have no employees, however, you can skip the key person coverage. The sad fact is that if you die, your business is very likely going down with you. To protect your family against the risk of losing your income, buy a personal life insurance policy instead.

Web Insurance

Some insurance companies offer Web insurance policies, which protect businesses with websites against a variety of risks, including theft, copyright infringement, and interruptions of service. These policies used to be so expensive and difficult to qualify for that they were out of reach for all but the largest companies, but times have changed. Today, you can get insurance for a simple site for anywhere from $500 to $3,000 a year, according to Mike Mansel. An insurance professional can help you decide whether your cyber-risks are great enough to justify this expense.

Consider a Package Deal

Many insurance companies offer package policies geared to the needs of small businesses. If you run a home business, you may be able to get less expensive coverage through an in-home business policy. These policies typically also cover business property and liability, and some also provide business interruption protection. According to the Insurance Information Institute, an in-home business policy will cost something in the range of $250 to $400 a year for about $10,000 of coverage. However, your business will have to meet the insurance company's requirements for coverage, which may include having very few employees, bringing few business visitors to your home, or purchasing your homeowners' insurance from the same company.

If your home business can't meet these requirements, or if you run a business outside of your home, you should look into a business owners' policy or BOP. These packages typically include business property insurance, liability protection, and some business interruption protection. According to Chad Berberich, director of Executive Products at RLI Corporation Insurance (www.rlicorp.com), a "mom and pop" home-based business with revenues up to the low six figures can expect to pay an annual premium of anywhere from $1,500 to $4,000 for a BOP.

Typically, neither a BOP nor an in-home business policy provides coverage for professional liability (malpractice), employment practices liability (often referred to as EPLI) to protect you from lawsuits brought by current or former employees, workers' compensation, or other employee benefits (health or disability insurance, for example). Also, you will almost certainly have to pay separately for automobile coverage if you use your car for business.

What You Need If You Have Employees

When you hire employees, you take on some financial obligations. In addition to paying wages and Social Security and Medicare taxes for each employee, you'll also have to pay for unemployment insurance and, in a handful of states, disability insurance. And if you have more than a few employees, you'll probably have to purchase workers' compensation insurance.

Workers' Comp Coverage for Yourself?

Even if you don't have employees, you may have to pay for workers' comp insurance to cover your own work-related injuries. This often comes up for business owners who perform services at a client's location—for example, plumbers and contractors. Particularly if your work creates a risk of injury, clients may insist that you have your own workers' compensation coverage to make sure that you won't make a claim against their policy—and that they don't have to pay extra to cover you on the policy they carry for their own workers.

Workers' compensation insurance. This insurance pays your employees for work-related injuries and reimburses them a portion of lost wages if they cannot work due to injury. You buy it either by paying into a state fund or by buying a policy from a private insurer. Some states don't require employers that have only a few employees to get this coverage; contact your state insurance or labor department to find out your state's rules.

Unemployment insurance. If you have even one employee, you will probably have to pay for unemployment insurance (UI). UI is a joint program of the state and federal governments. It's funded by a payroll tax on employers, which goes into a fund from which workers who are laid off or fired for reasons other than serious misconduct can draw money while they're unemployed. The amount you have to pay will depend on how many employees you have and how many unemployment claims your former employees have made (if any). For lots of information on UI, including details on state requirements, go to the website of the federal Department of Labor's Employment and Training Administration, at www.doleta.gov. Choose "Business & Industry" for a list of topics for employers, including UI.

Disability insurance. Five states (California, Hawaii, New Jersey, New York, and Rhode Island) provide temporary disability insurance to workers who are temporarily disabled and unable to work. In California and Rhode Island, employees pay the cost of this insurance through payroll deductions; in Hawaii, New Jersey, and New York, employers pay into the plan. If you do business in one of these states, go to your state labor department's website to find out more about your obligations.

DON'T

Don't count on your homeowners' insurance to cover your home-based business. According to the Insurance Information Institute (www.iii.org), a typical homeowners' policy provides only $2,500 in coverage for business equipment. And it won't provide any coverage at all for business-related liabilities, such as theft of business property, injuries suffered by customers or employees, or damage caused by your products or services.

Despite these facts, 60% of home-based businesses don't have business insurance coverage, according to the Independent Insurance Agents & Brokers of America (www.iiaa.org). Why? Most of them thought they were already covered by some other type of insurance.

Getting Group Insurance Through an Association

If you belong to a trade organization, professional group, or other business association, you may be eligible for special rates on certain types of insurance. For example, if you become a member of the National Association for the Self-Employed (www.nase.org), your business may be entitled to insurance discounts for your home office. There are specialized membership organizations for every field of business—and some of them may provide specialized or group insurance plans. For example, the Association of Pet Dog Trainers (www.apdt.com) offers members access to group liability insurance policies, and the American

Institute of Certified Public Accountants (www.aicpa.org) makes a variety of insurance programs available to its members. And if you practice acupuncture and are in the market for malpractice insurance, group rates are available through the American Association of Oriental Medicine, www.aaom.org.

You'll have to do some comparison shopping to decide whether the policies offered through a membership organization will work for you and provide all of the coverage you need. Some are available only to businesses that meet specified criteria; some offer only limited coverage and low policy limits; some offer a type of protection that you could buy elsewhere as part of a package, for a lower overall bill. Even if you ultimately decide not to purchase insurance through one of these groups, you can use its policy information as a starting point when deciding what type of coverage you need for your business. After all, others in your field are the experts on the true risks of running your type of business.

Who Needs Malpractice Insurance?

In the not-so-distant past, just a handful of professions (including doctors, lawyers, and accountants) really needed professional liability insurance—a special type of liability insurance designed to protect against claims that the policyholder made mistakes or acted carelessly in providing professional services. Today, however, anyone who sells professional services (those that require advanced education or training) could conceivably be sued for harming someone by providing services that don't meet the standards of the profession. For example, a masseuse whose poor technique injures a client or a website creator who delivers a site that is immediately hacked could face a claim for professional negligence, often referred to as malpractice.

Of course, the fact that you can be sued for something doesn't necessarily mean you should insure against it. A good insurance professional can help you figure out whether you're really at risk for this type of lawsuit.

INTERNET LINK
You can find links for all the resources in this book at www.nolo .com/wowbusiness.

Tips for Saving Money on Insurance

One way to save money on insurance is simply to work with the right professional—someone who will help you figure out what coverage you need and offer you a competitive price. An agent or broker is paid by the insurance company, by commission. Some of them are independent— that is, they shop around among various companies to find the right policy. Others work exclusively for one insurance company and are called captive or direct-writing agents.

Generally, you'll want to avoid agents or brokers who work with only one company, for the obvious reason that they'll be trying to sell you that company's products, even if they don't provide the best coverage for your business or offer you the best price.

An independent agent or broker is also paid by commission, but will shop around to find you the right coverage at the right price.

The process of finding the right insurance pro is a lot like finding the right accountant, lawyer, or other professional. The best place to start is by asking for recommendations from others who do business in your field, your mentor, friends, or coworkers from your day job. You can also get lists of insurance specialists from business organizations, such as your local chamber of commerce or a trade group. However, Scott Simmonds says you'll often get a better referral if you ask members or officers of the group for the name of the person they actually do business with, not who the organization recommends. If you are working with a lawyer or accountant, you might also ask them for leads.

There's no magic formula for finding the "right" insurance professional —you simply need to find someone you trust to do a good job for you.

Will the agent or other professional:

• periodically provide you with information about new policies you might want to consider?

• give you quotes from other companies from time to time?

• help you if you have to file a claim?

You're looking for someone who will do all of these things, "not someone who will put your file in a drawer and hope never to hear from you again," says Mike Mansel.

Here are some more tips that will help you lower your insurance bills.

Assess your true risks. How much business property do you own? Do you sell products—and if so, what are the chances that they might cause someone injury? Will you carry a large inventory of completed products or valuable raw materials? If you sell services, could a client suffer major harm (physical or financial) if you made a mistake? Will you have employees, and if so, how many? Your answers to questions like these will help you and your insurance pro figure out what kind of coverage you really need.

Will Your Clients' Insurance Cover You?

In some business fields, your clients may have to provide the insurance. For example, Mike and Carrie McAllen, who run Grass Shack Events & Media (www.grassshackroad.com), a company that plans events mostly for corporate clients, find that their clients often supply the insurance for their events. Many of their events are held in hotels and similar facilities. Because the client books the venue, Mike says, it is the client who has to show proof of adequate insurance for the event. Of course, this doesn't meet all of Grass Shack's business insurance needs, but it helps lower the bills.

Reduce your risk. Risk management will minimize your insurance claims and bring your premiums down. Depending on your business, there may be things you can do to reduce your likelihood of suffering a costly loss. Consider getting out of high-risk fields or activities, if possible—for example, an athlete who wants to turn a passion for sports into a business might decide to focus on developing a clothing line, not on creating technical safety equipment that could cause serious injuries if produced or used improperly. Or, you may want to implement procedures to make sure that you aren't taking on risky employees—for example, by checking the driving record of anyone who will drive for you. You can also transfer risk to others. One way to do this is to minimize the materials for which you will be responsible—for example, don't store a lot of supplies or finished products on your premises, but leave them with others who will have to pay for and insure the loss if there is one. (Of course, this strategy will work only if the person or company you store things with is adequately insured.) This will add up to lower initial premiums, fewer claims, and lower premiums in the future as well.

Start your shopping with required insurance. If you are legally required to carry certain types of insurance (such as workers' compensation), make sure you set aside the money for it. Similarly, if you have to carry certain types or levels of insurance for other reasons—for example, because your commercial lease obligates you to carry a certain amount of property insurance—shop for that first. You will have to show proof of these types of coverage to get your business off the ground.

Prioritize your greatest risks. Once you've dealt with required coverage, spend your money where you need it the most. If you face a serious risk of a loss that could wipe you out, put your insurance dollars there first. For example, many artisans whose work requires heavy machinery and lots of room rent space in warehouses or other industrial buildings, often in areas of town that have a high crime rate. These entrepreneurs probably won't have a lot of visitors and won't create products that risk injuring someone—but they do have valuable business property to protect. Your insurance pro can help you figure out what your priorities should be.

Consider higher deductibles. When you purchase a policy with a higher deductible, you'll pay lower premiums. This can be a financial lifesaver for a business struggling to get off the ground. If you suffer a loss, however, you'll have to pay more money out of pocket before the insurance company starts chipping in.

Ask your insurance pro about discounts. Many companies offer lower premiums or discounts to policyholders who take certain safety precautions. Installing smoke detectors or a security system are a couple of steps you can take that may get you a lower-priced policy. Find out whether any of these discounts are available through the companies you're considering—then take the necessary steps to lower your insurance bills.

Don't duplicate the coverage you already have. Carefully review your homeowners' or renters' insurance policy, for example. If you have only a few relatively inexpensive pieces of business equipment, your existing property coverage may be adequate. Or, you may be able to purchase an inexpensive endorsement to increase your coverage.

Consider riders to your existing policies. Home-based businesses that have few business-related visitors can get a relatively inexpensive liability endorsement. You can also add an endorsement to increase coverage for business equipment. If you use your personal car for business and your existing auto insurance policy doesn't cover business use, you may be able to get the coverage you need through an endorsement. However, if you use a car solely for business, you'll have to buy a separate business/commercial auto policy.

Online Insurance Resources

- The **Insurance Information Institute**, www.iii.org, offers lots of free information on insurance and a glossary of common insurance terms.
- The **Federal Small Business Administration** offers a free primer on business risk and ways to transfer that risk (including insurance) at www.sba.gov. Type "business risk" into the site's search box.
- **Insure.com** offers extensive insurance information for small businesses, at http://info.insure.com/business. Be sure to check out the "Small Business Liability Tool," (under "Small Business Insurance Tools") which allows you to choose a profession, from gun shop owner to Web designer, then view common risks and recommended types of insurance.

Don't pay for more than you need. Sounds obvious, but it's a common small business mistake, according to Chad Berberich. Don't have a lot of business visitors? You might be eligible for an endorsement to your homeowners' insurance that will cover your liability issues. The same is true if you don't have much business equipment or other property. You may end up paying for a bit more coverage than you need if you purchase a BOP or other business insurance package, but the lower price of getting a package deal might be worth it. (Of course, you can always try to negotiate an even lower price for a reduced package, but you may not be successful.)

Always read the fine print. Before you write your premium check, make sure you understand exactly what you're getting for your money; your insurance pro should help you with this. Check the terms, exclusions (what isn't covered), limits, and so on. Make sure you know exactly what is covered, and to what extent. Many insurance companies place a limit on how much you can collect per item, per incident, per person, or per year—and may further break these limits down depending on what caused the loss, what type of property was damaged, and so on.

Make sure you can collect if you need to. If you need to make an insurance claim, you'll have to prove the extent of your loss. For property, you should photograph and keep records of the value of your business equipment, inventory, and so on. If you have very valuable items—for example, if you sell fine art or antiques—consider having them valued by an independent appraiser.

Keep your coverage up to date. Most experts suggest that you set aside a time once a year to consider whether you need to increase your coverage. Have you purchased property, expanded your business substantially, gotten another vehicle, expanded into a different business? These are all things you should discuss with your insurance provider, to find out whether they warrant changes to your existing policies.

Don't Count on Customers' Liability Waivers

If you're in a high-risk business (for example, you teach skydiving or run rock-climbing clinics), you might think you can shift some risk to your customers by asking them to sign liability waivers—agreements that they are responsible for their own safety and cannot sue you if they are injured. The problem is, these waivers don't always work. Because of legal rules that limit how far people can go to dodge responsibility for their own carelessness or wrongdoing, "the bottom line is that a good lawyer can break a liability waiver, indemnification, or hold-harmless agreement pretty easily," says Mike Mansel.

Your insurance pro may advise you to ask clients to sign these waivers anyway, as a first line of defense. However, if a dispute arises over who's responsible for a serious injury, you should be prepared for the possibility that a court might throw out the agreement.

Raising Money for Your Business

What's the Difference? Equity vs. Debt Financing 66

Borrowing With Credit Cards 68

Signature Loans 69

Bank Loans 70

What Motivates a Bank to Lend Money? 71

    Questions to Ask Before Seeking a Bank Loan 72

SBA Loans 73

State Lending Assistance 74

Borrowing From Family and Friends 75

Social Lending Networks 75

Angel Investing 76

    Why Do Angels Invest? 76

    How Much Do Angels Want? 77

    Watch Out for Fraudulent Angel Brokers 78

What People With Money Want to Know About Your Business 80

Venture Capital 82

Selling Stock to the Public 82

As the owner of a fledgling business, you probably need money. Maybe you've exhausted your savings and you need a few thousand dollars to cover marketing or accounting costs. Perhaps you need more, maybe five to ten thousand dollars to bridge the gap between when you will get paid and when your bills are due. Maybe you need even more than that to buy equipment or lease space.

If you're like the vast majority of small business owners, you won't get that money from your local bank or from investors. Less than 20% of business start-ups are able to fund themselves from these sources. Instead, you should expect that initially your money will come from credit cards, signature loans (small loans from large financial institutions), or family and friends. Later, after a few years in business, you may be able to tap into sources such as angel investors, bank loans, or even venture capitalists.

In this chapter, we'll give you the lowdown on borrowing money, whether from a credit card company, a wealthy uncle, or your local bank.

What's the Difference? Equity vs. Debt Financing

There are two ways to fund your business: loans (debt financing) or investments (equity financing). When someone lends you money under the terms of a loan agreement (sometimes referred to as the "note"), you are obligated to repay the amount borrowed (the principal) along with interest. Someone who invests in your enterprise, on the other hand, acquires partial ownership, usually in the form of stock in your corporation. So, in order to explore equity financing, you must have a business entity that can accommodate investment—generally, a limited liability company or corporation.

The advantage of a loan is that it is not an investment. In other words, you are not giving up any ownership in your enterprise, and the lender has no management say or direct entitlement to profits in your business. Your only obligation to the lender is to repay the loan on time, and you can deduct the interest payments at tax time.

The disadvantage of a loan is the debt—the looming monthly payments and the potential for personal liability (if you guaranteed the loan), loss of property (if you secured the loan), or a lawsuit if you default on the loan payments. In a worst-case scenario—one in which you secured the loan or guaranteed it—defaulting could result in the loss of your business, attachment of your wages, or a judgment that could be used against your property.

The advantages of equity financing are that you will not have to repay investors if your business goes under and your personal property is unlikely to be at risk. You may also get advice and guidance from those who have a vested interest in your business's success.

The disadvantage of equity financing is that you get a smaller piece of the pie because you are giving up a share of the business. And if an investor seeks to control your business, it may be more of a nuisance than a help.

The trick with either type of financing is convincing someone that your business is stable enough to merit a loan or investment. We discuss that issue in more detail below.

	DEBT FINANCING	EQUITY FINANCING
WHAT IS IT?	You borrow money from an individual or institution.	You sell an ownership interest in your business.
ADVANTAGES	You don't give up an ownership interest in your business.	You don't have to repay investors if the business fails. Investors may offer you helpful business advice.
DISADVANTAGES	You're in debt. You may face personal liability if you personally guarantee the loan and fail to pay it.	You give up a portion of your ownership interest. You may also lose some control over how your business is run.

> ### Borrowing Basics
>
> If you're unfamiliar with borrowing money, here are a few basic definitions.
>
> **Amortization** is a system for calculating the total amount due on the loan—interest and principal—as it is paid off over a period of time. You can calculate these numbers yourself by using an amortization calculator. (Type "amortization calculator" into an Internet search engine.)
>
> Some loans come with a **prepayment penalty**. This is your punishment for paying back a loan before it's due. In states where these penalties are permitted, it's often not worth paying off the loan early.
>
> If you **personally guarantee a debt**, you will have to pay if the loan goes bad. In other words, the buck doesn't stop at your business; it can stop at your home or personal bank account. If you personally guarantee a loan, having an LLC or a corporation won't protect your personal assets from creditors.
>
> A **secured loan** is one in which you pledge property as part of the loan agreement—for example, you take out a second mortgage on your house. If you fail to honor the loan agreement—for example, you miss several payments—the lender can take the secured property (collateral) and sell it to recover the amount you owe.

Borrowing With Credit Cards

Perhaps you've gotten one of those credit card offers that promise, "We can lend you enough money to get you completely out of debt." Alas, the reality is that whenever you borrow, you always go deeper into debt.

The average U.S. consumer has access to $12,190 from credit cards, so it's easy to see why half of the nation's start-ups are funded with plastic. We don't need to dwell on the downsides—you're probably already aware that credit card companies charge high interest rates and extraordinary penalties. And if you miss a payment on one card, all of your cards can raise their interest rates. You can easily get in over your head. When you take a cash advance, there are more unbearable fees and usually no grace period, which means you pay interest from the day you take the advance, even if you pay off your balance within a month. Is there any way to alleviate the negatives of credit cards? Here are a few suggestions.

When shopping for a card, be wary of teaser rates (low introductory rates that jump after a few months) and check the grace period (the number of days you're charged interest on purchases). Many companies have been shortening their grace period for purchases from 30 to 20 days. Shop around for perks—airline miles, travel discounts, or other purchasing credits. Always compare the periodic rate that will be used to calculate the finance charge. You can find rates at websites comparing current credit offers (type "credit card compare" into a search engine).

DON'T

Don't charge business expenses if your credit card balances are greater than 80% of your credit limits; you've already got a credit card problem. One other thought: Bankruptcy laws effective in October 2005 make it much harder to get rid of credit card debts even if you file for bankruptcy—particularly if your income is greater than the median income for your state.

Signature Loans

Signature loans—loans for $5,000 or less—are often available from your bank, credit card company, or from a large financial company, based on your credit rating and your history with the lender. (The name refers to the fact that you may get a loan offer in the mail or from a bank; all that is required is your signature to make it binding.) These loans are not much different than taking a cash advance with a credit card. You pay high interest rates on monthly payments, along with an assortment of fees.

Usually, if your credit history is good or you own a home, you can borrow a few thousand dollars using a signature loan without pledging collateral. However, be aware that many signature loans can create enormous personal financial risk (see "Avoid Predatory Lenders," below). Read the fine print on the loan document.

Bank Loans

The old saying about bank loans—that you can qualify for a bank loan only when you don't need it—unfortunately rings true. The more speculative your business—that is, the more it requires imagination to envision its success—the less likely you will get a loan unless you have assets beyond the amount of the loan. However, the more evidence you have pointing to your eventual success, the more likely you'll obtain the loan. But if your business is just taking off, it's going to be challenging to get a bank loan.

And if you're in a region dominated by large banks (those with more than $5 billion in assets), your chance of getting a loan drops by 25%. Why? According to one study, loan approval is often based on a personal relationship between bank officers and business owners, and unfortunately, in these days of megabank mergers, those relationships are disappearing.

Types of Bank Loans

Term loans are your typical loans, made for a period of years and requiring regular payments of principal and interest based upon an amortization schedule.

Lines of credit are loans commonly used in cash flow crunches—for example, you owe suppliers and employees but haven't received income from sales. Generally, interest on a line of credit is paid monthly, and the lender can demand the total amount of the loan at any time (this is called a "demand loan"). Sometimes the line of credit is temporary—for example, for one-time projects—and sometimes it lasts up to 36 months, after which the line of credit becomes a term loan.

Swing loans, sometimes called "bridge loans," are commonly used when businesses need money to close a deal, usually over the concurrent purchase and sale of real estate.

What Motivates a Bank to Lend Money?

Banks, like all lenders, will check out you and your business before handing you money. The decision is traditionally based on the five "C's" of credit, described below. Practically, you're much more likely to qualify if you can personally guarantee the loan or you can secure the loan with property equal to the value of the loan. You're less likely to qualify if your cash flow is erratic or the forecast for your industry is poor.

Capacity. Usually the most important factor, capacity refers to how you intend to repay the loan. The bank looks at your business's cash flow and your payment history on existing credit relationships—personal and commercial.

Collateral. The lender ideally wants collateral or "guarantees" that equal the value of the loan. Business assets (equipment, buildings, accounts receivable, and, in some cases, inventory) and personal assets can be sources of collateral.

Character. The bank's loan officer will form an opinion as to whether or not you are trustworthy and will run credit checks and background checks—for example, to determine whether you have a criminal record.

Capital. Capital refers to how much you personally have invested in the business. Banks believe that if you have a significant personal investment in the business, you are less likely to default on the loan.

Conditions. Conditions focus on the economic climate within your industry. Loans are more difficult to obtain when the forecast for your industry is grim.

CRM. The 6th "C." The five C's of credit are slowly being replaced by a mathematical standard known as credit risk modeling (CRM) that uses software to predict when a firm's assets will fall below liabilities. It looks at financial ratios and historic records of defaulting businesses and predicts—based on your finances—whether your venture will succeed or fail (and when). Though currently in use by only a few banks, you can expect that this methodology will eventually trickle down to many more loan decisions.

Questions to Ask Before Seeking a Bank Loan

Before filling out a loan application, here are a few questions to answer.

Do you understand collateral? Sometimes a loan is rejected because the person starting the business doesn't understand collateral. Collateral refers to the assets that you pledge for the repayment of a loan. These assets can be your business's accounts receivable, inventory, or business equipment, and they are used to secure the loan (versus an "unsecured" loan, which has no collateral). In the event you default on the loan, the lender can acquire and sell the collateral. If a business does not have any assets worth securing, a lender will look to personal assets—for example, stocks or bonds—or some other form of personal guarantee. A personal guarantee means that the borrower guarantees repayment from personal assets, rather than from business assets.

Are you asking for enough? One of the most common errors people make when borrowing is that they underestimate the situation and borrow less money than they should. If you borrow too little, you may have a hard time convincing the bank to loan you more.

Do you have a checkered personal credit history? For the most part, the small business owner is going to have to personally guarantee the loan, so a checkered personal history will have a negative impact, as will the amount of time the business has operated. (Businesses under two years old tend to be viewed critically.) Do you know your credit score? You can't fix it if you don't know what it is. You can learn your credit score through services such as Dun & Bradstreet (www.dnb.com) and Experian (www.experian.com).

Do your financials match up? Don't provide financial reports that were printed at 3 a.m. the night before your meeting. Proof and review any financial documents used for a loan application with an accountant or financial adviser.

Are you prepared for loan guarantees? Chances are good that someone will have to personally guarantee your loan. If you sign a guarantee, try and limit it to a one-year guarantee that can be renewed if necessary. Avoid having your spouse sign the guarantee unless he or she is active in the business. If you have friends or relatives who are willing to guarantee your business loan but they're not willing to guarantee the whole loan, it could be because the guarantee requires them to be "jointly and severally" liable, meaning they must pay the entire loan if there is a default. To avoid this result and to encourage multiple guarantors, a guarantor can sometimes simply provide collateral or security for the portion of the loan he or she is guaranteeing. So if there are three guarantors, for example, each may guarantee only one-third of the loan.

SBA Loans

If you're interested in a bank loan but you're not sure if you qualify or how to proceed, you may want to check out the Small Business Administration (SBA). The SBA does not make loans; it guarantees up to 85% of the amount you borrow from someone else in the event of default. Beware, though: Despite SBA support, lenders sometimes require collateral or guarantees from the business owner for all (or a portion) of the loan. In other words, getting an SBA-guaranteed loan is often as difficult as getting a regular bank loan. To find out more, check out the SBA website (www.sba.gov). The most helpful resource for preparing an SBA loan application is *SBA Loans: A Step-by-Step Guide*, by Patrick O'Hara (Wiley).

The SBA has several loan programs and similar services. The 7(m) microloan program provides short-term loans (due in a year or less) of up to $35,000; the average amount is $10,300. All small businesses are eligible for microloans, but it's probably easier to qualify if you are one of the businesses for which the program was created—that is, businesses run by women, minorities, or people with disabilities; or companies in economically depressed areas. Proceeds cannot be used to pay existing debts or to buy real estate.

7(m) loans are made by several hundred nonprofit microlenders who have been given grants by the federal government. Interest rates vary but are not supposed to be higher than 4% over the prime rate. Unfortunately, politics may have something to do with how the money is distributed. The four states that initially received the bulk of grants were those represented by the ranking members of congressional small business committees. To find out if there is a nonprofit lender of microloans in your area, contact your local SBA.

The 7(a) program is really an umbrella for many types of SBA loans. The average 7(a) loan is approximately $240,000. Interest can be fixed or variable—usually not more than 2.75 points above the prime rate. You can't get one of these loans if you're a nonprofit or if you're engaged in an enterprise involving creative works, such as book publisher, music distributor, movie theater, magazine publisher, or greeting card manufacturer. If you're interested in the 7(a) program, the SBA also has a loan prequalification program, which can help you analyze your loan application.

The 504 program guarantees larger loans (an average of over $300,000). These loans are usually for a business that is trying to expand and are commonly used to finance real estate or equipment purchases.

State Lending Assistance

Your state may provide small business lending assistance in several ways, including:

Business Development Centers (BDCs). Approximately 20 states offer SBA-style loan assistance to their residents. Check your state government website to find out whether your state offers BDC help.

Local development funds. Many communities offer small loans or grants to businesses in order to encourage development. Check with your city or county government.

State loans. Some states lend money directly to small businesses to encourage certain industries within the state. For example, Hawaii intends to encourage technology companies by offering loans through the Hawaii Strategic Development Corporation (HSDC). Check your state's website for more information.

Borrowing From Family and Friends

Family and friends are usually more comfortable lending money than buying an interest in your company. A loan is a straightforward matter. But ownership (often in the form of shares in your corporation) may seem abstract and risky. If you're going to borrow from family and friends (or from any individual, for that matter), make sure you do it with the appropriate formalities: Sign a promissory note, calculate interest and principal, and set up a payment schedule. If you don't, you may find yourself embroiled in money disputes over Thanksgiving dinner.

You can easily draft your own promissory note (forms are available from Nolo, the publisher of this book, as well as from other providers on the Internet). You can calculate interest and payments using amortization calculators that are easily found online.

You can also get help making a loan more businesslike from Virgin Money (www.virginmoneyus.com). Virgin Money doesn't lend money—it facilitates loans. A Virgin Money loan specialist examines your loan, helps to prepare a legally binding agreement (with secured collateral, if required), and then creates a repayment schedule. The company also manages the payment process through automatic electronic debits and credits and will send payment reminders to the borrower. Virgin Money must be doing something right: The company has managed over $200 million in loans.

Social Lending Networks

What if obtaining a business loan was as simple as posting an item on eBay? That's the goal of social lending network sites such as Prosper (www.prosper.com) and LendingClub (www.lendingclub.com). Unlike sites like Virgin Money, which facilitate loans between family and friends, social lending networks allow the business seeking money to post its needs at the site (usually up to $25,000) and then—assuming the borrower meets certain credit standards—lenders can make offers at various interest rates.

INTERNET LINK
You can find links for all the resources in this book at www.nolo .com/wowbusiness.

Angel Investing

Angel investors don't lend you money—they acquire equity in your business. (The name comes from the wealthy individuals known as "angels" who fund Broadway shows.) Angel investment—if we can demystify the terminology—merely refers to an investment from an individual, usually a stranger.

Angel investing is a hot topic on the Internet and is sometimes portrayed as a magic bullet for companies that need money. Don't be fooled. There's nothing particularly angelic about the relationship. Basically, it involves finding and convincing a wealthy individual— someone willing to take a risk—to buy a chunk of your business (but not enough to take it away from you). An angel investor usually invests close to home, insists on direct involvement in the business, and wants a high rate of return (20% to 50%). Angels are also looking for a great team in much the same way that a gambler looks at the horse, the jockey, the trainer, and the owner.

Why Do Angels Invest?

Unlike venture capital companies that must invest on behalf of their shareholders, angel investors don't have to invest. So why do they take chances on unproven businesses?

Profit is obviously one motivator. Angels understand that one out of three of their investments will fail. As for the others—the successes— they expect to cash out within seven years (often less) and they expect a minimum 25% annual return on their investments. Usually, they're hoping this will happen in one of two ways—your company will be acquired by another or will graduate to an initial public offering (IPO) in which the public is offered shares.

Excitement is the other major motivator. Angels love to participate in high-risk equity investments for the thrill of the game.

Speed Dating With Angels

Looking for a way to speed-pitch your funding request to several angel investors in a short period of time? You may want to consider the new generation of angel brokers, online companies that will help you shape your pitch (or business plan) and screen it for investors. Companies such as FundingUniverse (www.fundinguniverse.com), PlanHeaven (www.planheaven.com), FundingPost (www.fundingpost.com), and Go4Funding (www.go4funding.com) offer variations on this angel brokering theme.

At FundingUniverse, for example, the company will help you tweak your business plan and prepare a video presentation, then circulate your offer to its pool of investors. Some of these sites charge subscription fees, some offer free posting, and some, like GoBIGnetwork (www.gobignetwork.com) act as classified ad services.

Although many of these sites have reported success facilitating investments, no major media success stories have emerged from this new approach, and in a 2008 *Wall Street Journal* article, serious angel investors discounted the services.

How Much Do Angels Want?

Angels want a piece of your business—usually represented by corporate shares. On average, angel investors typically receive about 20% equity in the businesses in which they invest. The actual amount an angel pays to your company for an ownership interest depends on how your business is valued. So, if your business is valued at $100,000, an angel would, as a very general rule, expect to pay $25,000 for a 25% ownership interest.

Obviously, there are a few challenges here. One is to determine the market value of your business—a difficult task considering the speculative nature of many businesses. Another challenge is to predict what its value will be when the angel plans to cash in—for example, when the company is sold in five years.

For example, an investor who puts in $25,000 for a one-quarter interest of a business valued at $100,000 may expect to cash out in five years with a 40% per year return. For that to happen, the business would have to be worth $540,000 in five years.

If you're on a quest for angel investment, check out the books recommended below and review the material at Active Capital (formerly ACE-NET) (www.activecapital.org), one of the oldest and most well-established sites for entrepreneurs seeking private investment, and Angel Capital Association (www.angelcapitalassociation.org), an umbrella alliance of many angel groups. Click on "Directory" on the home page for a thorough listing of links to angel groups and resources throughout the U.S. Two of the best books are *Angel Financing: How to Find and Invest in Private Equity*, by Gerald Benjamin and Joel Margulis (Wiley), and *Angel Investing: Matching Start-Up Funds with Start-up Companies*, by Mark Van Osnabrugge and Robert J. Robinson (Jossey-Bass).

Watch Out for Fraudulent Angel Brokers

The popularity of angel financing has spawned a business for angel brokers, finders, or intermediaries—companies that, for a fee, find angel financing. Unfortunately, many of these brokers are scams. Watch out for brokers who charge large up-front fees. When a finder starts talking more than a few hundred dollars, you're probably wasting your money.

You should also beware of brokers who make **repackaging pitches**. These finders or brokers may want to charge you a large fee to create a business plan and other marketing materials. That's a waste of your time.

Another sign of a scam is if a finder or broker is pressuring you to act quickly; they're probably just rushing you to get their fee. And, as always, beware of dealing with anyone who cannot furnish references.

Funding: A *ReadyMade* Solution

The initial funding for *ReadyMade* magazine (www.readymademag.com) came from family and friends. But after the magazine launched and was generating a buzz, CEO and publisher Grace Hawthorne knew it was time to "jump to the next level." She explored debt financing in the form of a Small Business Administration (SBA) loan but abandoned that plan when she realized she'd have to use personal assets for collateral.

As Grace puts it, "As an entrepreneur, you're already giving up your life working on your business, and you're thinking, what else do you want me to give up?" Next, she sought equity funding from investors and large media companies, but their take was negative. "No new magazine survives after three issues," she was told.

It became apparent to Grace that *ReadyMade* was too small for the media giants to take seriously. The magazine continued to fund itself for another two years and then had the good fortune to attract the attention of a mid-sized media company that made an equity investment in the spunky magazine. The investment was especially fortuitous because the investor company didn't bring just money to *ReadyMade*, it also brought guidance and experience. "There's smart money and there's dumb money," says Grace. "Smart money brings added value to the investment because you're also getting knowledge and wisdom."

"They had built their company in a similar way and understood the value we had created," says Grace. "They said, 'We know how to do X, Y, and Z.' We didn't have that expertise or money to buy the expertise that was so important to the growth of our business." The lesson: If possible, seek financing from someone who can offer experience and guidance.

What People With Money Want to Know About Your Business

Just as you wouldn't buy a house without an inspection, investors and lenders will not open their checkbooks without performing "due diligence"—an investigation of the risks and potential value of your business. This includes:

- **Verifying facts.** Lenders and investors will want to see all supporting information and may conduct their own investigations and prepare their own financials.

- **Interviewing your managers, friends, and associates.** They may want to speak with everyone associated with the business and people with whom you have worked in the past.

- **Digging up background information about you.** A lot of personal information—including criminal records, judgments in civil lawsuits, and bad debts—is available to anyone willing to pay $50 to $100 for an Internet background check. There's little sense trying to hide any of that from potential lenders or investors.

- **Studying the competition.** Investors and lenders will study your actual and prospective competitors and examine the channel in which you compete—for example, to determine whether there may be problems with distribution.

 DON'T

Don't conceal, lie, or exaggerate about investment opportunities. Always give potential investors everything that is available for them to make a knowledgeable decision. When in doubt, disclose, disclose, disclose. There are two reasons for this: It's unethical and illegal to dupe someone into investing in your business, and falsifying investment claims violates federal and state securities laws.

For more information about securities law rules and exemptions, visit the SEC website (www.sec.gov). A quick way to research your state's exemption rules is to go to the home page of your state's securities agency, which typically posts the state's exemptions rules and procedures. To find your state securities agency, go to your secretary of state's website. If in doubt, speak with an attorney.

Avoid Predatory Lenders

Predatory lending is any unfair credit practice that harms the borrower or supports a credit system that promotes inequality and poverty. Avoiding predatory loan practices is often easier said than done. Here are tips on how to avoid getting burned:

Seek more than one opinion on your borrowing status. The most common predatory practice is to place a borrower into a higher interest rate than the credit risk calls for—for example, you qualify for a 6.5% loan but the lender charges you a 10% rate. (Studies indicate that 63% of borrowers who pay high rates would qualify for lower conventional rates.) The people who facilitate these loans often get bonuses for placing borrowers into higher rates, so there's a great incentive to act in a predatory manner. You don't have to accept the interest rate offered.

As a general rule, **a loan in which the fees exceed 5% of the loan is probably predatory** and you should avoid it, if possible. A predatory loan may include a 10% "loan origination" fee and exorbitant penalty fees if you try to pay the loan off early. (Why? If the borrower can't pay off the loan, that makes it more attractive on the secondary market—reselling loans to insurance companies, pension plans, mutual funds, and other investors.)

Don't be pressured into signing documents without reading them. Some lenders switch the terms of the loan—meaning that you sign paperwork for fees and interest rates that may differ from the initial proposal made to you.

Venture Capital

It's unlikely you'll be dealing with venture capitalists—at least not in your early stages of development. Venture capitalists (VCs) are an institutionalized version of the angel investor, except they have a lot more cash. Unlike angel investors, who invest their own money, VCs invest money acquired from financial institutions and wealthy individuals. Angels don't have to invest (they can bank their money if they wish), VCs do; their business is to earn profits for their investors. VCs are exceptionally discerning, choosing to invest in fewer than 2% of the proposals that come their way. When they do invest, it's usually because they determine there is a very experienced management team, an untapped niche, and a chance for remarkable returns. They expect a minimum return of 40% annually on their investment and won't hesitate to withdraw funding if they change their minds about the prospect of success. For more information, look at the National Venture Capital Association (www.nvca.com).

Selling Stock to the Public

An initial public offering (IPO) is the sale of stock to the public to raise cash to expand your business. The process is expensive—anywhere from $250,000 to $1 million—and it is always a gamble, because there is no assurance that the public will buy the stock that you're offering. Unlike selling stock in a small corporation, selling to the public (meaning investors whom you don't know and will probably never meet) is strictly regulated by the Securities and Exchange Commission. If you get to the lofty heights where an IPO seems doable, you will also be able to pay for the hundreds of thousands of dollars worth of professional advice needed.

Do You Need a Business Plan?

How to Create a Business Plan in 24 Hours 84

The Elements of a Business Plan 93
    Executive Summary...93
    Company Summary 93
    Products or Services...94
    Market Analysis 94
    Strategies 95
    Management Team..95
    Your Financials 95

f you expect to ask investors or banks for money, you're probably going to need a written business plan. A business plan describes your business and explains how and why it will become profitable. It contains summaries of your company, your industry, and your competitors, and it provides financial forecasts. Even if you're not seeking money, there are a couple of elements of a business plan that can benefit every company, particularly the financial forecasting tools that let you analyze your break-even point and your profits and losses.

It would be nice not to have to spend the time preparing a plan. Business guru David Gumpert feels your pain. In his book *Burn Your Business Plan* (Lauson Publishing), he argues that business plans are a bunch of mumbo jumbo with crazy projections. Moreover, he says that investors routinely disregard them because they really want to see only one thing: evidence of demand for your products and services. That said, investors and bankers still find something comforting about that stack of papers, and they routinely request business plans when you put your hand out for money. Don't worry—as with everything else in small business management, there are people and products who can simplify the business plan process.

How to Create a Business Plan in 24 Hours

If you need a plan quickly (or just want to get it over with), you can do it with some off-the-shelf help. Start by looking at business plans for companies similar to your own. There are many, many plans available online—everything from an artificial flower importing business to a wedding consultant business. The place to start is Bplans.com, where 60 sample plans created with *Business Plan Pro* software are posted. Once you've got an idea of what your plan should look like, map out your own using do-it-yourself products or by hiring a pro to help you.

If you're on a limited budget ($35 or less), buy *How to Write a Business Plan*, by Mike McKeever (Nolo), a comprehensive guide that can help you evaluate profitability, estimate operating expenses, prepare your financial forecasts, and find potential sources of financing (up-to-date sources are provided). The book includes a CD-ROM with some sample plans and fill-in spreadsheets that calculate cash flow, financial statements, sales revenue, and profit and loss.

If you have more money to spend, buy *Business Plan Pro*, business plan-creation software from Palo Alto Software ($100 or less). It contains more than 400 sample business plans and uses a question-and-answer format to get you going. The program allows you to present your plan via Microsoft *PowerPoint* and contains a database that lists over 1,200 venture capital firms.

If you have more money to spend on the project ($200 to $1,000), you may want to consider paying a freelance writer or a bookkeeper with small business experience to help you polish your plan. Business plan writing services can be found on the Internet and probably in your local yellow pages. To get an idea, type "write business plan" into your search engine.

Below is an excerpt from a business plan from a service company reprinted with permission from Mike McKeever's *How to Write a Business Plan*.

CENTRAL PERSONNEL AGENCY

By: Eleanor Buss
November 3, 20xx
Executive Summary

My sole proprietorship, Central Personnel, will specialize in providing South City employers with secretarial, clerical, and computer (word processing) skilled personnel. I am presently a junior partner in Mid-Mountain Personnel Services, a similar type of personnel agency with headquarters in North City. I manage the branch office in South City. Mid-Mountain provides me with an office in a good downtown location and a moderate salary. I like what I do and feel that helping people find work is a creative and satisfying activity.

I will be competing with my former employer, Ms. Jackie McCabe (dba Mid-Mountain Personnel Agency), to some extent, even though her headquarters is, and will remain, in North City. To minimize any hostility that could hurt business, I have kept Ms. McCabe informed of my plans. She supports them, has agreed to allow me to take over the lease on the South City Office, and is enthusiastic about working out a referral plan under which we will work cooperatively when we are dealing with employers located in each other's prime geographical area.

My best estimate of sales revenue and cash flow (both of which are spelled out in detail in this plan) shows that even using conservative estimates, I will earn a significant profit once my new business has been underway six months. My background experience in the personnel agency field and past record of success support my view that I will succeed. I am eager to begin.

Experience and Background

As my resume sets out in detail, since 19xx I have worked for three different employment agencies in this area, successfully finding jobs for many people. This has given me the opportunity to learn the personnel agency business thoroughly, including how to find employers needing workers and how to locate and screen desirable employees.

During the years I was acquiring this valuable experience, I always planned to open my own business. Last year, in the hope of achieving this goal, I formed a partnership with Ms. Jackie McCabe, who has operated Mid-Mountain Personnel Service in North City for several years. As a junior partner, my responsibility was to open a South City branch office, which I did. My goals were to increase my income and to have more control over business decisions than I had as an employee. While the personal relationship between Ms. McCabe and myself is cordial, the partnership has not worked to our mutual satisfaction. This has been largely because Jackie's main office in North City has grown so fast it has consumed all of her energy. This has left me operating the South City branch largely by myself, at the same time that a substantial portion of the profits I have generated go to Jackie under the terms of our partnership agreement.

As part of terminating our partnership agreement, Jackie and I have agreed that I will retain the lease on the present Mid-Mountain office in South City. In addition, we have signed a written agreement (available upon request) which provides that we will share all fees and commissions when one of us places an employee with an employer in the other's primary market area. Having made this agreement, I need accomplish only two more tasks before I can open my business. The first is to take and pass the state personnel agency license examination. I expect to do this in January with little difficulty, as I have received top grades in the preparatory course given by North State Community College. My other task involves the purpose of this proposal. I need to borrow enough money to begin business.

Company Summary

Central Personnel will specialize in secretarial, clerical, word processing, and computer operator jobs, a field in which there is constant turnover. I will also provide services for technical and mid-management jobs, but expect it to take several years before these latter areas provide a substantial portion of my income.

My particular specialty will be women reentering the workforce after completing family-raising responsibilities. In this connection, I have developed a successful liaison with the South City Women's Resource Center. This group, which is partially funded by grants from local businesses, provides training, seminars, and counseling for reentry women and will provide me with a source of many highly motivated potential employees.

Because of my two-year history in the personnel business in South City, I have placed many employees and expect that the already-developing trend in which much of my business comes from repeats and referrals will continue. Also, in cooperation with the Women's Resource Center, I shall continue to provide detailed counseling to applicants (especially those who have been out of the labor market for several years or more) on how to compose resumes and take interviews, as well as on which jobs to seek. In addition, I plan to work closely with employers to assist them in determining what type of employee they need, how much they should pay, etc. I want employers to feel that my prescreening is honest and thorough and that by dealing with me, they can save time by not having to interview clearly unsuitable candidates.

Market Strategies

The secret to success in the personnel business in South City is finding high quality employee applicants. Because of the relatively rapid turnover among clerical employees, and because the South City economy is expanding, it is relatively easy to place highly motivated employees with good skills once they have been identified. Because of my prior two years in this business and this area, many of my initial candidates will come from repeats and referrals from people I have placed. Others will be referred as part of my work with the Women's Resource Center.

In my experience, there are several other effective marketing techniques to develop a wider community base. Classified advertising of job openings develops many prospective employees. Also, maintaining an active presence in the Chamber of Commerce and other traditional business and civic organizations enables prospective employers to recognize me as a person of integrity and stability. In addition, as discussed above, I shall continue to expand by association with the South City Women's Resource Center, a group that counsels women reentering the labor force. I also intend to provide free seminars of my own on "How to Find a Satisfying Job." Finally, I will regularly mail a brief newsletter to all major area employers listing all the job areas for which I have qualified applicants.

Competition

South City has three active personnel agencies in addition to the branch of Mid-Mountain, which I now run and which will close as part of the opening of my new business.

Bill's Personnel Services: This is the oldest and largest in the city. Recently, Bill's has suffered from its own high employee turnover, largely because it is run by an absentee owner. Bill's traditionally advertises heavily and depends on aggressive pricing policies to compete. They provide little employee counseling and, in my opinion, do not screen potential employees with sufficient thoroughness. At Mid-Mountain, I have already demonstrated that my personal approach to the needs of both employers and employees as opposed to Bill's high-volume approach is welcomed by the South City marketplace.

Strictly Business: This firm was recently acquired by an experienced professional counselor who heads a staff of three good counselors. Its primary emphasis is on technical management people and it handles clerical and computer operator jobs only as a sideline. Eventually, Strictly Business will be a competitor as I develop more mid-level management clients, but initially, they will not be a problem as our markets are so different.

The Woodshaft Organization: This agency has a staff of three and is directly competitive. Woodshaft spends about $1,000 per month on advertising, but does little work with community organizations such as the South City Women's Resource Center. The owner's husband died recently and as an understandable result, the business seems to lack energy. I believe that the Woodshaft Organization will offer the most competition over the next several years. However, because of the expanded South City job market, my own proven track record at Mid-Mountain, and my commitment to hard, creative work, I feel there is plenty of room for my new enterprise to prosper.

Market Growth

South City has a large number of the type of jobs I specialize in, with plenty of growth potential. Most of the other agencies are more interested in technical job categories. South City's growth as a regional financial and market center will ensure commensurate growth in job openings and should encourage the trend for women to reenter the job market. My approach to counseling both employers and employees is unique locally and I expect a continuing growth from my commitment to individual service, because this approach saves everyone time and expense in the long run.

My new downtown location (the office I will take over from Mid-Mountain) is already established, convenient, and close to the Women's Resource Center, with which I work closely.

Financial Projections

The key to the prosperity of Central Personnel Agency lies in quickly getting the business into the black and then building on that initial success.

The profit and loss and cash flow forecasts in this section show a significant profit and positive cash flow from the beginning of operations. These results depend on my ability to generate revenue at the rate of $4,000 per month for the first two months and $5,000 for each month thereafter. I have no doubt about my ability to do this based on the job orders already on the books. This is because I have most of the employee applications necessary to fill these jobs on file and know how to locate the rest. And even if my revenue forecasts for the first two months are off by as much as $1,500 per month (37.5%), I will still be able to pay business expenses, service loans, and cover my basic living expenses.

Profit and Loss and Cash Flow Forecasts

Most items of equipment will be leased or rented, so there will be little need for capital beyond working capital and some fees and printing costs:

Printing/stationery	$500
Initial advertising	1,000
License application fee	250
Employment agency license fees	250
Business license	50
Insurance deposit	50
First and last months' rent and deposit	1,030
Phone installation	200
New furniture	500
Working capital	2,000
Total Capital	$5,830

Other capital items and most of the furniture have already been paid for. The office building provides a receptionist and copy service as part of the rent.

CENTRAL PERSONNEL AGENCY: PROFIT AND LOSS FORECAST—YEAR ONE

	MAR	APR	MAY	JUN	JUL	AUG	SEPT	OCT	NOV	DEC	JAN	FEB	YEAR TOTAL
1. PLACEMENT REVENUE	4,000	4,000	5,000	5,000	5,000	5,000	5,000	5,000	5,000	5,000	5,000	5,000	58,000
2. FIXED EXPENSES	—	—	—	—	—	—	—	—	—	—	—	—	—
A. RENT	515	515	515	515	515	515	515	515	515	515	515	515	6,180
B. ADVERTISING	300	300	300	300	300	300	300	300	300	300	300	300	3,600
C. TELEPHONE	30	30	30	30	30	30	30	30	30	30	30	30	360
D. SUPPLIES/POSTAGE	10	10	10	10	10	10	10	10	10	10	10	10	120
E. INTEREST	150	150	150	150	150	150	150	150	150	150	150	150	1,800
F. TRAVEL/ ENTERTAINMENT	50	50	50	50	50	50	50	50	50	50	50	50	600
TOTAL EXPENSES	1,055	1,055	1,055	1,055	1,055	1,055	1,055	1,055	1,055	1,055	1,055	1,055	12,660
3. PROFIT BEFORE TAXES	2,945	2,945	3,945	3,945	3,945	3,945	3,945	3,945	3,945	3,945	3,945	3,945	45,340

CENTRAL PERSONNEL AGENCY: CASH FLOW FORECAST—YEAR ONE

	PRE-OPENING	MAR	APR	MAY	JUN	JUL	AUG	SEPT	OCT	NOV	DEC	JAN	FEB	YEAR TOTAL
1. USES OF MONEY														
A. LICENSES/DEPOSITS	1,100	—	—	—	—	—	—	—	—	—	—	—	—	1,100
B. WORKING CAPITAL	2,000	—	—	—	—	—	—	—	—	—	—	—	—	2,000
C. FIXED EXPENSES	1,500	1,055	1,055	1,055	1,055	1,055	1,055	1,055	1,055	1,055	1,055	1,055	1,055	14,610
D. PRINCIPAL REPAYMENT	0	50	50	50	50	50	50	50	50	50	50	50	50	600
E. FURNITURE/ TELEPHONE	700	—	—	—	—	—	—	—	—	—	—	—	—	700
F. OWNER'S DRAW	700	1,200	1,200	1,200	1,200	1,200	1,200	1,200	1,200	1,200	1,200	1,200	1,200	15,100
2. TOTAL USES	6,000	2,305	2,305	2,305	2,305	2,305	2,305	2,305	2,305	2,305	2,305	2,305	2,305	33,660
3. SOURCES OF MONEY														
A. LOAN	6,000	—	—	—	—	—	—	—	—	—	—	—	—	6,000
B. REVENUE	—	4,000	4,000	5,000	5,000	5,000	5,000	5,000	5,000	5,000	5,000	5,000	5,000	58,000
4. TOTAL SOURCES	6,000	4,000	4,000	5,000	5,000	5,000	5,000	5,000	5,000	5,000	5,000	5,000	5,000	64,000
5. NET CASH (LINE 4 – LINE 2)	0	1,695	1,695	2,695	2,695	2,695	2,695	2,695	2,695	2,695	2,695	2,695	2,695	30,340

The Elements of a Business Plan

The purpose of a plan is to sell your business, so first impressions matter. If your plan does not look and read like others—that is, it doesn't include the typical headings and subject matter—the reader will presume that something is lacking. Here are the elements of a typical plan.

Executive Summary

The executive summary summarizes the plan—and is often the only part read by busy investors. It includes an introduction to your business, your objectives, and your mission. What's your mission? It's the main purpose for which your company exists—for example, to provide the finest quality knitwear at the best prices, or to provide access to the law for all people. Here's the mission statement for a fictitious business, FlightTime Audio, that sells recordings of vintage airplanes:

> Our goal at FlightTime Audio is to create the highest quality, most accurate recordings of modern and vintage airplanes, as well as related sound effects. In doing so, we hope to both preserve the audio aviation experience and to provide a realistic standard by which all aviation recordings are made.

Company Summary

The company summary describes the ownership and history of your business and describes its facilities and location. If you are a start-up that has not yet opened its doors, include a summary of your start-up activities and expenses. Here's where you get a chance to tell the story of how you became a businessperson. Below is an example:

> I started FlightTime in 2005 with approximately $4,000 worth of recording equipment. Over the first year, I invested another $3,000 to pay for the manufacture of FlightTime's first two releases, "Sounds of the Piper J-C" and "Sounds of the Australian Tiger Moth."

I was pleasantly surprised when both products sold out their initial pressings and have since sold over 5,000 units each. Currently, FlightTime offers 35 recordings, and our particular specialty—vintage biplanes—affords us an excellent niche and an easily targetable market. Currently our biggest sellers are "Sounds of the Curtiss Robin," "Sounds of the Stearman," and "Sounds of the Piper J-2," the latter of which was licensed for use in the motion picture "Sahara."

In 2005, FlightTime's gross revenues were $189,000, of which $101,000 was profit. As explained below, I expect profits for the coming year to exceed $250,000. In 2006, my wife became a full-time employee of Flight-Time, managing the manufacturing and sales side of the business. I will now focus solely on creating new recordings.

Products or Services

Next, describe whatever it is you're selling and explain the technology, source, or origin of your products or services. Also set out ideas you may have for the prospects of these products or services.

Market Analysis

In the market analysis, you analyze your industry and explain current business conditions—for example, if you sell cell phone accessories, you would note that the market for these items has been increasing for the past three years. You also need to name, describe, and differentiate yourself from competitors. This section may prove challenging—for example, you may have to describe patterns of distribution or selling or other unique factors for your industry. Don't worry if you are unclear about your particular industry. Business plan tools (including sites such as www.bplans.com) can help you research your industry.

Strategies

Here you can expound on your strategies for success—for example, what gives your business a competitive edge. You may need to discuss the aspects of your pricing, promotion, sales, and distribution that will put you ahead of competitors—that is, your basic strategy for reaching more customers and fending off competitors.

Management Team

This section of your business plan is basically a résumé, setting forth your business accomplishments and those of anyone who's working with you. Here's an example:

> As my résumé sets out in detail, below, my employment history as a cargo pilot, and later as a recording engineer, made me ideally suited to create and run FlightTime Audio. My flying experience—particularly my years working for UPS—allowed me to meet many pilots and learn a great deal about modern and vintage planes. My experience as a recording engineer, particularly my experience recording live performances, taught me the basics of microphone technique and recording technology.
>
> My wife, Doris, who now manages manufacturing and sales, previously worked as a manufacturing liaison for Hewlett Packard, overseeing Asian production of scanners and printers. She has a business degree from Greenlaw University in Chicago. Prior to working for HP, Doris was an accountant for a chain of laundries. Doris brings much-needed business knowledge to the business and allows me the freedom to concentrate on creating new recordings.

Your Financials

Ah, the guts of your plan! Here you provide your best estimates of start-up costs, revenues and expenses, and your estimate of profitability. These financial projections will tell you the cost of your products or services, the amount of sales revenue, and profit you can anticipate. If your business is not already off the ground, it will explain how much you'll have to invest or borrow.

We explain how financial forecasting works and how forecasts are prepared in Chapter 2. As we explain there, financial forecasting is a matter of making educated guesses as to how much money you'll take in and how much you'll need to spend—and then using these estimates to calculate whether your business will be profitable. Most business plans include a break-even analysis, a profit and loss forecast, and a cash flow projection

Both of the resources mentioned earlier—*Business Plan Pro* and Mike McKeever's *How to Write a Business Plan*, can simplify this procedure. McKeever's book comes with a CD-ROM with spreadsheet templates. With both products, you enter the numbers and the software calculates the results. (With *How to Write a Business Plan*, you will need to own a copy of Microsoft *Excel*.) You'll need to determine and add in details such as whether you will be making credit sales and how much time is granted—for example, you grant 90 days to pay a bill (net 90) on your invoices. That helps determine when you can expect payments.

 DON'T

Don't play with your numbers to create a rosier picture for investors. Not only is it unethical, it can result in a lawsuit (and the end of your business) if you intentionally mislead investors with doctored financials. Also, always suggest that potential investors check with their own financial and legal advisers to evaluate the investment. Although different investors are comfortable with different degrees of risk, you should disclose all the relevant information to them so they can make informed choices.

Getting Paid

Invoiced Accounts 98

Checks..100

Credit Cards..100
    Going Online With Credit Cards...101
    Credit Card Fraud 101

Collections...102
    Get Busy and Stay at It...103
    Read About Collections...103
    Don't Harass Creditors...103
    Be Direct and Listen 103
    Look for Creative Solutions...103
    Write Demand Letters..104
    Deal With Excuses...104
    Offer a One-Time Deep Discount...104
    Turn the Account Over to a Collection Agency....................................105
    Consider a Lawsuit..105
    International Sales...106

ometimes the biggest challenge for a small business owner comes in the final stages of a transaction—when the customer must give you the money. If there's a problem or delay in the payment, then your business has to devote time and energy to correcting the situation. You may have to delay payments to suppliers, contractors, and to yourself.

You didn't go into business to manage billing, chase customers, or pursue insolvent clients. In fact, it's a little embarrassing to have to call someone and try to collect a debt. What's a small business owner to do?

Get over it.

As Carol Frischer says in *Collections Made Easy* (Career Press), the debtor is the one who should be embarrassed, not you. "Shame on the person who puts you in the position of having to ask for your money."

Getting paid is part of doing business, and you'll have to master the details. Fortunately, with a little preparation, you can minimize late payments, bounced checks, and credit card fraud, and develop the business radar that lets you know when an account is headed for collections.

Keep in mind that most of the problems related to payment are solved by effective communication. In a sense, getting paid is actually an element of your marketing. If you can work with financially troubled clients as they make their way through a rough patch, you may end up with devoted customers for life.

Invoiced Accounts

If you're a professional service provider—for example, a lawyer or an accountant—or you sell products to a wholesaler (a company that places your goods in retail accounts), then you probably invoice your customers. An invoice is a bill that sets the terms for payment. Most invoices require payment within 30, 60, or 90 days.

When you invoice a customer, your business is extending credit. You may not feel like you're extending credit—after all, you're just waiting for payment—but from a legal perspective, you're making an unsecured loan. (A secured loan is one which the borrower would pledge property as a collateral for the loan.) The problem with unsecured loans is that they're … unsecured. If the business doesn't have the money, it won't do any good to sue, because there will be nothing to recover. If the business goes bankrupt, you're out of luck.

Most of the time, extending credit isn't risky. If you do have doubts about a new customer, you can check on creditworthiness by having them complete a credit reference form (and checking the results). A good credit reference form should require information about who is in charge of the business, who to contact when problems develop, how much credit the applicant is seeking, other firms with which the company has done business on credit, and any other financial information required for making your decision. If it's a big account and you're investing a lot of resources in it, it may be worth it to pay for credit research from a company such as Dun & Bradstreet (www.dnb.com), BusinessCreditUSA (www.businesscreditusa.com), or Equifax (www.equifax.com).

When you get the information back, how do you tell whether the customer is a credit risk? That will be a personal call based on the size of the business and its history. Collections expert Timothy Paulsen suggests separating patterns from single events. If a customer has one or two minor credit blemishes—perhaps the result of an unexpected growth spurt—that should not necessarily be the basis of denying credit. That is different from evidence that indicates the client or customer just doesn't like to pay bills.

The greatest risk in extending credit is when you throw all of your business to one big account. The obvious problem with that strategy is that you're at risk of losing a lot of money if the big account has financial problems or goes bankrupt. For that reason, don't ditch your smaller accounts because of large orders from one customer. Loyal smaller accounts give a business a constant, reliable source of income.

When you write your invoice, provide an accurate, clear statement of the transaction and request that the customer contact you if there are problems. That request may make it harder for a slow-paying account to later excuse its delinquent behavior.

Got Cash?

Outside of a bank wire transfer, cash is probably the most reliable way to get paid. Worried about counterfeit bills? No need. According to the Department of the Treasury, only nine out of every million bills are counterfeit.

Checks

You're probably aware of the typical precautions to avoid bounced checks, but since 450 million rubber checks appear each year, we'll remind you anyway. Don't take checks without seeing some ID; if the check lacks the person's name; if the check is postdated; or if it is a two-party check (a check written by someone other than your prospective buyer).

DON'T
Don't accept a check for less than the full amount owed that says "Payment in Full." In some states, if you deposit the check, especially if the amount owed is in dispute, you may have wiped out the balance owing.

Credit Cards

If you're operating a brick-and-mortar business (not online) and want to accept credit cards, you'll need to establish a merchant account, set up through a bank associated with a credit card processing company. The latter handles the actual credit card orders. You must pay application fees, which can range from $200 to $600.

The percentage you have to pay Visa or MasterCard (usually 2% to 3% of sales)—depends on your expected sales revenue and the bank. Although the percentage takes a cut from your revenue, there's an upside to it—payments by credit cards don't require collections or a credit check. Because banks may reject your merchant application if it seems suspicious (you're estimating way-high sales revenue), it's wise to estimate conservatively. Expect bank approval to take one to two months.

Going Online With Credit Cards

If you're taking credit card orders online, you'll need an e-commerce provider who manages your shopping cart and credit card acceptance. The credit card processing is handled by the provider's credit card transaction clearinghouse, a company that collects money from a customer and then pays the credit card companies their percentage of the sales. The balance is then deposited into your bank account within three days. For more about setting up credit card payments online, see Chapter 18.

Credit Card Fraud

What happens when you're defrauded with a credit card? In bank lingo, it's called a chargeback. The bank that issued the card instructs your bank to take the disputed payment out of your account.

In the real (offline) world, it's much easier to avoid chargebacks and credit card fraud because the person must show you the card. You have an opportunity to judge the customer's demeanor and (in most states) to verify with identification, that the customer and card owner are one and the same. If in doubt, you can call the issuing bank and check that the credit card is in good standing.

For online retailers, there's good news and bad news. The bad news is that chargebacks are nine times more frequent in online transactions than in traditional store transactions.

The good news is that your credit card transaction clearinghouse may have fraud prevention systems that can flag risky transactions—for example, they may use Card Identification Codes, the three- or four-digit numbers that are printed on the back of the credit card in addition to the 16-digit embossed number. Ask your e-commerce provider or credit card transaction clearinghouse about its antifraud protection.

DON'T

If you're a wholesaler selling to a large retailer, don't be swayed by promise-you-anything orders. Large retail customers may make sweetheart offers to get your merchandise under a net 30 or 60 arrangement. That's because the store may have an "asset-based" loan with its bank. Under this arrangement, the more merchandise in the store, the more money the store can borrow. Don't play into a failing store's problems by extending credit when you have doubts.

Collections

Late-paying customers usually fall into three categories:

- customers who want to pay but, because of real financial problems, can't do it on time
- customers who prefer to delay or juggle payments, and
- customers who will do whatever possible to avoid any payment.

For the first two categories, there is hope. You may be able to manage these debts and to convince the debtors to make partial or full payment. This is especially true if you have encouraged customer loyalty and your customers sincerely want to support you. As for the last category, you need to recognize this type as quickly as possible and take serious action—perhaps turning the account over to a collections agency.

Most professional bill collectors agree that payment problems are solved by effective communication. Sometimes getting paid can even be viewed as an element of your marketing. If you can work with financially troubled clients as they make their way through a rough patch, you may end up with devoted customers for life.

Here are some suggestions for managing your collections.

Get Busy and Stay at It

According to a survey by the Commercial Collection Agency Association (www.ccascollect.com), after only three months, the probability of collecting a delinquent account drops to 73%. After six months, it's down to 57%. After one year, the chance of ever collecting on a past due account is a dismal 29%. Send bills promptly and rebill monthly. There's no need to wait for the end of the month. Send past due notices promptly once an account is overdue.

Read About Collections

Debt collectors can offer helpful tips and you can learn many of them by reading either *Collections Made Easy*, by Carol Frischer (Career Press), or *Paid in Full*, by Timothy R. Paulsen (Advantage), both of which are friendly, succinct, and helpful.

Don't Harass Creditors

It's rarely a successful strategy and it's sometimes illegal. If a customer asks that you stop calling, then stop calling. If a customer asks you to call at another time, find out the right time to call, and call then. Don't leave more than one phone message a day for a debtor, and never leave messages that threaten the debtor or contain statements that put the debtor in a bad light.

Be Direct and Listen

Keep your calls short and be specific. Listen to what the debtor says and keep a log of all of your collections phone calls.

Look for Creative Solutions

If the customer has genuine financial problems, ask what amount they can realistically afford. Consider extending the time for payment if the customer agrees in writing to a new payment schedule. Consider entering into a simple promissory note with the debtor that details the new payment schedule. Call the day before the next scheduled payment is due to be sure the customer plans to respect the agreement.

Write Demand Letters

Along with phone calls, send a series of letters that escalate in intensity. You can find sample collection letters (sometimes referred to as "demand letters") online. Save copies of all correspondence with the customer and keep notes of all telephone conversations (in case you hand the matter over to collections or take the customer to court). You can also pay a collection agency a fixed fee to write a series of letters on your behalf. Take note: This is different than turning over the debt to an agency—for example, Dun & Bradstreet Small Business Solutions (http://smallbusiness.dnb.com) will write a series of three letters for $25.

Deal With Excuses

How can you tell if the customer is simply delinquent with a payment or whether the delinquency is a precursor of bigger financial problems? That is, how can you sift through the excuses given by a debtor without a lie detector? Carol Frischer considers excuses like a puzzle. You must solve each one and then stay a few steps ahead of the next one. If you're given an excuse—the person writing checks is sick this week—then you must determine whether it is true or not. If it turns out not to be true—that is, another excuse arrives the following week—then you should become less tolerant and more aggressive. Always maintain your sense of urgency. For example, if the company is "expecting a big check next week," insist on a partial payment this week and the remainder when the big check arrives.

Offer a One-Time Deep Discount

If an account is fairly large and remains unpaid for an extended period (say six months) and you're doubtful about ever collecting, consider offering in writing a time-limited, deep discount to resolve the matter. This way, the customer has the incentive to borrow money to take advantage of your one-time, never-again offer to settle. You can finalize this with a mutual release and settlement, a legal document that terminates the debt. You can find such forms at Nolo's website (www.nolo.com).

Turn the Account Over to a Collection Agency

Turning a debt over to collections is your last resort. A collection agency will usually pay you 50% (or less) of what it recovers. Of course, in some cases, half is better than nothing. You're likely to want the help of collection agency when the customer lies to you about the transaction or becomes a serial promise-breaker, assuring you on various occasions that payment is on the way, when it isn't. Dun & Bradstreet Small Business Solutions (http://smallbusiness.dnb.com) and other companies offer debt collection services. The Commercial Collection Agency Association (www.ccascollect.com) provides more information on collection agencies.

Consider a Lawsuit

You can also take the debtor to court. Small claims court is inexpensive, though it can take a good chunk of your time. Furthermore, any judgment that you receive may be worthless if the debtor lacks a job or bank account. For an excellent guide to using small claims court and collecting after you win, see *Everybody's Guide to Small Claims Court*, by Ralph Warner (Nolo). You can hire a lawyer for larger debts (say, over $5,000). But beware of filing a lawsuit to chase a debt; your legal fees may exceed the amount owed.

If a Customer Goes Bankrupt

The worse your customer's financial condition, the harder it is to recover any money. When a customer declares bankruptcy, you've got a big problem. A bankruptcy will effectively wipe out your debt unless you're a secured creditor (the customer promised some property to secure your debt). Pursuing a creditor into bankruptcy is often not worth the effort.

Competitors for Collections

If you're constantly stuck with small debts that aren't worth sending out to collections, why not get your competitors to collect the money? A Canadian company devised a system in which video stores work cooperatively to recover small bad debts. Here's how it works. The company maintains a centralized database into which all members report their deadbeat customers. If a customer owes a $25 charge to the Video Shack, the owner enters that debt into the system's database. If that same customer tries to open a rental account at Video-A-Go-Go, that retailer, finding the debt in the database, won't open an account until the debt is paid. Video-A-Go-Go keeps 25% of the recovered sum, the collection company gets 25%, and 50% goes back to the Video Shack.

International Sales

If you're selling outside the U.S., here are two tips: Get the payment up front, and get the payment up front. You don't have the ability to chase down rubles, drachmas, or pesos in a faraway land. These payments can be made by credit card, bank transfers, or bank letters of credit. To avoid confusion about currency conversion, keep your dealings in U.S. dollars. For more information on exporting goods, check out the U.S. Trade Information Center (www.trade.gov/td/tic).

 **INTERNET LINK**

You can find links for all the resources in this book at www.nolo.com/wowbusiness.

Hiring Help

What's the Difference? Employee vs. Independent Contractor 109

    Advantages and Disadvantages 111

Should You Hire an IC or an Employee? 113

Finding the Right Person 116

Legal and Paperwork Requirements: ICs 119

Legal and Paperwork Requirements: Employees 120

When you're hiring someone to work for your business, you have two basic options: You can hire an independent contractor (IC), sometimes known as a consultant or freelancer, or you can hire a full-fledged employee. This is an important decision for a variety of reasons. It affects your tax and legal obligations, the way you run your business, and your profitability. This chapter explains the rules.

Once you've decided which type of worker you want, you'll have to decide on someone and deal with tax forms and other paperwork requirements. This chapter will help you navigate the hiring process efficiently.

Take Care When Hiring Family or Friends

As a general rule, if you're trying to find the right person for the job, be cautious about hiring friends or family members who don't really fit the bill. Many of the business owners we spoke to had a sad tale to tell about hiring a friend or family member, only to find that their new worker—while pleasant enough in a social context—was never going to be a serious competitor for employee of the month. I learned this the hard way.

In 1995, I began playing bass with a San Francisco band that had just completed its major-label debut. The job, which lasted two years and included two trips to Europe, ended during a recording session when the leader took me aside and told me I was fired. I was stunned and pretty pissed off. The bandleader was my wife.

It wasn't that I was a poor musician—in fact, she hired me back the following week as her guitar player. It's just that I wasn't suited to playing bass. The moral of the story is pretty obvious: Don't hire anyone—especially someone whom you know and will have a hard time firing—unless you're confident he or she will do the job well. —Rich Stim

What's the Difference?
Employee vs. Independent Contractor

An independent contractor (IC) is a person who generally provides specialized services on a per-project basis for a number of businesses. Some common examples of ICs include plumbers, architects, bookkeepers, and piano tuners. You hire an IC to provide a service, usually one that requires a certain level of skill, experience, and sometimes licensing. You can hire an IC on an ongoing basis—for example, to maintain your website periodically or to do your accounting each year. ICs also work by the job—for example, to remodel a home office or help a business launch a product line.

An employee, on the other hand, is not running his or her own business. An employee follows the rules you set and meets the standards you require, often at your workplace. You can exercise a lot more control over an employee, from setting work hours to imposing a dress code to dictating exactly how the employee does every aspect of the job. Although you can hire an employee for a short-term project (such as helping you with a seasonal mailing crunch or gift-wrapping items during a holiday rush), it's more common to hire employees on an open-ended basis, until the work runs out or the employee quits or doesn't meet your expectations.

Sometimes there are gray areas where it's tough to tell how a worker should be classified, but it's usually pretty straightforward: If you're hiring someone who runs his or her own business, you're probably hiring an IC. If you're hiring someone to work for your business, subject to your control and your standards, you're probably hiring an employee.

There are plenty of ways you can get caught if you misclassify a worker. For example, if someone you hired as an IC applies for unemployment, your state's unemployment insurance agency might decide that the worker was really an employee—and is entitled to unemployment compensation. Something similar might happen with your state's workers' compensation board or tax agency.

However, the agency you need to be most concerned about is the IRS—both because it imposes hefty penalties for misclassification and because it will have more contact with your business (and more opportunities to look closely at how you classify your workers). The IRS test considers workers employees if the company they work for has the right to direct and control the way they work—including the details of when, where, and how the job is accomplished. In contrast, the IRS considers workers independent contractors if the company they work for does not manage how they work, except to accept or reject their final results.

DON'T

Don't treat workers as ICs if they are really employees. If you're attempting to avoid taxes and legal requirements, there are a number of government agencies that might call your bluff (no government agency is ever going to tell you that you should have classified an employee as an independent contractor). Even a mighty company like Microsoft has made—and paid for—this mistake. The company hired a pool of freelancers, who signed agreements stating that they were contractors and so were not entitled to employee benefits. The IRS disagreed, finding that the workers were actually employees, not independent businesspeople. The company had to pay taxes, penalties, and overtime pay. Then, several workers sued Microsoft for employee benefits. As a result, the software giant had to pay a small fortune to the misclassified workers. (*Vizcaino v. Microsoft Corp.*, 120 F.3d 1006 (9th Cir. 1997).)

If you're curious about how the IRS makes its consideration, here are some factors that they use.

FACTORS THE IRS CONSIDERS	
FACTORS THAT MAKE A WORKER LOOK LIKE AN IC	**FACTORS THAT MAKE A WORKER LOOK LIKE AN EMPLOYEE**
Worker can earn a profit or suffer a loss from the activity.	Worker is paid for his or her time, regardless of how well or poorly the hiring company is doing.
Worker furnishes the tools and materials needed to do the work.	Worker receives tools and materials from the hiring business.
Worker is paid by the job.	Worker is paid by the hour.
Worker decides how to do the work.	Worker receives instructions and training on how to do the work.
Worker decides when and where to work.	Worker has set hours, usually at the hiring company's place of business.
Worker hires and pays any assistants.	Worker's assistants (if any) are provided and paid for by the hiring company.
Worker pays for business and travel expenses.	Worker's job-related expenses are paid by the hiring company.
Worker works for more than one business at a time.	Worker provides services to only one business.
Worker does not receive employee benefits from hiring company.	Worker receives employee benefits from hiring company.
Worker can be terminated only for reasons specified in contract.	Worker can quit or be fired at any time.
Worker provides services that fall outside of the hiring company's usual operations.	Worker provides services that are an integral part of the hiring company's regular operations.

Advantages and Disadvantages

Your circumstances and the type of work you need done will largely determine what type of worker you should hire. (See "Should You Hire an IC or an Employee?" below, for factors to consider.) However, there are some general advantages and disadvantages of using each type of worker that apply pretty much across the board.

Advantages of hiring an IC. The advantages of hiring an IC all flow from the fact that the IC is an independent businessperson. Unlike an employee, who may need training and guidance from you, an IC is likely to have enough experience to jump right into a difficult project—which is especially advantageous if you don't know much about what you want the worker to do—for example, if you hire an electrician to wire your garage for use as a home office or you pay a Web designer to create a website where you can sell your ceramic dishware. Because ICs usually work on a project basis, you don't have to worry about finding work for them or laying them off; once the project for which you hired them is complete, they're gone. You won't have to worry about all of the laws that apply to employers, from overtime to rest breaks to antidiscrimination rules to providing time off. And, because you don't have to chip in for an IC's Social Security and Medicare taxes (or pay the other expenses of hiring an employee, such as providing tools, supplies, and a place to work), you'll probably save money by hiring ICs, even if you have to pay them a higher rate than you'd have to pay an employee.

Advantages of hiring an employee. The advantages of hiring an employee flow from the employee's status as your worker. You can exercise as much control as you want over your employees, within pretty broad limits. Unlike an IC, who will do the job as he or she sees fit (and may be juggling your project with a number of other commitments), you can tell employees exactly how, when, and where you want them to do their work. You are also getting a certain amount of consistency in your workforce. Of course, employees can always quit, but generally, they'll be on the job from day to day, unlike ICs who leave once they finish a project. And, if you're hiring someone to do creative work for you—design a logo, invent something, or take photographs, for example—you will automatically own anything an employee creates. This is not the case with ICs, who will own the rights to whatever they create unless they sign them over to you in writing.

Should You Hire an IC or an Employee?

There isn't a one-size-fits-all answer to the question of whether you should hire an IC or an employee—it depends on a lot of factors, including the type of business you run, the kind of work you need done, your cash flow, and your comfort level in dealing with paperwork. Here are some things to consider when you're deciding what type of worker to hire.

Does the work you need done require specialized knowledge, experience, or licensing? If so, an IC will probably be the better choice. Unlike an employee, whom you may have to train, an IC will be ready to go on day one—and will have the skill and background to do the job right. Of course, it's possible to find highly skilled and experienced employees, but they are more likely to be looking for long-term work; you stand a better chance of finding an independent businessperson who is willing to jump into a complicated short-term project. Because most ICs are paid by the project (unlike employees, who generally are paid for their time), ICs also have a stronger incentive to finish the work quickly.

How long will the work last? If you have a specific project or task you need done (for example, a one-time electrical job or help designing your packaging), you'll probably want to go with an IC. If you hire an employee to do a discrete project, you'll either have to find other work for that person or lay him or her off when the job is done.

Are you hiring someone to do creative work for you—artwork, inventing, or design, for example? If so, you'll automatically own the work an employee creates while on your payroll. An IC, in contrast, will own the creative rights to the work unless you make a written agreement signing the rights over to you.

Is the work you need done an integral part of your business? Generally speaking, employees are better suited to handle the ongoing work of your business. You'll have more control over the quality of the work—and a steady workforce to turn out a consistent product—if you hire employees. Also, the IRS takes a close look at this issue when it audits a business; if your workers are doing the work for which your company is known (for example, they make the products or perform the services you sell), the IRS is much more likely to classify them as employees, not ICs.

How much can you afford to pay? Your total cash outlay will probably be lower for ICs than employees. Although an IC is likely to charge you more to do a project than you'd have to actually pay an employee, employees are more expensive overall after you add on taxes, insurance costs, the price of equipment, materials, and workspace, and other cash outlays.

How's your cash flow? State and federal laws set strict guidelines for paying employees. You have to pay at least the minimum hourly wage, and you have to pay them according to a schedule set by state law (anywhere from once a week to once a month). If you don't follow these rules, you could face fines and penalties. For an IC, you and the IC will set the pay schedule yourselves. If your clients pay you by the project, you can pay the IC when you get paid. If you won't be able to pay for a while, you can work out an installment arrangement with the IC.

Are you looking for loyalty? If so, you're more likely to find it in an employee than an IC, who works for a number of clients. If you will count on your workers to be your eyes and ears or represent you to others—for example, to supervise other workers or oversee your operations—you will probably want a lot of control over how that person does the job. For example, when Christopher Lake, a carpenter and general contractor in the San Francisco Bay Area, needs a worker to take his place dealing with his clients and overseeing his projects and workers on job sites, he brings on an employee: "That way, I know he is representing my company, not his own."

How do you feel about rules and red tape? Unless you're ready to learn your legal obligations as an employer and set up a payroll system to withhold taxes and pay them over to the IRS, don't hire employees. You can run into trouble quickly if you don't handle employee matters by the book; for an IC, on the other hand, the paperwork is minimal. Keep in mind, however, that government agencies will take a close look at ICs to make sure they shouldn't have been classified as employees. This means you may be a more likely target for an audit if you hire ICs.

Ramp Up Quickly With ICs

Mike and Carrie McAllen run a production company. Doing business as Grass Shack (www.grassshackroad.com), they are hired by businesses that want to communicate their corporate message in a creative and interesting way—through video, digital media, graphic presentations, and more. Sometimes, Mike and Carrie's work involves putting on a large corporate event, such as a sales meeting or conference, designed to showcase a company's accomplishments and get the audience excited about the company's plans

So how does one couple manage to throw a sophisticated corporate soiree? By hiring ICs. Although Mike and Carrie oversee each project (and pitch in to help as needed), they bring in experienced professionals to handle much of the work. "Using contractors keeps our company lean and our overhead low. Once we know what a particular project will require, we can bring in professionals who have the expertise we need—and can give our clients the best possible experience. We don't have to train them beforehand or find things for them to do once the project is over. And because we use the same people again and again, we know that they'll do a great job for us."

Although using ICs offers a lot of flexibility, it can also be a bit precarious. To bring on people on a per-project basis, you need to have a lot of contacts, Mike and Carrie explain. "Every once in a while, we'll find that most of the people we know with a particular specialty—such as running complex computer presentation programs or doing elaborate lighting displays—are booked. That's when it helps to know a lot of people; it also helps that we know how to do it ourselves, just in case we can't find anyone on short notice."

Finding the Right Person

Unless you are lucky enough to get a referral for the perfect worker from a friend or colleague, your first step is to post the job. The trick to using a help-wanted ad is not only what you put in it, but also where you post it. Your goal is to put your ad in front of the people you want to attract. Once you figure out what these people read, where they hang out, and where they look for work, you'll know where to post your job. Here are some examples:

- **Colleges and universities.** If you're looking for some basic help with graphic design, marketing, academic research, or anything else someone might learn in a degree-granting program, post your job at a local college or university. Students are eager to do a good job—after all, they want solid job references for the future. And they probably have access, through their schools, to equipment and technology that will be useful.

- **Job boards at local stores.** Many stores that cater to particular industries have a bulletin board where you can post jobs. For example, if you're looking for a general contractor, carpenter, or other skilled tradesperson, you might be able to post a notice at a local hardware store or lumber yard. If you're looking for graphic design help, consider posting at an art supply store.

- **Online job listings.** When we asked business owners where they look for qualified workers, many of them gave us the same answer: Craigslist. This website (or "online community," as its founder calls it) offers local bulletin boards for about 70 locations in the United States, where people can post items for sale, personal ads, housing listings, input to discussion forums, and jobs. To look for workers, you can either search listings by people who want work or, for $75, post your own help-wanted ad. Craigslist offers 25 categories of jobs, from accounting to writing and editing. And because it's such a popular site, you can count on getting plenty of responses to your ad.

- **Trade journals and newspapers.** If you're looking for a professional in a particular field, consider posting an ad in a magazine, journal, or paper that caters to this group, such as a publication for Web designers, craftspeople, or hot rod enthusiasts. This approach has the advantage of targeting folks with the right interests and skills, but they might not be in the right geographical area to work for you. That's why posting in a local publication is usually your best bet.

- **Temporary agencies.** Depending on the type of help you need, you might find qualified people through a temp agency. These days, many agencies specialize in particular fields. For example, companies looking for skilled tradespeople often turn to Contractor's Labor Pool (www.clp.com), a nationwide company that matches skilled labor with employers seeking help. You can find agencies specializing in office work, graphics and art design, printing, Internet technology, and much more.

Once you have some ideas about where to post your ad, put something in writing. The best help-wanted postings are short and sweet. To write an ad, start by listing what you want the worker to do, focusing on specific tasks and duties. If the worker must have particular experience—for example, using a certain computer program or working with specific machinery or customers—include that, too. Don't forget to tell applicants how to contact you and what to send (for example, a resume, work sample, or references).

DON'T

Don't use terms in your ad that could be considered discriminatory—for example, words like "youthful" or "energetic" appear to screen out older applicants, while "skilled tradesman" may not sit too well with a female carpenter. The best way to avoid legal problems when writing an ad is to focus squarely on the abilities necessary to do the job well—not on personality issues or character traits. This will not only help you stay out of legal trouble, but also spare you the pain of sitting through interviews with candidates who are trying hard to appear "peopleoriented," "eager," or "self-starting."

Want Free Help? Consider an Internship Program

What's better than hiring a well-trained, highly motivated student? There are probably a few right answers, but one that ranks high on the list is getting the same person to do the work for free. You can do this by setting up an internship program in partnership with a local college, vocational school, or graduate program. In exchange for on-the-job training, you receive free help—and a first look at people you might want to hire for a full-time position.

If you want help from interns, you'll have to do your part. You'll have to create a job experience that offers them training, meaningful work, and exposure to various aspects of your business. This means you can't just require your interns to do menial tasks, like cleaning the office and making coffee (although many interns will happily handle some of your grunt work). Interns should come away from your business with a solid understanding of your field.

The best way to establish an internship program is to work with a local school and arrange for students to get credit for working for you. Start by contacting the department or program that best fits your business needs or a professor who teaches classes in a relevant field. Many colleges and universities post information about creating an internship program online. Or you might be able to get internship information from your state's labor department website or your local chamber of commerce. For examples, see www.indianaintern.net, a program of the University of Indianapolis and the Greater Indianapolis Chamber of Commerce, or http://careerservices.class.umn.edu/employer, a website that offers internship information from the University of Minnesota.

Once you start getting responses, you'll need to screen applicants, check references, conduct interviews, and make a hiring decision. These topics are beyond the scope of this book. For help in hiring, check out Nolo's website, www.nolo.com, where you'll find plenty of free information, and the Business Owner's Toolkit, at www.toolkit.cch.com (click "People Who Work for You"). Other helpful resources include

The Employer's Legal Handbook and *Hiring Your First Employee*, both by Fred Steingold (Nolo), *Hiring the Best: A Manager's Guide to Effective Interviewing*, by Martin Yate (Adams Media), and *How to Compete in the War for Talent: A Guide to Hiring the Best*, by Carol Hacker (DC Press).

INTERNET LINK

You can find links for all the resources in this book at www.nolo .com/wowbusiness.

Legal and Paperwork Requirements: ICs

There are only a couple of legal rules you have to follow when hiring an IC—and they kick in only when you pay an IC $600 or more in one year.

Complete and file IRS Form 1099-MISC, *Miscellaneous Income.* This form is very straightforward—you simply enter identifying information about your business and the IC, then enter the amount you paid the IC in the box marked "Nonemployee compensation." You must provide copies of the form to the IC no later than January 31 of the year after you made the payment. You also have to file copies of the form with the IRS and your state taxing authority (you have to file with the IRS by February 28 of the year after you made the payment; check with your state tax agency to find out its filing deadline). When you file the 1099 with the IRS, you must send along IRS Form 1096, *Annual Summary and Transmission of U.S. Information Returns.* Form 1096 is essentially a cover letter on which you add up all payments you reported on 1099 forms for the year.

FINDING THE FORMS

Although you can download both Form 1099 and Form 1096 from the IRS website, www.irs.gov, you cannot file these copies. Instead, you must file an original of each, which you can get by contacting your local IRS office (you can find a list of offices at the IRS website) or calling 800-TAX-FORM.

Get the IC's taxpayer identification number. The IRS knows that many ICs work under the table—they're paid in cash, which they don't report (or they underreport) to the IRS. To put a stop to this, the IRS requires those who hire ICs to get a copy of their taxpayer ID—their employer identification number or Social Security number that they use on their tax returns. If an IC won't give you an ID number or the IRS informs you that the number the IC gave you is incorrect, you have to withhold taxes from the IC's pay and remit that money to the IRS. (The IRS calls this "backup withholding.") Obviously, you want to avoid this extra chore—and you can, by requiring the IC to fill out IRS Form W-9, Request for Taxpayer Identification Number. If the IC doesn't have an ID number yet, you don't have to start withholding until 60 days after he or she applies for one.

DON'T

Don't hire an IC to do anything other than a very minor project without signing an agreement. An IC agreement helps you and the IC clarify the terms of your deal, creates a written record of exactly what you agreed upon, and can help convince the IRS and other agencies that you and the IC did not intend to create an employer-employee relationship. For help creating a written IC agreement, take a look at *Consultant & Independent Contractor Agreements*, by Stephen Fishman (Nolo).

Legal and Paperwork Requirements: Employees

There are more forms to fill in—and rules to follow—when you hire an employee than when you hire an IC. Fortunately, most of the paperwork is fairly simple, and you can find the forms online.

When you hire an employee, you must do all of the following.

Have the employee complete IRS Form W-4, *Employee's Withholding Allowance Certificate*. On this form, the employee provides basic identifying information and tells you how much money to withhold from each paycheck. You must have this form in your files, but you don't have to send it to the IRS.

Set Up a Payroll System

Once you become an employer, you'll be responsible for withholding and paying a variety of taxes on behalf of your workers. For example, you'll have to withhold federal income tax, Social Security tax, and Medicare tax from your employees' paychecks and periodically pay that money (along with your own contribution for the employee's Social Security and Medicare) to the IRS. In most states, you'll also have to withhold and periodically pay state income tax. A handful of states also require you to withhold and pay taxes for state-run disability insurance programs (and, in California, for paid leave to care for a sick family member). And you'll have to generate end-of-the-year paperwork, such as IRS Form W-2, showing your workers how much they earned and how much they paid in taxes.

As you might imagine, it would be somewhat difficult to do all of this math yourself—and generate an itemized pay stub detailing all of the withholding for your employees. Fortunately, there are plenty of options for small business owners, including relatively inexpensive software and Web-based payroll services that do the work for you. A couple of the most highly recommended are the *QuickBooks* series (from Intuit), which offers a range of payroll options including Inuit's system (www .intuit.com), and Paycycle, an online payroll service (www.paycycle.com). The advantage of using a *QuickBooks* product is that it will integrate with the company's accounting and tax software—if you use an entire suite from Intuit, you can track all of your financial records in one program.

FINDING THE FORMS

You can download W-4 forms from the IRS website, www.irs.gov, or get them by contacting your local IRS office (you can find a list of offices at the IRS website) or calling 800-TAX-FORM.

Complete USCIS Form I-9, *Employment Eligibility Verification*. This form confirms that the employee is eligible to work in the United States. The employee must complete a portion of the form and then give you documentation of his or her eligibility. The form tells you what kinds of documents are acceptable; a U.S. passport or a driver's license and birth certificate or Social Security card are the typical showing for U.S. citizens. You don't have to file this form, but you must keep it on hand for three years after you hire the employee or one year after the employee quits or is fired, whichever is later.

FINDING THE FORMS
You can download I-9 forms from the website of the United States Citizenship and Immigration Services (USCIS, formerly the INS), at www.uscis.gov. You can fill in the form on your computer or print out a blank copy and fill it in by hand. I-9s can now be completed and stored entirely electronically, signatures and all; check the USCIS website for more information on this.

Report the employee to your state's new hire reporting agency. Employers must submit basic information on new employees to the state, which uses that information to track down parents who owe child support. You will have to submit your employee's name, address, and Social Security number; some states require additional information, such as the employee's date of birth or first day of work.

FINDING THE FORMS
To get the information and forms you need, start at the website of the Administration for Children and Families, a subdivision of the federal Department of Health and Human Services. Click the tab for "Working with ACF," then scroll down to the heading "Employer Info." This will lead you to several publications about the new hire reporting program as well as a list of state requirements and links to the agency in each state that administers the program. Go to your state agency's website to download the required form and find out what information you have to provide.

Get an employer identification number (EIN) from the IRS. You've probably done this already, but if you haven't, check out the instructions in Chapter 13.

Register with your state's labor department. Once you hire an employee, you will have to pay state unemployment taxes. These payments go to your state's unemployment compensation fund, which provides short-term relief to workers who lose their jobs. Typically, you must complete some initial registration paperwork, then pay money into the fund periodically. Unemployment compensation is a form of insurance, so the amount you pay in will depend, in part, on how many of your former employees file for unemployment (just as your insurance premiums depend, in part, on how many claims you file against the policy).

FINDING THE FORMS

Start at the federal Department of Labor, which administers federal/state unemployment programs. Go to http://workforcesecurity .doleta.gov/map.asp, which provides a link to each state's unemployment agency. Once you get to your state agency's website, look for a tab or link on unemployment, or find the material for employers or businesses. Many states provide downloadable forms and online information on your responsibilities.

DON'T

Don't forget workers' compensation insurance. Many states require all employers to have workers' comp coverage, either by paying into a state fund or buying a separate policy. Some states exempt employers with no more than two or three employees from this rule, but it might make sense to purchase coverage anyway. Beyond the legal requirements, having workers' comp coverage can save you a bundle if one of your employees is hurt on the job.

Hang up required posters. Even the smallest businesses are legally required to post certain notices to let employees know their rights under a variety of workplace laws. The federal government wants you to put up a handful of notices; many states have additional posting requirements.

FINDING THE FORMS

The Department of Labor's website, www.dol.gov, lists workplace posters. (Search for "posters" in the A-Z index to find what you need.) Your state's labor department probably also has any required posters on its website. If you're having trouble figuring out which requirements apply to you (or you don't want to post a dozen different notices), you can get an all-in-one poster that combines all required state and federal notices from your local chamber of commerce for about $20.

Working With or Bringing in Family Members

What's the Difference? Family Business vs. Nonfamily 126

A Few Pointers for Family Businesses 127

Avoiding Problems If You Ever Divorce 129

Tax Benefits of Hiring Your Children or Parents 130

Hire Your Children 130

Hire Your Parents 132

Incorporate the Family Business 132

amily businesses are weird. They hire based on nepotism, they blur the distinction between home and work, and they're prone to dysfunction. But despite these obstacles, family businesses work. They have a better chance of survival over the first five years than nonfamily businesses. They make up a third of companies on the S&P 500 and contribute more than half of the national payroll. They also stay connected to the community. The average annual charitable donation from a family business is $50,000.

No wonder many people with a growing business turn to a spouse, child, or other family members for help. As Tony Soprano can attest, there's something to be gained by bringing the family into the business—for example, loyalty, respect, and a sense of mission. But it can also trigger emotional, legal, and business issues. In this chapter we'll explain how you can make it happen without mangling the family tree.

What's the Difference? Family Business vs. Nonfamily

Family businesses operate under the same legal rules as other businesses with a few differences. Since by their nature, family businesses are owned and run by people related by birth, marriage, or adoption, they trigger estate planning issues. Having relatives on the payroll and being married to your co-owner also allows you to take advantage of some tax breaks, discussed in this chapter.

But what's really different about family businesses—and what you should seriously consider before inviting relatives in—is the emotional effect when family members appear in the workplace. There's more chance for volatility when family members disagree about how to deal with a new competitor or a dip in sales. Fortunately, there is a lot of help and advice available for those who want to avoid or resolve family dysfunction.

Before You Ask

Here are some questions to think about before asking a family member to join the business:

- **Is the family member qualified?** Relatives are easy to hire and hard to fire. Neil Koenig, author of *You Can't Fire Me, I'm Your Father* (Hillsboro Press), suggests a simple standard. Just ask: "Is this person hirable at our competitors?" If not, don't consider the relative for a job. If you're unsure about qualifications, business counselor James Hutcheson suggests asking family members to come in for a short specified period of time to avoid painful terminations if things don't pan out.

- **How will it affect family finances?** Don't bring in a spouse (or other relative) until you project the short- and long-term impact on your family balance sheet. If your spouse leaves a day job, it may cast a shadow over the family's financial picture and affect your personal relationship, credit rating, tax deductions, and benefits. For more information on the effect of leaving a day job, review Chapter 19.

- **Does the family member share your vision?** You can't expect your family to share your rabid interest in the business, but it helps if the person you're asking to help believes in what you're doing. A shared vision can unify your family business; a lack of interest can cause dissent.

A Few Pointers for Family Businesses

Some conflicts may be healthy in a family business, but major disputes can distract or even derail a business or marriage. The key to avoiding problems in some cases is to separate the family from the business.

Provide a realistic estimate of the time commitment and clearly explain what help is needed and how it will be accomplished. You must accurately estimate how much time is required for the assigned tasks. Don't underestimate. Time the activity with a stopwatch, if that's feasible. You should also be able to explain to your spouse or child how long and how often their help will be needed—for example, weekly, monthly, or seasonally.

You must accurately describe the work and spell out the type and variety of tasks. Says business author Jill Lublin, "In the case of spouses working together, it's crucial that the division of duties is clear. Each spouse should do their job and then get the heck out of the other one's way."

Provide reasonable compensation. You can pay your relations with equity (an ownership interest) or with cash. Either way, the compensation must seem as reasonable as it would to an investor or unrelated employee. If not, you'll likely trigger resentment or disputes that will soon spill over to the dinner table.

Establish boundaries. For most people, the boundary between work and family is clear, but that's not always the case when a family member joins the business. "If you can't turn it off at home," says business counselor Dr. Rachna Jain, "your whole relationship rises and falls with the business." There are many ways to turn off work discussions (see "Turning on the Band Light," below), or you can simply establish no-biztalk-zones or ban business discussions during certain times (such as dinner).

Get expert help. If one family member sees a problem—even if others refuse to acknowledge it—it's probably time to bring in a family business counselor for expert help. Lots of good advice is available in books. Two popular texts are *Keep the Family Baggage Out of the Family Business*, by Quentin Fleming (Fireside), and *Working With the Ones You Love*, by Dennis Jaffe (Aspen Family Business Group). Many family therapists have subspecialties dealing with family businesses. You can locate these counselors on the Internet (use "family business counselor" as a search term) or get a referral from a local therapist.

> ### Turning on the Band Light
>
> My wife and I have a band business (www.angelcorpuschristi.com). Both of us were sick of nonstop business discussions, so we designated a table lamp in the dining room as the "band light" and agreed that we could talk business only if the light was on. The physical business of turning the lamp on made us think before bringing up the subject, and its presence reduced discussions and made them more efficient. When away from home, we prefaced discussions with "Is the band light on?" —Rich Stim

Avoiding Problems If You Ever Divorce

Husband-and-wife teams run 1.2 million American companies. Many of these couples will eventually divorce—for example, chef Wolfgang Puck and his wife, Barbara Lazaroff, divorced after 20 years developing their restaurant and food business empire, valued at $300 million. Apparently, their split had little effect on the smoked salmon pizzas; the company remains robust, and the website features glowing profiles of both founders.

Unfortunately, not all business divorces resolve as well. One study estimated that a third of all divorced couples remain hostile several years after the divorce. So it's easy to see why the "D" word can have an unfavorable impact on the business's employees, customers, and contractors. Here are some things to consider when spouses split.

Even if only one spouse operated the business, the ownership will likely be split between both after divorce. Unless there is an agreement to the contrary—for example, a prenuptial or buyout agreement—divorce laws generally require that the value of the business ownership be split by the separating spouses. In community property states (Arizona, California, Idaho, Louisiana, Nevada, New Mexico, Texas, Washington, and Wisconsin), each spouse is entitled to an equal share unless the business was acquired with one spouse's separate property. In other states, a similar rule makes each spouse entitled to an equitable (fair) share of the business.

Most ownership issues can be anticipated with a buyout agreement (also known as a buy-sell agreement). Buyout agreements are like a prenuptial agreement for your business. They can require that a person sell an ownership interest back to the company or to other co-owners, according to a valuation method provided in the agreement. Preparing the valuation can be tricky, which is why a buyout agreement can be helpful. It establishes a way to put a value on the business and usually requires that the value of the business be calculated on two dates: marriage and divorce. An attorney can assist in preparing a buyout agreement or you can prepare one yourself by reading *Business Buyout Agreements: A Step-by-Step Guide for Co-Owners*, by Bethany Laurence and Anthony Mancuso (Nolo).

Watch Out for "Triangles"

Business author Dennis Jaffe points out that competitive spouses operating a business together sometimes form "triangles"—bringing in a third individual, such as a child or another employee, to use to side with them and as a means of pressuring the other spouse.

Tax Benefits of Hiring Your Children or Parents

Bringing in a family member may lower your taxes. Your accountant or tax preparer can help you with some of the strategies discussed below.

Hire Your Children

If you hire your children, you can deduct salaries you pay them. Your children, particularly those under age 18, probably pay taxes on this income at a lower tax rate (starting at 10% for amounts under $8,025) than you pay on your business income. Not only that, a minor child who performs services for the family business does not have to pay any taxes on the first $5,450 in wages earned in a year (as of 2008). If your child is under 18, you don't even need to pay payroll taxes—that is, payments such as FICA (Social Security and Medicare) and FUTA (federal unemployment) that are required for all other employees. Even more tax can be saved if the child establishes an IRA, the contributions for which are tax deductible up to $5,000 per year. In that case, your working offspring won't have to pay taxes on the first $10,450 of earned income. For more information on employing your child, see IRS Publication 929, *Tax Rules for Children and Dependents.*

Keep in mind that these rules don't apply for hiring anyone's kids— only your own. If the IRS questions you, the primary concern will be whether the child does real work and is paid reasonable wages. In general, as long as you are paying for a task you would pay someone else to do—for example, sweeping up the studio, putting stamps on promotional postcards, running errands, doing clerical tasks, entering data into a computer, or answering the phones—and as long as the payment is commensurate with what you might pay an outsider, the IRS will likely accept the categorization.

Of course, many tasks require skills or training. The IRS is not likely to accept that your five-year-old, however gifted, actually does data processing. To further enhance your position with IRS auditors, it helps to maintain a payment schedule for your child that is tied to work performed and not make periodic lump-sum payments.

Live Long and Prosper

Are you interested in longevity for your family business? One suggestion is to avoid the big city. In a study by *Family Business* magazine, only seven out of the 50 oldest family businesses in America were in large cities (defined as cities big enough to host a major league sports franchise).

Hire Your Parents

If you hire your retired parents, you can deduct the expense, lowering your taxable income. Your parents will probably be taxed at a lower tax rate than what you pay. But before Mom and Dad punch the time clock, check what effect the extra income will have on their Social Security. In some cases—for example, for parents under 65, income from your business could reduce their Social Security income.

Community Property States and Spouse-Owned Businesses

If spouses own the business in a community property state (Arizona, California, Idaho, Nevada, New Mexico, Texas, Washington, or Wisconsin), they can report their business income on a Schedule C (as a sole proprietorship) as part of the joint return. This doesn't save money but it does save the time and hassle of filing a K-1 partnership return, which is required of spouses who co-own a business in a non-community property state. If one spouse owns the business and the other works for it, however, it's a sole proprietorship, and income is reported on the individual family member's tax return.

Incorporate the Family Business

Incorporation has extra benefits when family members work in the business. If you incorporate the family business, you can shift income from higher tax brackets to lower ones (known as "income splitting") by giving stock to family members in lower tax brackets—for example, giving stock to kids under age 14.

Family Limited Partnerships

It's possible that you've heard talk about family limited partnerships (FLPs), a business form popularized in the 1990s that shields a business from many liabilities and provides tax benefits, especially when you're transferring assets of the business to another generation. In the typical FLP, the parents act as the general partners. The children are the passive limited partners, who cannot run the business and are prevented from transferring their interest to others outside of the family. (See Chapter 3 for an explanation of limited partnerships.) If the parents are sued, the business assets of the limited partners can't be touched by creditors. Using FLPs, savvy accountants and lawyers have helped family businesses achieve nearly tax-free transfers of millions of dollars of money and business property to their heirs.

Chances are that you won't need to think about FLPs for your family business because the tax benefits usually won't kick in unless your family has millions in assets. In any case, the IRS is suspicious of FLPs. In 2004, a federal tax court knocked out a Texas FLP, obligating heirs to pay over $2 million in taxes. In another 2004 case, however, a court of appeal upheld an FLP, though it stated that a transaction between family members will be scrutinized more thoroughly to assure that the arrangement is not a sham transaction or a disguised gift. (*Kimbell v. U.S.*, 371 F.3d 257 (5th Cir. 2004).) In short, tread carefully and with the sound advice of an attorney or accountant before forming an FLP.

Who's Afraid of Contracts?

Check 'Em Out 137

Oral Agreements: Legal But… 138

Using Form Agreements 138

   Don't Go for the Cheap Stuff 139

   Consider Industry Organizations and Guilds 139

Find the Bias 139

Drafting and Formatting Your Agreement 140

Who Signs the Agreement? 142

Common Contract Provisions 142

   Confidentiality 142

   Warranties, Covenants, and Representations 143

   Indemnity 143

   Audit 144

   Term and Renewal 144

   Termination 144

Boilerplate 145

   Entire Agreement 145

   Waiver 146

   Severability 146

   Governing Law 146

   Jurisdiction 146

   Force Majeure 147

Dispute Resolution 147

    Attorney Fees.. 147

    Arbitration and Mediation... 148

When You Have to Review a Contract.. 149

    Step 1. Read... 149

    Step 2. Compare 149

    Step 3. Prepare 149

Maintaining Paperwork 150

Do You Have a Fear of Negotiating Contracts?........................ 151

Signing a contract may arouse your suspicion and concern. After all, contracts bind your business (or you), they're written in legalese, and they sometimes contain unexpected legal landmines. But bringing in a lawyer every time you need to write or read one is expensive. The trick is to know when you can do it yourself and when to pick up the phone for help. You may be surprised how much you can manage on your own.

Check 'Em Out

As any lawyer will tell you, a contract, no matter how carefully drafted, cannot completely insulate you from the dishonest acts of an individual or company. That's why it's crucial to know something about the people with whom you contract. So find out what you can about the experiences of others with the company. Find out the company's record regarding payments and other issues that matter to you, and see if you can locate any Internet items about any lawsuits that the business has been involved in. Here's an example of how this type of investigation can work.

Steve works full-time for an animation company. He's also a cartoonist in his spare time, and his characters, Sam & Max, have been the subject of a successful video game and a television series. Steve was approached by a California company that wanted the rights to release the Sam & Max television series on DVD. It seemed like a good proposal, especially since fans of Sam & Max had expressed an interest in getting a DVD. But before proceeding, Steve's lawyer suggested they spend a little time checking out the company. The research was disheartening. The company had recently released another TV series and it had been a disaster; fans had even set up websites complaining of a rip-off. Further investigation showed that the person behind the company had been the subject of other complaints and lawsuits. Disappointed, Steve turned down the deal. A few months later, the owner of the company was arrested on fraud charges.

Oral Agreements: Legal But...

You've got a legally enforceable contract whenever two parties are in agreement—an offer has been made by one party and accepted by the other. In a few situations, a contract must also be in writing to be valid. For example, a contract for a real estate transaction or an agreement that will last more than one year must be in writing.

Oral agreements have obvious advantages—simplicity, efficiency, and a sense of trust that's missing from 20-page contracts. But the advantages of oral agreements can also be their problems. The uncertainty and vagueness of oral deals leave the doors wide open for protracted disputes in which the wealthier party has an inherent advantage. For that reason, we recommend that you always "get paper," as they say in the music business—that is, get it in writing. If you do enter into an oral agreement, preserve any documentation—from letters to cocktail napkins—that detail its terms, and write a letter confirming your understanding.

Using Form Agreements

Start with the concept that lawyers don't actually write contracts from scratch —they build them around existing templates or borrow pieces from other agreements. In this way, legal agreements are inbred, nicked from other documents, and passed along over the transom. There are probably fewer than six degrees of separation between the lease drafted by your landlord's lawyer and the one that Donald Trump uses for Trump Towers.

When you need to write a new contract or review an existing one, it helps to start with a form agreement. But where can you get one? Until the age of desktop computers and the Internet, contract templates were the exclusive province of lawyers and legal publishers. But thanks to the do-it-yourself legal movement (led by Nolo, the publisher of this book), an industry now exists that provides form agreements for just about every small business need.

It's very important to carefully select which one you'll use, because there's a wide range of quality, from the legally enforceable to the dangerously unreliable. Here are some tips for finding the best legal self-help materials.

Don't Go for the Cheap Stuff

The quality is remembered long after the price is forgotten. Every bargain software bin contains a "1,000 Legal Forms" disk. These low-end products usually don't provide instructions, explanations, or follow-up advice. Instead, focus on top-of-the-line stuff; it's easier to use and understand. How do you know what's top of the line? Check consumer reviews at Amazon.com and ratings by companies such as CNET, *The New York Times*, or *The Wall Street Journal*. Look for a company that regularly updates its products with new editions, update notification services, and so forth. (Check the publication dates, too.) Finally, visit a company's website and find out how long it has been in business.

Consider Industry Organizations and Guilds

Professional and trade organizations such as the American Institute of Architects (AIA), the Graphics Artist Guild (GAG), and the American Trucking Association (ATA) provide standardized, high-quality contract documents for members. If you're a member of a trade organization, find out if it provides form agreements.

Find the Bias

Many form agreements favor one party or the other. If you find one that favors your position, fine, but the instructions should also explain which provisions reflect that bias. Otherwise you won't be prepared to argue for your point of view if the other party challenges the agreement. Many quality legal forms provide clauses that are fair to each side and explain how to use them to create an agreement that both sides are happy with.

Electronic Agreements

Electronic contracts and signatures are as legally valid as paper contracts thanks to a federal law enacted in 2000. An electronic contract (or e-contract) is an agreement created and "signed" in digital form—no paper copies. For example, you write a contract on your computer and email it to a business associate, who emails it back with an acceptance ("I accept this"). An e-contract can also be in the form of a "click to agree" contract (the user clicks an "I agree" button). Although electronic agreements are binding, like oral agreements, you can enforce them only if you have proof of the contract. So always keep records, preferably paper, of these electronic transactions.

Drafting and Formatting Your Agreement

Find a quality form agreement that's directly on point and you won't need to do any writing, except your signature. But in many cases, the form agreement will need some work. Here are some drafting suggestions.

Avoid legalese. Using legalese—uncommon phrases and wording that seem like a secret language—can make your agreement ambiguous. Instead of "whereas" and "heretofore," use words with common and everyday meanings. Set out each party's rights and obligations in as clear a manner as possible.

Don't contract for something illegal. Just because both parties agree on something doesn't mean a court will enforce the agreement. Contracts that violate laws or public policy will not be enforced—for example, an agreement to charge an illegal interest rate or to conspire to limit commerce unfairly. By the way, you can find each state's legal interest rate at Virgin Money (www.virginmoneyus.com). Choose "Business Loans," then click "Tips & Tools."

Be specific. To create a legally enforceable agreement, you must agree on the material terms, which are the important things people bargain for—the who, what, how much, how many, where, and when questions. Having a written agreement isn't, by itself, enough to make it enforceable. For example, a publisher had a written agreement to publish a collection of John Cheever stories, but the contract didn't specify the content of the book, and it didn't establish when the manuscript was to be delivered, when the book would be published, or what happened if the book was no longer in print. When Cheever's widow wouldn't cooperate with the publisher, a court would not enforce the contract because it lacked these essential terms. (*Academy Chicago Publishers v. Cheever*, 144 Ill. 2d 24, 578 N.E.2d 981 (1991).)

Anticipate problems. Lawyers earn big bucks for anticipating contract disasters and providing a means—ahead of time—of resolving them. Focus on the most likely and most damaging potential problems. For example, what happens if goods aren't delivered on time? Will you provide a period to correct the problem? How (and where) will you resolve disputes? And be sure to anticipate the biggest problem—the other side is untrustworthy (more on that later).

Use standard provisions. There is common ground in every written agreement, regardless of the specifics of the deal. It's usually in the form of the standard contract clauses discussed later in this chapter. If you understand these commonly used provisions, you're on your way to understanding most contracts.

Pay attention to appearance. Whether it's a letter agreement or a 30-page license, the look of your contract matters. True, there's no law that says your contract must look like it came from a lawyer. But your contracts should reflect a professionalism that instills trust. Number the contract provisions, provide boldfaced titles, and use a clear, formal font.

Who Signs the Agreement?

Only someone with the necessary authority can sign an agreement.

- **Sole proprietor:** You sign, of course, and you're personally liable.

- **Partnership:** Any general partner or person given authority by a general partner can sign. All of the owners will be personally liable for the obligations under the agreement unless the agreement excludes them from liability.

- **Corporation or LLC:** Only a person authorized by the business can sign contracts—usually the president, CEO, or an executive. The name of the corporation or LLC should appear above the signature line, and the name and title of the person signing should be included below the signature line. The signing party for a corporation or LLC won't be personally liable unless the agreement says so.

Common Contract Provisions

Before you sign (or click "I Agree") for your next contract, familiarize yourself with these common contract sections.

Confidentiality

A confidentiality provision requires each party to preserve the other's trade secrets—and allows each to sue for breach of contract if the other slips up. Usually, it starts with language such as, "The parties acknowledge that each may have access to confidential information that … "

WATCH OUT
Be careful when dealing with a confidentiality provision that doesn't adequately define the trade secrets it covers—ditto for a provision that requires you to keep trade secrecy for five years or more after the agreement terminates. (See Chapter 11 for more on trade secrets.)

Warranties, Covenants, and Representations

These provisions are special promises or assurances that, if untrue, allow the other party to sue for damages. For example, you may warrant that your new invention doesn't infringe other inventions. If it does, the other party can get out of the deal and sue you to get compensated for its losses. A typical warranty clause starts, "Company warrants and represents that …" followed by the specific promise—for example, that a product will not infringe or that you have the power to enter into this agreement.

WATCH OUT
Beware of a warranty that is beyond your knowledge—for example, a warranty that the use of your product will not violate any laws or that all of your suppliers will abide by certain labor standards. If possible, narrow these down with "the best of my knowledge."

Indemnity

An indemnity provision acts like a powerful shield against problems that may arise with a third party. For example, if you do home repair work and indemnify a homeowner against losses caused by your unsafe actions, you will have to pay for damages and legal fees if someone is injured because of your unsafe actions. Indemnity provisions are also sometimes referred to as "hold harmless" provisions because the language for an indemnity provision often states "Company A shall hold Company B harmless from any losses. … "

WATCH OUT
Avoid indemnity provisions that are unusually broad. For example, stay away from a provision that indemnifies the other party for any breach of the agreement. Like warranties, try to rein in an indemnity clause so that it is for specific injuries to third parties. If possible, only provide indemnity for disputes that result in lawsuits. (Some companies seek indemnity for any threatened claim or dispute.)

Audit

An audit provision allows you to examine the other side's books if you ever have an accounting dispute—for example, if you believe that the other side is not accounting for all sales under a license agreement. Usually these audits can be held during regular business hours and with reasonable notice.

 **WATCH OUT**
Avoid a provision that allows you to bring only a CPA to an audit. CPAs are expensive, and you may prefer to bring your regular accountant.

Term and Renewal

These provisions set the time limit for the agreement and establish the terms for renewal.

WATCH OUT
Be careful when dealing with automatic renewals. In these cases, you must terminate an agreement within 30, 60, or 90 days before the end of the term. If you don't have the date calendared and you fail to cancel on time, you'll be stuck for another year.

Termination

A termination provision establishes the basis for ending the agreement. Even without a termination provision, either party can terminate an agreement if the other party commits a material breach—that is, a major breakdown of the agreement. Because parties may differ in their opinions as to what constitutes a material breach, a termination provision can define the conditions—for example, a failure to pay on time or to fix the failure within 30 days.

WATCH OUT

Avoid a one-sided termination provision (one side can termi-nate at will; the other cannot). Also avoid a termination provision with too many triggers—for example, a right to terminate for seemingly minor infractions. Don't be lulled into a sense of security if the agreement provides that you can terminate an agreement if the other side goes bankrupt. You can't. Bankruptcy law takes precedence over contract law, and you will not be able to terminate without permission from the bankruptcy court. For example, your publishing agreement may establish that in the event of the publisher's bankruptcy, the agreement terminates and all rights to your book will revert to you. Surprise! In the event of the publisher's bankruptcy, the bankruptcy court will decide whether the agreement terminates and what happens to your rights.

Boilerplate

The following "boilerplate" or standard provisions are found at the end of most agreements. These provisions, created by lawyers to deal with odd and usually uncommon contingencies, are really noticed only if they're omitted from the agreement.

Entire Agreement

This provision (sometimes referred to as the "integration" provision) establishes that the agreement is the final version and that any modification must be in writing. It prevents parties from later claiming, "But you told me such-and-such." When this is included, one party will have a harder time convincing a court that the other promised something that's not in the agreement. You can usually recognize this clause as something like, "This is the entire agreement between the parties. It replaces and supersedes any and all oral agreements between the parties. ..."

Waiver

By including a waiver provision, neither side can claim that the other set a precedent by deviating from the agreement in some way—for example, accepting payment later than usual. ("But you didn't object when I was late before, so that changed the terms of the deal.") Usually you can identify it by language such as "The failure to exercise any right provided in this agreement shall not be a waiver of prior or subsequent rights…."

Severability

This provision (aka "invalidity") permits a court to sever (take out) a portion of the agreement that's no good while keeping the rest of the agreement intact. In this way, one legal error in a contract won't torpedo the whole transaction. Usually you can identify it by wording such as, "If a court finds any provision of this agreement invalid or unenforceable, the remainder of this agreement will be interpreted so as best to carry out the parties' intent. …"

Governing Law

This provision (also known as a "choice of law") determines which state's laws should be followed in the event of a dispute. For most basic contract and corporate matters, state laws are fairly similar, so this isn't usually a major issue.

Jurisdiction

Jurisdiction provisions—sometimes called forum-selection clauses—require you to consent in advance to the jurisdiction of a specific court and give up the right to complain about jurisdiction later or bring a lawsuit anywhere else. In other words, if you or the other party bring a lawsuit arising out of or relating to the contract, you'll both have to bring it in the agreed-upon court.

Two states, Idaho and Montana, refuse to honor these provisions. In other states, courts have required that the parties have some contact with the state beyond the contract provision—for example, they must do business with the state's citizens. If possible, you want to avoid a jurisdiction clause that forces you to travel out of state to bring a lawsuit.

Force Majeure

Back in the old days, if you contracted to deliver ten saddles, it didn't matter if all of your leather was destroyed by a flood and you were kidnapped by Druids. You still had to deliver. Today, courts are more forgiving. Performance is often excused if it's rendered impractical by a supervening event—for example, a fire that destroys your studio. To guarantee that you aren't obligated or in breach after a disaster strikes, most contracts include a force majeure provision (sometimes known as an "Act of God") that excuses or delays performance if it's virtually impossible.

Dispute Resolution

The following provisions—attorney fees and arbitration—have the potential to level the playing field in the event of a dispute. And that's why some companies with superior bargaining power oppose inserting them.

Attorney Fees

In the event of a legal dispute over the contract, the attorney fees provision establishes that the loser must pay the winner's legal fees. Since attorney fees can exceed the value of the lawsuit, this provision can be especially helpful in preventing pyrrhic victories.

SAMPLE ATTORNEY FEES PROVISION: The prevailing party shall have the right to collect from the other party its reasonable costs and necessary disbursements and attorney fees incurred in enforcing this agreement.

Arbitration and Mediation

Mediation and arbitration are referred to as alternative dispute resolution or ADR. Both methods are often cheaper and faster than a lawsuit, so it's usually a good idea to include one or both.

If you include a mediation provision then a mediator will try to help you settle your dispute. "Try" is the key word here, since the mediator can't make a decision or bind the parties. An arbitration provision is more decisive. It allows the parties to avoid a lawsuit, and instead hire one or more arbitrators—professionals trained to evaluate disputes—to rule on a dispute.

Both have drawbacks. Mediation works only if both parties have a good faith desire to resolve their problems. Arbitration, unlike a court ruling, is not appealable (that's why it's called "binding arbitration") and can be set aside by a judge only if the arbitrator was biased or the ruling violated public policy. Also, arbitrators must be paid, and their fees may run $10,000 or more. Finally, participants in arbitration usually hire attorneys, so you may not avoid having to pay legal fees.

SAMPLE COMBINATION MEDIATION/ARBITRATION PROVISION:

If a dispute arises under or relating to this agreement, the parties agree that the dispute shall be settled first by a meeting of the parties attempting to confer and resolve the dispute in a good-faith manner. If the parties cannot resolve their dispute after conferring, any party may require the other parties to submit the matter to nonbinding mediation, utilizing the services of an impartial professional mediator approved by all parties. If the parties cannot come to an agreement following mediation, the parties agree to submit the matter to binding arbitration in the state of _____ or another location mutually agreeable to the parties. The arbitration shall be conducted on a confidential basis pursuant to the commercial arbitration rules of the American Arbitration Association. Any decision or award as a result of any such arbitration proceeding shall be in writing and shall provide an explanation for all conclusions of law and fact and shall include the assessment of costs, expenses, and reasonable attorney fees. An arbitrator experienced in business law shall conduct any such arbitration. An award of arbitration may be confirmed in a court of competent jurisdiction.

When You Have to Review a Contract

Lawyers believe that you're more likely to get what you want if you write the first draft of the contract. For that reason (or simply because the other side likes to use its own familiar agreement), a company or individual may give you their contract to use. Reviewing someone else's agreement is the flip side of writing one. Be prepared to spend an hour or two making your analysis. Here are some suggestions on how to proceed:

Step 1. Read

Make a photocopy of the agreement and read it through. If you can understand everything, great—you may not need an attorney. If you can't understand something, flag the number of the confusing provision or section.

Step 2. Compare

Compare the agreement to similar ones you've executed in the past or to a form agreement. Look for glaring differences—for example, their agreement says that the photographer owns the copyright, while your agreement says that the client owns the copyright.

Step 3. Prepare

Prepare a table listing the number of any section you want modified and explaining your concerns and the changes you want made—for example, add a new provision, strike this section, and so forth.

Here's an example:

SECTION	COMMENT
INTRO	Please revise the address for my business. The correct address is 14 Lincoln Road, Wikedia, California 94366
2 TERM	Please modify this section so that the agreement is only for one year, as we agreed.
8 LATE PAYMENTS	Please modify the second line so that the interest rate for late payments is 1.5% per month.
10 INDEMNIFICATION	I'm not comfortable requiring my company to absorb 100% of the indemnification costs. I think it would be fair to limit indemnification to sums that have been paid under the agreement.
11.2 TERMINATION	Please strike Section 11.2. It was my understanding that my company had the right to terminate during any year if you stopped distributing the products for a period of six continuous months.
14 JURISDICTION	I could not afford to travel to New York for litigation. Either strike the jurisdiction section or provide for jurisdiction in both New York and California.

You can later convert this chart into a response letter to the other side or you can use it as the starting point for talking with an attorney.

Maintaining Paperwork

Maintaining your contracts is an essential element of your business recordkeeping. Your contract files should contain, in addition to the signed contract:

- correspondence and copies of email regarding the contract
- drafts with changes made by the parties (this will help to show what you intended, if there's ever a disagreement), and
- whatever documentation exists, especially in the case of oral contracts, to prove the existence of the agreement—receipts, notes, and, if possible, your own memo to the file detailing the terms.

Chapter 2 provides tips on organizing your records.

Test your legalese. Sometimes the biggest challenge when reading a contract is sorting through the jargon. Here's a test of your knowledge of legalese. Can you match the term with the meaning?

TERM	MEANING
1. herein	a. previously
2. hereinafter	b. considered as
3. heretofore	c. in spite of
4. notwithstanding	d. from this point on
5. foregoing	e. in this document
6. deemed	f. preceding

Answers: 1e, 2d, 3a, 4c, 5f, 6b

Do You Have a Fear of Negotiating Contracts?

Many books teach how to negotiate a contract, but most people agree that the classic *Getting to Yes*, by Roger Fisher and William Ury (Houghton Mifflin), is the best of the bunch. Fisher and Ury emphasize:

- separating the people from the issues (removing the emotion)
- looking beyond the negotiating parties to see who or what is the real interest or influence affecting each party
- generating options to create a problem-solving environment, and
- neutralizing conflict by sticking to objective and easy-to-justify principles of fairness.

If you're new to business and negotiation, you may be stuck for the right things to say while discussing a deal. Try creating scripts ahead of time. Below, (in the right-hand column) are examples of how to use five "magic phrases" gathered by writer Jenna Glatzer ("Those Magic Phrases—How to Negotiate Like a Pro," *Home Business*, Sept. 1, 2004). The left-hand column indicates what you might actually be thinking.

NEGOTIATING LIKE A PRO	
YOU THINK	**YOU SAY**
That's ridiculous. I can't believe they're even offering that.	That sounds a little low.
There's no way I can do that work at that price. My hourly rate would be a joke.	To make it worth my time, I would need at least ...
They're being completely unrealistic. Their offer doesn't even include the cost of goods.	Considering the amount of _____ required, can we agree to ...
They must be used to dealing with low-quality outfits and they're obviously not familiar with my standards.	I'm expecting more for this work.
There's absolutely no hope for this deal.	Can we work on that?

SEE AN EXPERT

You should pick up the phone when an agreement is too complex or too important to go it alone, or if you don't trust the other side. An agreement may be too complex if your legal needs aren't met by mass-marketed legal forms. You'll know when an agreement is especially important to your business—for example, a "big deal" contract with a major client or a contract that affects your company's long-term viability.

11

Protecting Business Ideas

Four Steps to Protect Your Ideas.. 154

    Step 1. Record Your Ideas... 154

    Step 2. Identify What's Proprietary 155

    Step 3. Ensure Your Rights 155

    Step 4. Enforce Your Rights.. 155

What Ideas Have You Got?.. 156

Ensuring Rights: Registration and Other Measures................................... 158

    Copyright 158

    Utility Patents.. 159

    Design Patents.. 160

    Trademarks.. 160

    Trade Secrets 160

Chasing People Who Rip Off Your Ideas.. 162

Licensing or Selling Your Rights 163

What If You Copy Somebody Else's Ideas?.. 163

Ideas Your Employees or Contractors Come Up With 165

Two Companies That Made Money From Great Ideas.............................. 166

Every business starts with an idea. From that idea, many others often follow. For example, in the 1950s, the McDonald brothers wanted their hamburger stand to operate like a manufacturing plant, mass-producing burgers and pricing them cheaply. While competitors provided long menus, the brothers limited their selection to nine items. They also eliminated glass and china, preferring disposable packaging.

They didn't own these ideas—other businesses could copy them freely. But McDonald's combined these clever ideas with consistent quality, fast customer service, franchising, and aggressive marketing. The result is a small business that, under the direction of innovator Ray Kroc, became a global phenomenon.

Sometimes, however, a business succeeds because it has ideas that others cannot copy. These are known as proprietary ideas because they are the exclusive property of the business, which can stop competitors from using them. These types of ideas are the innovations and creative thinking we associate with inventions, new processes, books, artwork, crafts, or similar creative products. If your business plans on exploiting these kinds of ideas, you'll be looking to seek the maximum legal protection in the form of a copyright, patent, trademark, or trade secret.

Four Steps to Protect Your Ideas

As you can see from the steps below, the key to protecting ideas is recording them accurately and knowing your rights.

Step 1. Record Your Ideas

This may seem obvious, but we'll say it anyway: Having an idea is never enough. No matter how you come up with your business idea—while exercising, driving, or perhaps standing in the shower (see "Ideas While Showering," below)—you can't protect it unless you have expressed it in a manner that can be judged, recorded, and registered. In the case of books, art, and music, it's simply a matter of recording your work—for example, putting your image on canvas or your words on paper. In the case of a patentable invention, you must manifest your idea with a written description that clearly explains how to make and use your invention, or, alternatively, create a working prototype. For example, you may have an idea for improving pizza delivery boxes. But unless you can express that idea in a manner that meets the standards of patent protection, your idea will have little value. That makes sense under the law, since without this fixed expression or manifestation of your idea, it would be difficult for the government to offer protection, provide systems of registration, or resolve disputes.

Step 2. Identify What's Proprietary

You need to determine if you have any "Rembrandts in the attic," as one popular book on business ideas puts it. "What Ideas Have You Got?," below, points you toward the things that qualify as proprietary and protectible.

Step 3. Ensure Your Rights

Register your valuable ideas with the agencies that oversee copyrights, patents, and trademarks. If you have trade secrets, take steps to maintain the confidentiality of the information. We explain the basics later in this chapter.

Step 4. Enforce Your Rights

Perhaps an ex-employee has taken your customer list; maybe a competitor is imitating your trademark in order to siphon customers. Going after these people ("infringers") can be expensive and disappointing—for example, you may win a lawsuit only to learn that the infringer has closed up shop and disappeared. We'll offer you some tips on when to pursue infringers and when it's not worth the effort.

What Ideas Have You Got?

You can't protect your ideas unless you can categorize them. Lawyers refer to this process as an "intellectual property audit" (protectible expressions of ideas are referred to as "intellectual property" or "IP"). It's often performed before the sale of the business. Like any audit, you create an inventory; as new IP is created, licensed, or acquired, you add that to the inventory.

Here are some questions to help you uncover your IP:

Have you developed new products, formulas, recipes, technologies, or processes? Functional devices, technologies, formulas, or processes that were invented by your business within the past few years may be protected under trade secret or patent law.

Does your business create original works, such as crafts, music, artwork, film, or publications? Artistic and/or creative products or publications are protected under copyright law. Copyright even extends to some unexpected places—for example, software programming and architecture. Some art may also be protected under design patent law—for example, furniture, jewelry, or toy designs.

Have you created business plans, financial projections, marketing plans, sales data, or similar strategy directives? The results of your business strategy brainstorming sessions are protected under trade secret law, provided you keep them confidential. (Tips on doing that are provided, below.)

Have you created new ways of doing business? You can get a patent (sometimes referred to as a business method patent) on a way of doing business. For example, Netflix, the online movie rental service, has a patent on its "method and apparatus for renting items" that covers the process used for its subscription service.

Have you prepared a website, advertising, or marketing or promotional materials? Promotional efforts like websites and advertisements are usually protected under copyright law.

Have you created names and logos to identify your business, products, or services? The ways in which the public identifies your products and services—commercial signifiers like names, logos, and choice of color schemes—are protected under trademark law. For more on trademark protection, read Chapter 12.

Do you have customer lists or other industry database information? You might not think of a database or customer list as something you can stop others from using, but under certain conditions, described below, they can be protected under trade secret law. A customer list is more likely to qualify as a trade secret if the information in the list is not easily ascertainable by other means and if the list includes more than names and addresses—for example, pricing and special needs.

Ideas While Showering

NASA scientists were stymied by how to fix a defective mirror on the Hubble space telescope until engineer James H. Crocker was taking a shower in a German hotel room and came up with the idea for mirrors perched on automated arms.

Maybe the best place for you to come up with brilliant business ideas is in the shower. Why? Researchers offer various reasons. Some believe that the routine activities of showering—scrubbing, shampooing, rinsing—combined with the white noise of the shower and the repetitive sensation of water hitting the skin relax the body into a nonaroused "alpha" state in which it's common to daydream. Others maintain that showers are idea generators because of the "enclosure" or "incubation" effect—that is, being away from normal life.

Some believe that you get more oxygen while showering because water falling from the showerhead ionizes the air, which enables you to take in a higher percentage of oxygen.

Or, it may be simpler than that. James Crocker's brilliant idea to fix the Hubble telescope was inspired by the adjustable shower head he observed in his German hotel shower.

DON'T

Don't assume that your customer lists are proprietary information or that you can automatically stop an ex-employee from using them. For example, a salesman worked for an insurance company selling life insurance to automobile dealers. When he moved to a competing insurance company he took his customer list and contacted these customers at his new job. A court ruled that the customer list was not a trade secret because the names of the automobile dealers were easily ascertainable by other means and because the salesman had contributed to the creation of the list. (*Lincoln Towers Ins. Agency v. Farrell*, 99 Ill. App. 3d 353, 425 N.E.2d 1034 (1981).)

Ensuring Rights: Registration and Other Measures

With the exception of trade secrets, if you plan to enforce your rights in your IP, you'll have to file some papers with the federal government. Here's the scoop.

Copyright

Copyright protection begins once a work is created and generally lasts for the life of the creator plus 70 years. Works made for hire (discussed below) are protected for 120 years from their date of creation or 95 years from their first publication, whichever is longer. For example, if you want to sue an infringer, you'll need a copyright registration.

We recommend using the U.S. Copyright Office website (www.copyright .gov), where you can download copyright application forms or copyright publications that explain copyright laws and rules in plain language. For additional help, check Nolo's copyright resources and products at www.nolo.com. The filing fee for registration is currently $45 ($35 if filing electronically), and the registration process takes approximately six months. If you have to do it in a hurry—for example, you want to file a lawsuit—you can expedite the registration for an added fee (over $500). If you can't afford to register all of your copyrighted works, register your most popular items—that is, the ones most likely to be copied.

Utility Patents

Obtaining a patent is a time-consuming process that can be quite expensive—often costing more than $10,000. Be sure you have cleared a few hurdles before you consider it.

The **first hurdle** is to check whether a similar invention or method already exists. You can do a basic search of patent records on the Internet at the USPTO website (www.uspto.gov). Nolo's *Patent Pending in 24 Hours*, by Richard Stim and David Pressman, and *Patent It Yourself* by David Pressman explain how to do basic searches.

The **second hurdle** is to determine whether your idea is marketable. For several hundred dollars, you can perform your own marketability studies—for example, interviewing potential customers, retailers, or distributors to gauge interest in your product. A small number of universities evaluate inventions for inventors at a very reasonable price—for example, the WIN Innovation Institute (www.innovation-institute.com), affiliated with Southwest Missouri State University charges approximately $250 to determine how probable it is that your invention will be accepted in the marketplace.

The **third hurdle** is to verify your invention's novelty by paying for a professional patent search. This search will give you a more realistic idea than your basic search as to whether previous inventions or publications (known as "prior art") will prevent you from getting a patent. You can locate patent searchers over the Internet or find one through a patent lawyer. A professional search ranges in cost from $300 to $1,000.

If you're wary of this whole process but want to preserve your place at the USPTO for one year, you can file a document known as a provisional patent application. It's not expensive (under $100) and once you've filed, you can claim your invention as "patent pending" and test it in the market before seeking a patent. For more on provisional patent applications, use Nolo's online filing procedure or read *Patent Pending in 24 Hours*.

If you decide to apply for a utility patent, you can pay a professional or learn how to file the application yourself. For some people, the expense of hiring a patent attorney is the biggest barrier. If your funds are limited (or if you just can't stand the idea of paying an attorney), consider doing it yourself—or doing as much as you can and then bringing it to an attorney to review or help. You may well want help with the most important and difficult-to-draft section, the claims. The claims set the boundaries for what's protected by the patent.

Once you get a patent, you may exclude others from making, using, or selling the patented subject matter throughout the U.S. for 20 years from the filing date of the patent application. In reality, this means a patent lasts for approximately 17 to 18 years because it takes the USPTO—the agency that oversees patents—a few years to examine and approve the application.

Design Patents

Design patents protect new and "nonobvious" ornamentation of a useful object, from the flickering icon on your computer screen to the shape of your MP3 player. Preparing and filing a design patent is fairly simple— especially compared to preparing and filing a utility patent. If you're a self-starter with a do-it-yourself mindset, you can, with a bit of work, prepare your own design patent application and save anywhere from $500 to $1,000 in lawyer's fees. A design patent lasts for 14 years.

Trademarks

If you want to stop others from using your name, logo, or some other commercial signifier, register your trademark at the USPTO. We discuss trademark registration and enforcement in Chapter 12.

Trade Secrets

Trade secret law allows your business to protect material that you keep confidential. The protection lasts as long as you can keep a secret. Once the information is generally known or can be learned by the people within an industry, it loses its special status and is no longer protected. For example, a federal court ruled that a blood bank's list of blood donors was not a trade secret because it posted the list on a computer bulletin board accessible to its competitors. (*American Red Cross v. Palm Beach Blood Bank, Inc.*, 143 F.3d 1407 (11th Cir. 1998).)

So the key to getting trade secret protection is to take reasonable precautions to keep the information confidential. In general, a business is considered to have taken reasonable steps if it uses a sensible system for protecting information—for example, locking its facilities, monitoring visitors, and labeling confidential information. A crucial part of your company's trade secret maintenance should be to require contractors, employees, investors, and others exposed to confidential information to sign a nondisclosure agreement (NDA). A person who reveals or misuses your protected information after signing a nondisclosure agreement can land in serious legal trouble. You can not only seek a court order barring further disclosure or misuse of your information, but you can sue for financial damages as well.

Asking employees or contractors to sign an NDA may seem burdensome or out of character. But the American Society of Industrial Security estimates that U.S. businesses lose at least $24 billion a year because of stolen trade secrets, most of it from the transfer of secrets by employees. Using a nondisclosure agreement may prove to be the most effective method of protecting your business and its confidential information. For free copies of nondisclosure agreements and more on trade secrets, check out www.ndasforfree.com.

"Protection" May Not Really Protect You

Once you have a copyright, trademark, trade secret, or patent, you're protected, right? Wrong. You're protected only if you're willing to sue people who use your ideas without permission. Considering that lawsuits over these issues commonly cost $50,000 or more in attorney fees (and there's no guarantee that you'll get it back), it's no wonder that many people find it too expensive to enforce their rights.

Chasing People Who Rip Off Your Ideas

If someone rips off your trade secrets, copies your copyrighted or patented work, or steals your trademark, you can make them stop and perhaps get compensated for the damage they've done. Not every dispute over ideas ends fairly or happily. Edwin H. Armstrong, the man who pioneered and patented modern radio communications, claimed that RCA and other communication companies had stolen his innovations. Eventually, he was so beaten down by the decades of litigation that he jumped to his death. It wasn't until 32 years after his patents had been granted that his widow eventually settled the cases with RCA, Motorola, and Emerson.

On the other hand, not every dispute over property rights turns into a lawsuit. Sometimes, a letter from your lawyer along with evidence of registration of your trademark, copyright, or patent will be enough to halt the infringement. In other cases, you may have to file a lawsuit and hope for a quick settlement. Your attorney can advise you on litigation—but beware that some attorneys are eager for litigation simply because they can make a lot of money from it. Proceed cautiously before filing a lawsuit.

Here are some things to consider:

Most people don't get rich over infringement lawsuits. With the exception of egregious patent or copyright thefts, you're unlikely to earn a windfall by winning an infringement lawsuit. Usually, you're awarded the infringer's profits (or your lost profits) and not much else. In many cases, the costs of the lawsuit exceed the amount recovered.

Most people don't get awarded attorneys fees. The judge will order the losing party to pay your attorney's fees only if the infringer acted willfully or intentionally. This excludes many, many infringers who were unaware they were infringing or who stopped once notified of the infringement.

You risk losing your rights. Infringers commonly argue that the patent, copyright, or trademark at issue is invalid, or that the information wasn't a trade secret. If the infringer proves invalidity—for example, someone invented your device before you filed your patent—your golden goose will be dead.

Investigate the financial stability of the person you're suing. It's foolish to sue someone who can't pay or who will disappear into cyberspace. And generally, avoid filing a lawsuit unless the infringement is likely to affect your bottom line.

Avoid filing lawsuits solely based "on principle." Attorneys love clients who fight on principle. That means the battle will continue much longer than if the client's decisions were based on business realities—for example, that it's cheaper to settle than litigate. This isn't to say you should abandon your ethical principles; just don't let this be the primary motivator for filing a suit.

Licensing or Selling Your Rights

You can make money selling your rights to someone else, either temporarily (a license) or permanently (an assignment). In return for letting a company use proprietary rights, you earn a percentage of the revenue generated (a royalty). For example, the artists who created Cabbage Patch dolls earned millions from licensing their creation. Similarly, Ray Dolby's company was built upon licensing its noise reduction patents to audio manufacturers.

What If You Copy Somebody Else's Ideas?

It's possible that someone may accuse your company of stealing ideas. The opening salvo in these disputes is usually a letter from an attorney demanding that you "cease and desist" from any further uses. To minimize any potential damages, you should:

- respond immediately, saying you received the letter and are investigating the claims
- investigate the claims and, if necessary, request further information from the owner of rights, such as proof of ownership
- if possible, stop using or distributing the device or work (for example, remove the photo from a website or stop selling a book) until the claim has been fully investigated, and
- contact an attorney knowledgeable in intellectual property law.

Not all legal threats are valid, so you will need an attorney's opinion. Be sure to ask your attorney for an estimate of the legal expenses for fighting the dispute.

DON'T

Don't assume that you can use portions of a work on the basis of "fair use," a copyright principle that permits you to copy small portions of a work for purposes such as parody, scholarship, or commentary. In one case, a company published a book of trivia questions about the events and characters of the Seinfeld television series. The company believed it had a fair use right to include questions based upon events and characters in 84 episodes and used dialogue from the show in 41 of the book's questions. A court ruled it was not a fair use; the company had to stop publishing the book and pay financial damages. (*Castle Rock Entertainment, Inc. v. Carol Publ. Group*, 150 F.3d 132 (2d Cir. 1998).)

SEE AN EXPERT

If your IP is key to your business success—particularly if your business relies on the sale or licensing of technology—you should contact an attorney specializing in intellectual property. In the case of patentable innovations, it is essential that you consult an attorney early on, since there are time limits (starting with when you first sell or publicly expose or publish your innovation) that can prevent you from obtaining patent protection. In the case of copyrightable innovations like music, books, movies, and art, you should contact an attorney whenever you have concerns about infringement or ownership. Note that there are many low-cost attorney services for arts-related issues. Check the Volunteer Lawyers for the Arts website (www.vlany .org) to see if there is an organization in your state. There are two groups of IP attorneys: patent attorneys who are licensed to practice before the United States Patent and Trademark office (USPTO) and IP attorneys who cannot file patent applications but who can advise on trademarks, copyrights, and trade secrets.

Ideas Your Employees or Contractors Come Up With

Who owns the ideas created by your workers? That depends on whether the worker is classified as an independent contractor or employee. Here are some basic principles:

- You automatically own everything—patents, trade secrets, and copyrights—created by employees in the course of their employment. Even so, it's preferable to have written agreements stating this with employees, particularly in the case of patents and trade secrets.

- You do not own things created by an independent contractor unless you both agree to it in writing. These agreements usually transfer ownership to you (known as an "assignment"), although in the case of copyright, your business may acquire ownership from an independent contractor under a principle known as a "work made for hire."

- An employee or independent contractor can never own the rights to your trademarks. The owner is always the business that first uses that trademark in commerce, regardless of who created it. However, if the trademark involves artistic elements (other than choice of font), it may be separately copyrightable, and an independent contractor may own rights under copyright law.

What's a Release and When Do You Need One?

If you want to use someone's name or image for business purposes, you may need a signed release. A release is a contract in which someone forgoes a right to sue you. Without it, the person might be able to bring you into court for various violations of personal rights.

Whether you need to obtain a release depends on why you want to use a person's name or image. If your use is for commercial purposes—for example, using a person's photo in an advertisement—always gets a release. When in doubt, we recommend that you obtain a signed release. It is best to keep the release as short and simple as possible. That's because most people asked to sign a release do so on short notice and often balk if it is complex or intimidating.

Two Companies That Made Money From Great Ideas

Here are two examples of companies that succeeded by exploiting intellectual property.

The sounds of silence. Ray Dolby had an idea for a business: Get rid of noise on recordings. In the early 1960s, the recording industry was plagued by noise, particularly the hiss from recording tape. Dolby created the first successful noise reduction system, eventually used in millions of professional and consumer tape machines, and later in film and digital recording devices. Other companies had devised and patented noise reduction processes, but Dolby's ideas—protected by more than 50 patents—gave the company its edge. When his company finally went public in 2005, Dolby, as the primary shareholder, collected $306 million in cash and kept shares in the company valued at $1.65 billion.

The lonely bull market. Jerry Moss and musician Herb Alpert had an idea for a business: Independently sell and distribute Herb's (and other artists') recordings. They each invested $100 to form a partnership. Their first recording on A&M Records, "The Lonely Bull," sold 700,000 copies, netting the two partners $180,000. Over the next 25 years, the duo signed numerous artists, from the Carpenters to Janet Jackson. Many companies have had the idea to sell recordings and own songs, but not every company had the skills to spot the artists with great musical ideas. The recordings and songs owned exclusively by A&M under copyright law enabled the company to outdistance competitors. In 1989, Alpert and Moss sold A&M Records for $300 million. They later sold their publishing company, which owned the copyrights for thousands of popular songs, for $12.5 million in cash and stock valued at $350 million. ●

Using Names and Trademarks

What's the Difference? Legal Name vs. Trademark 168

Choosing or Changing a Name 168

    Sometimes the Obvious Choice Is the Best Choice 169

    Pick a Name That Distinguishes You 169

    Avoid a Name That's Similar to Competitors 169

Perform a Simple "Knockout" Search 170

Federally Registering a Trademark 170

Staying Out of Trouble 174

Choosing a name for your business, products, and services is fun—but also a little scary. Should you pick something clever and daring like Yahoo! or Google, or stick to the folksy, like Ben & Jerry's? There's no one right answer. But whatever way you go, you need to know enough about business names and logos—collectively known as trademarks—to stay out of trouble.

What's the Difference? Legal Name vs. Trademark

Your trademark is the name (or logo or other signifier) that consumers see when purchasing your products and services. (If you sell services, it's technically a "service mark," but for our purposes we'll refer to both as trademarks). A business can have many trademarks.

Your legal name is the name you use when communicating with the government or other businesses—that is, it's the name you use to buy property, file tax returns, and write checks. You must get clearance for your legal name from your state government as part of the incorporation or LLC formation process. State government clearance is not required for sole proprietorships or partnerships, though they often must file fictitious business name documents with a county government office. This clearance has nothing to do with your right to use your name as a trade name or trademark, as described below. For example, getting corporate clearance for your business name will not shield you from trademark disputes from another company with a similar name.

Choosing or Changing a Name

If you're choosing a name or you believe that a name change will give your business a fresh start in the marketplace, consider some of the factors below.

Sometimes the Obvious Choice Is the Best Choice

PepsiCo wanted a hip name for its hip new blue cola. Like many big companies in a similar situation, it turned to a high-priced marketing company specializing in creating product names. The marketing company analyzed the blue Pepsi product, debated over 1,500 suggested names, and ultimately recommended ... "Pepsi Blue"—the nickname by which Pepsi had referred to the product internally.

Pick a Name That Distinguishes You

You don't need to be clever, just distinctive. The point here is to create a name that differentiates you from competitors. For example, Pompeii Pizzas is distinctive enough from competitors Joe's Pizza, Roundtable Pizza, or Saul's Deep Dish Pizza.

Avoid a Name That's Similar to Competitors

This is the flipside of the previous point. As we'll discuss later in this chapter, choosing a name similar to a competitor may trigger a dispute. And if the competitor's been using the name longer than you have, you'll lose the battle of the names. A similar name is one that is likely to confuse consumers—for example, you see a camera named "Polarad" and think it is a Polaroid. To create a legal problem, the similar name must be used on similar goods or services.

Determining the degree of similarity is part science and part witchcraft, and sometimes depends on the sophistication of the consumers. If you're in doubt as to whether a name you are choosing is too similar, put yourself in the competitor's shoes and look at the choice from that perspective. Would you feel ripped off? To determine if your name is similar to national competitors, check the Internet using Google or another search engine for competitors with similar names. Also check the database of federal trademark registrations at the U.S. Patent and Trademark Office (www.uspto.gov). Click "Search" under "Trademarks."

Perform a Simple "Knockout" Search

You cannot register or use a trademark that's confusingly similar to an existing trademark used in a similar class of goods or services as yours. You should search the USPTO trademark database (www.uspto.gov) when changing or choosing a new name. Look for current and pending trademark registrations using the USPTO's TESS (Trademark Electronic Search System) database. If your search yields a mark that you think conflicts with your mark, check its status via the USPTO's TARR system (Trademark Applications and Registrations Retrieval) database. Many trademarks in the database are abandoned or "dead" and should not pose a problem for your application. This type of search (called a knockout search) will uncover the most obvious marks similar to yours. Attorneys traditionally recommend that you follow this up with a professional trademark search as provided by companies such as Thomson & Thomson (www.thomson-thomson.com).

DON'T

Don't assume you get any trademark rights by creating a clever name. You don't get legal rights because you create a name. You get rights only when you use the name in commerce. You can reserve name rights with the federal government—and we'll explain how later in this chapter—but these rights don't exist until you use the mark in commerce.

Federally Registering a Trademark

Should you file a federal trademark application? Even without registering, you still have rights under state laws. You can always stop someone with a similar name from competing in your area for similar products or services, provided you can prove you used the name first. Always keep in mind that name rights are awarded because you were the first to use the name in commerce in connection with those products or services.

And having a federal registration does not automatically prevent someone from using a similar name. You will still have to pay an attorney to chase those who infringe on your trademark.

Consider filing a federal trademark application if you consistently sell products or services across state lines or plan to expand nationally. Registering a trademark with the USPTO makes it easier for the owner to protect it against would-be infringers and puts the rest of the country on notice that the mark is already taken.

The registration process involves filling out a simple application and paying an application fee. As of March, 2008, the fee was $275 per class of goods if filing electronically using TEAS Plus (a simplified version of the Trademark Electronic Application System), $325 per class of goods if filing electronically using TEAS (Trademark Electronic Application System), and $375 per class if filing a paper application.

However you file, you must also be prepared to work with an official of the USPTO to correct any errors in the application. To qualify a mark for registration with the USPTO, the mark's owner first must put it into use "in commerce that Congress may regulate."

This means that the mark must be used on a product or service that crosses state, national, or territorial lines—for example, a catalog or Internet business that sells products to customers in different states, or a restaurant or motel that caters to interstate or international consumers.

If you're not using the mark in commerce yet you can file an intent-to-use application, which is used when the applicant intends to use the mark in the near future but hasn't begun using it yet. If you file an intent-to-use application, another document—a statement indicating your actual use of the mark—must be filed later, along with an additional fee once the actual use of the trademark begins. And you must show the USPTO that the mark is now being used in commerce.

Once the USPTO receives your trademark application, it determines the answers to these questions:

- Does the application have to be amended (because of errors)?
- Is the mark the same as or similar to an existing mark used on similar or related goods or services?
- Is the mark on a list of prohibited or reserved names?
- Is the mark generic—that is, does the mark describe the product or service itself rather than its source?
- Is the mark descriptive—that is, does it consist of words or images that are ordinary or that literally describe one or more aspects of the underlying goods or services?

Once you satisfactorily provide the answers to these questions to the USPTO, the agency will publish the mark in the Official Gazette (an online publication of the U.S. Patent and Trademark Office) as being a candidate for registration.

Existing trademark and service mark owners may object to your registration by filing an opposition. If this occurs, the USPTO will schedule a hearing to resolve the dispute.

If there is no opposition, and use in commerce has been established, the USPTO will place the mark on the list of trademarks known as the Principal Register.

Probably the most important benefit of placing a mark on the Principal Register is that anybody who later initiates use of the same or a confusingly similar mark will be presumed by the courts to be a "willful infringer," and therefore liable for any losses or injuries you suffer as result of their unauthorized use of your trademark.

The federal registration lasts for ten years. During that time, you have certain obligations to maintain your trademark registration—for example, you must file a Section 8 Declaration of Continued Use form between the fifth and sixth anniversaries of the registration. You can find information about the registration procedure as well as the maintenance requirements at the USPTO website (www.uspto.gov). For more on trademark registration procedures, check *Trademark: Legal Care for Your Business & Product Name,* by Stephen Elias and Richard Stim (Nolo).

INTERNET LINK

You can find links for all the resources in this book at www.nolo .com/wowbusiness.

Generics and Weak Trademarks

You can't register a generic name that describes an entire group or class of goods or services. For example, if you were to call your truck sales business "Trucks," you couldn't register it as a trademark. You can, however, register a mark such as "Geek's Hi-Tech Trucks" for a truck business, but the USPTO requires that you give up exclusive rights to the word "truck" by itself.

The USPTO will reject an application for a "weak" (descriptive) trademark, but you can register it later if you can prove that the name has achieved sufficient recognition among consumers—usually indicated by three or more years of use or relatively large sales or advertising dollars spent. A name is weak if it describes the nature or quality of the goods— for example, Park 'n Shop describes a place where you park and then shop. A made-up term like Kodak, or an arbitrary name such as Apple for computers, is strong because it doesn't describe the goods.

Trademark Symbols

Typically, the symbols ®, TM, or SM are used with trademarks—for example, IBM® or Happy Boy Music Store™. The symbol ® indicates that a trademark has been registered with the USPTO; it is illegal to use it if the trademark has no USPTO registration. If your trademark or service mark hasn't been federally registered, you can use the TM symbol or SM symbol. The TM and SM have no legal significance but indicate that the owner is claiming trademark rights.

Staying Out of Trouble

You've probably read about disputes in which one company sues another over its trademark. Or maybe you've heard about a big company pushing around a smaller business—for example, McDonalds stopping a company from using "McSushi" or "McSoup." Do you need to worry about a dispute over your business name?

Probably not. It's estimated that fewer than 4,000 lawsuits are filed each year in federal courts over trademark issues. And many of these lawsuits aren't even about the right to use a name. They're about the abuse of names by counterfeiters or by consumers—for example at "gripe sites" (websites such as Ballysucks.com, which disparage a company).

Even if someone does hassle you over your name, chances are good that you can resolve the dispute efficiently with a few letters or a call to a lawyer (see "The $200 Name Dispute," below).

For most small business owners, the odds of getting a letter from an attorney about a business name are slim to none. Here are some factors that help you determine whether your business is more or less likely to have name problems.

What will your competitors think of your name? Most name disputes are turf battles between competitors. The more your name or logo resembles a competitor's, the more likely you'll have a dispute. For example, the company that owns Victoria's Secret chased Victor and Cathy Moseley for five years—all the way to U.S. Supreme Court—after they named their novelties shop Victor's Little Secret. (Victor eventually changed the business name to Cathy's Little Secret even though the Supreme Court ruled in their favor.)

How far away are your customers? You're less likely to run into name problems if your customers are local, not regional or national. This means businesses that rely substantially on the Internet for revenue are more likely to run into name problems, primarily because their customers are spread around the nation (or world).

Do you want to be big? You're more likely to have name problems if you want to expand into new territories or franchise your business.

Are you trading off the popularity of a famous business? Even if you're not a competitor, you may run into a problem if your name conjures up a famous company's name or logo. For example, American Express wasn't amused when a condom company began using the trademarked slogan "Don't Leave Home Without It." Amex stopped the use under a trademark principle known as dilution—the tarnishing or blurring of a famous trademark by another business, even though the two aren't competitors.

The $200 Name Dispute

Richard owns Comet Building Maintenance, a janitorial service in Northern California. A Texas-based dry-cleaning chain, Comet 1-Hour Drycleaning, demanded information on Richard's use of the term "Comet," including how long he had been using it, and whether he was selling any products or services under that name. The implication was that Richard's right to use Comet—which he'd been doing for 18 years—was now in jeopardy.

Richard contacted me, and I called the Texas company's attorney and explained that Comet Building Maintenance offered janitorial services, not products, and that in Richard's 18 years of business, his company had never been confused with the Texas company. The Texas company backed off, and Richard never heard from it again. Richard's cost was $200 in attorney's fees. —Rich Stim

DON'T

When it comes to using another company's trademarks, there are several "Don'ts."

Don't mislead consumers when selling reconditioned goods. A company customized Rolex watches by replacing internal elements and adding diamonds. The company sold these as Rolex watches, and the Rolex company sued to stop the sales. The court ruled that because the reconditioning was so severe, it was unfair to call the watches "Rolex." (*Rolex Watch U.S.A. Inc., v. Michel Co.,* 50 USPQ 2d 1939 (9th Cir. 1999).)

Don't assume you can use trademarks from ratings or awards. Most companies that provide ratings or give awards provide guidelines for the use of their marks in advertising. Some require written permission; some, like Consumers Union, publisher of Consumer Reports, prohibit any use of their trademark in advertisements.

Don't advertise trademarked ingredients without permission. If you sell homemade candy featuring Grand Marnier brand liquor, don't give undue prominence to this (or any other) trademarked ingredient. For example, avoid saying "Intel Inside" if you assemble computers, unless you meet the conditions for use of the Intel trademark posted at the Intel website.

Don't confuse the source when selling complementary or add-on products. The Apple iPod has spawned an industry of products that complement the popular player, such as amplifiers, recording devices, and holders. It's okay to state you're selling an iPod holder, for example, but don't create the impression that it's endorsed or sold by Apple.

Don't mislead consumers on the Internet. There are many ways for a business to mislead consumers on the Web, and new ones keep popping up. For example, ShoesforSale.com puts the name of a competitor, Zappos.com, in its website code (in a form known as a metatag). When a consumer searches for Zappos, ShoesforSale.com turns up in the search results. The courts have not consistently resolved how to deal with these issues, but regardless of whether you will win or lose in court, you still face the costs of defending yourself in a dispute.

Don't assume you can sell trademark parodies. Sometimes it's permissible to parody a trademark. Parody is imitation that pokes fun at the mark—for example, by selling caps printed with the words, "Mutant of Omaha." But offensive parodies are often likely to trigger lawsuits. For example, lawsuits were filed over lewd photos of the Pillsbury doughboy and of nude Barbie dolls. Although the artist in the case involving Barbie dolls eventually won his claim, it required substantial legal effort and expense. (*Mattel Inc. v. Walking Mountain Productions*, Inc., 2001 U.S. App. LEXIS 2610 (9th Cir. 2002).) A trademark parody is less likely to run into problems if it doesn't compete with the trademarked goods and services and doesn't confuse consumers—that is, they get the joke and do not believe the parody product comes from the same source as the trademarked goods.

 SEE AN EXPERT

Call a lawyer ...

- if you receive a request from another business or its attorney asking you to stop using a trademark
- if you believe a competitor is using a confusingly similar name to your business
- if you file a trademark application and receive a notice of opposition from another trademark owner, or
- if you file a trademark application and are unsure of how to proceed when you receive an office action or rejection from a trademark examiner. ●

Licenses, Permits, and Other Paperwork

Basic Registration Requirements 180

Register Your Fictitious Business Name 183

If You Sell Goods, Get a Seller's Permit 184

Permits and Licenses for Specialized Fields 186

ven the smallest home-based business can't fly beneath the government's radar. For example, in the city of San Francisco, fortune-tellers have to post their rates, get fingerprinted, offer customers a written receipt, and get a fortune-telling permit from the city's police department. Although the San Francisco measure was billed as a way to protect consumers from charlatans, the real reason seems clear—it's a way to increase the city coffers. The city controller's office estimates that the city could net more than $46,000 annually if its estimated 130 fortune-tellers pay the permit fee.

As you can see, no matter what kind of business you run, you'll have to register with—and perhaps pay fees to—the federal, state, and local governments where you do business.

For most business owners, these registration requirements are easy to meet—you just have to fill out a few simple forms. However, while the paperwork is pretty straightforward, it's not always obvious exactly what you have to file and with which government agency. This chapter will help you cut through the red tape and get the licenses you need to run your business legally.

Basic Registration Requirements

There are a few forms that most businesses have to file. They include:

IRS Form SS-4, *Application for Employer Identification Number.* Despite its name, this form is required for many businesses that don't have employees. You must file it to get an employer identification number (EIN)—a nine-digit number that the federal government uses, like an individual's Social Security number, to identify your business for tax purposes. Your business must have an EIN if you have at least one employee. Even if you have no employees, you must get an EIN if:

- you have a partnership, limited liability company, or corporation (the EIN is necessary to identify your business on your tax returns), or

- you are a sole proprietor and have a Keogh retirement plan (a plan for self-employed people), buy or inherit an existing business, or file for bankruptcy.

FINDING THE FORMS

The IRS has made it very easy to apply for an EIN. You can download Form SS-4 from the IRS website, www.irs.gov, then mail or fax it to the IRS. If you want to speed things along, you can complete your form online and submit it electronically (follow the instructions at the IRS website) or provide the required information to an IRS representative over the phone (800-829-4933). If you file electronically or by phone, you will immediately receive a provisional EIN, which will become your permanent EIN once the IRS verifies your application information. Don't forget to write the number down and store it someplace safe; if you file online, print a copy of the form for your records.

State business license. A few states require any business within their borders to get a general business license. However, it's much more common for a state to require only certain types of businesses to get a license. If you work in a field that requires specialized training (engineering, nursing, or child care, for example) or deals extensively with consumers (such as home repair or tax preparation), you are more likely to need a state license. If you must get a license, expect to pay a fee and submit proof that you have the necessary education, training, or work experience. Fees range widely—in California, for example, a manicurist must pay an initial fee of $35, then $40 every two years after that; if you want to train guide dogs, however, you'll have to pony up $250 at the outset, then pay another $100 every year. Depending on your field, you may also have to take a test, post a bond, allow the state to fingerprint you, show proof of insurance, or meet other requirements.

FINDING THE FORMS

To find out whether you have to get a state business license, go to your state's website. You can find a link to it at State and Local Government on the Net, www.statelocalgov.net; also check out the list of links to state Web pages that offer business license information at the website of the federal Small Business Administration, www.sba.gov/hotlist/license.html. Many states have small business centers online (these often have "one-stop" in their title) or links to state agencies and publications that deal with business matters.

Local business license. Many cities and counties require those who do business within their limits to file a registration form. This form may be called a tax registration certificate, business license, business tax application, or something similar. No matter what the form is called, its purpose is the same: to tax your business. You may have to pay a flat fee or a rate that depends on your annual revenue. If your business is very small (as measured by its revenues), you may be exempt from a city or county licensing requirement.

FINDING THE FORMS

If you do business in a city, contact your city government to find out about licensing requirements and get the necessary forms. If you do business in an unincorporated area, contact your county government. Many local governments have websites—and some post information for small businesses and make their forms available online. You can find a comprehensive list of links to online local government agencies at State and Local Government on the Net, www.statelocalgov.net. If you're looking for county ordinances online, go to the website of the National Association of Counties, www.naco.org. Click "About Counties." Then you'll be able to search county codes and ordinances or look for a link to your county's website.

Make sure you meet local zoning requirements. When you register for a local business license, your local government will almost certainly check to make sure that your business meets the zoning requirements for the address you provide for your business. If your business isn't in compliance—because it's industrial in an area zoned residential, because it has too many employees, or because it will attract too much traffic, for example—you won't get a license. What's more, you can probably expect a city or county inspector to drop by and start issuing citations (or perhaps even shut you down) in fairly short order.

DON'T

Don't blow off local registration requirements. Although you might think that your local government doesn't know about your business, you might be in for an unpleasant surprise—one that comes with a hefty bill and penalties attached.

That's what happened to small business owners in Oakland, California. Using state tax records, the city of Oakland uncovered plenty of small businesses—many of them home-based—that had not applied for city business licenses or paid local business taxes. In 2004, these business owners were hit with demands for back taxes and penalties going back to 2001. Business owners raised a protest, many of them claiming that the charges were unfair because they didn't know they were supposed to pay a tax and never received a tax bill from the city. So far, however, the city has refused to budge—perhaps because the unpaid amounts add up to $6 million.

Register Your Fictitious Business Name

If you do business under a fictitious name (often called a "DBA," for "doing business as"), you probably have to register that name with your state or county government. A fictitious name doesn't refer only to a completely made up moniker, like Xerox or Kodak. Any name that doesn't precisely match your corporate, partnership, or limited liability company name is considered fictitious. And if you're a sole proprietor, any name that doesn't include your last name (or in some states, your full legal name) or seems to suggest that other people are involved in your business (such as John Brown & Associates) is fictitious.

In most places, you register a DBA with your county government. You will probably have to file a registration certificate (along with a fee, of course) with the county. You may also have to run a statement in a local newspaper for a set period of time, stating your DBA and your true name.

The state wants you to register your name so it can track you down if your business does something wrong, such as ripping off consumers or skipping out on loans or bills. But there's plenty in it for you, too. For starters, registering your DBA puts other companies on notice that the name is taken—and stakes your claim to use the name as of the date you registered. (It doesn't get you trademark protections, though—see Chapter 12 for more on that.)

There are also some practical reasons to register your name. For example, some banks won't let you open a business bank account under your fictitious name unless you show them a registration certificate. And you may not be able to enforce a contract you signed using your business name unless you can show that you registered it properly.

FINDING THE FORMS

For information on registering a fictitious name, go to your county clerk's website (you can probably find a link to it at State and Local Government on the Net, www.statelocalgov.net). If you can't find the information you need there, check your state's website.

If You Sell Goods, Get a Seller's Permit

In most states, if you're selling goods, you need a permit from the state authorizing you to make sales and collect sales tax from customers within the state. Sometimes, the permit lets you buy items from wholesalers (for resale to customers) without paying sales tax. Some states call this a seller's permit; others call it a resale permit or something similar. (Note: You might need a permit even if your state doesn't have a sales tax. Even in the handful of states that don't impose a sales tax—Alaska, Delaware, Montana, New Hampshire, and Oregon—local governments sometimes impose sales taxes, which you may be required to collect and pass on.)

If your business sells tangible goods—items you can touch, such as jewelry, clothing, or food—you'll almost certainly have to get a seller's permit. However, even if you sell services, you may need a seller's permit if:

- **your state taxes services.** A few states impose a sales tax on services. If you run a service business in one of these states, you may need a permit to collect tax from your customers.

- **you provide both goods and services.** For example, if you work as a caterer, you might sell both a product (prepared food) and a service (set-up and clean-up, waiting tables, and so on). In this situation, you may need a seller's permit—and you will have to separate what you charge for goods and for services so you can collect sales tax. If you occasionally provide goods in the course of doing your service work (as a plumber might supply a necessary fitting to repair a leak), you generally won't be required to charge your customers sales tax.

DON'T

Don't make sales unless and until you get a seller's permit, if your state requires one. If you're caught doing business without a permit, you could be subject to a number of penalties—such as having to pay the sales tax you should have collected from your customers, along with a fine. You could even face some jail time. That's what happened to a businessman in Sioux Falls, South Dakota. Convicted of doing business without a state sales tax license, he was fined $120, charged court costs of $45, and given 60 days in jail—to be suspended only if he paid all past due taxes, filed all delinquent tax returns, and had no violations of state tax laws for two years.

FINDING THE FORMS

You can find information on seller's permit requirements at the website of your state's tax agency. For a list of links to these agencies, go to the IRS website at www.irs.gov, choose "Business," then "Small Business/ Self-Employed," then "State Links." Or, choose your state's link at the list of tax agencies provided at the website of the federal Small Business Administration at www.sba.gov/hotlist/statetaxhomepages.html.

INTERNET LINK

You can find links for all the resources in this book at www.nolo .com/wowbusiness.

Permits and Licenses for Specialized Fields

Depending on the type of business you run, you might have to get any number of other permits from your state and local government. For example, you might need a permit from the fire department to run a day care center, a permit from the health department to sell food, or a permit from your state or local environmental agency to do work that involves hazardous chemicals. Your best resources for finding out whether you'll need to meet these requirements are the state and local agencies that regulate your profession. Give them a call or visit their websites—you can find comprehensive links to state and local websites at www.statelocalgov.net.

Marketing Basics

What's the Difference? Marketing vs. Advertising..................................190

Ten Marketing Tips..190

    You Can Avoid Advertising..190

    Drive Customers by Need, Price, and Access....................................191

    Market After the Sale 191

    Go Guerrilla 192

    Marketing Is a Sensory Experience..192

    Yes, the Customer Is (Almost) Always Right 193

    The Four Marketing Motivators 193

    Use Words That Sell 194

    Don't Rely on Market Research...194

    Measure Results...194

Your Marketing Toolbox..196

    Samples and Free Offers..196

    Personal Letters or Cards...197

    Telephone Marketing 197

    Postcards, Handouts, and Brochures 197

    Display and Classified Ads 198

    Yellow Pages..199

    Direct Mail...199

    Radio and Television 200

    Trade Shows..201

    Public Relations...201

    Online Advertising...203

Seminars and Product Demonstrations..203

Signs 203

Outdoor Advertising 204

Do You Need a Marketing Plan?...204

I f you ask five customers how they learned about your business and they say it was from satisfied customers, you can probably skip this chapter. There is no better, more cost-effective form of marketing than word-of-mouth. If new business comes by referral, then you already have a marketing team in action: your customers.

If you aren't getting new customers or keeping the ones you have, you may need a marketing fix. We'll provide some help in this chapter. As you read, keep a few things in mind.

Sophisticated marketing help is readily available. Cartons of books and hundreds of websites can advise you how to redo your packaging, get publicity, write newspaper ads, buy radio advertising, design new brochures, make television ads, or update your website with more pizzazz (though we're not really sure websites need more pizzazz). We recommend many of these resources throughout this chapter.

There are no one-size-fits-all rules when it comes to marketing. You may be able to handle all of your marketing with a well-designed booth at a national trade show or with a series of beautifully designed postcards. What works for you depends on your personality and your business. For example, a gregarious, extroverted business owner may be well-suited for live product demonstrations and similar public events. But an arty, introverted business owner may do a better job of reaching customers with personalized letters or customized mailings. Our advice is to explore the marketing resources available and choose what feels right for you and your business.

Think about marketing in a very broad way. It goes far beyond the tools discussed in this chapter. Everything you do in your daily business activity becomes part of your marketing effort: The way you greet customers, ship orders, handle refunds, or maintain your work space can have a greater influence on business success than your choice of business card or purchase of radio spots. Many small business owners have learned the hard way that the most successful marketing is working hard to maintain the integrity and credibility that are at the heart of your business.

What's the Difference? Marketing vs. Advertising

Marketing is any method of attracting and retaining customers. Marketing includes advertising. Advertising is when you pay to spread your message via the Internet, TV, radio, a newspaper or magazine, or any other medium. So, if you paint the name of your business on the side of your truck, that's marketing; if you pay someone to paint the name of your business on their truck, it's advertising. Think of advertising as one of many marketing tools. Why make the distinction? As you'll see, some marketing experts believe that advertising is the wrong route for small business owners.

Ten Marketing Tips

You want to formulate a marketing strategy that reflects your personality and your business. To help you achieve that goal, here are some ideas and suggestions.

You Can Avoid Advertising

If you buy only one marketing book, we recommend *Marketing Without Advertising*, by Michael Phillips and Salli Rasberry (Nolo), a book that changed the way many small business owners thought about marketing. Considering that the average American is exposed to 60% more daily advertising than 15 years ago, it's no wonder that Phillips and Rasberry want you to avoid paying for ad space. They point out that more than two-thirds of the profitable small businesses in the U.S. operate without advertising and urge you to concentrate on creating a high-quality operation that customers, employees, and other businesspeople will trust, respect, and recommend. Their key strategies are built around getting customers to spread the word, planning marketing events that keep customers involved, and encouraging the media to comment positively on your business. We'll discuss some of these strategies in more detail, below.

Drive Customers by Need, Price, and Access

As part of your marketing strategy, you need to consider the common factors that drive customers to a business. In *How to Run a Thriving Business* (Nolo), Ralph Warner advises that there are three elements:

- **Need.** When you're considering how to market or which tools to use, try to determine why customers need your products or services instead of your competitors'. For example, customers seeking computer repair may need house calls or evening maintenance—two qualities that could distinguish your business's marketing strategy.

- **Price.** In some cases, customers base purchasing decisions primarily on price; in others, people place perceived value over price. Figure out which rule applies for your business and price accordingly. Whichever drives customers, consumers like prices that are clear, easy to understand, and not hidden. Consumers dislike pricing surprises. And, if possible, give consumers some control over pricing. Retailers such as Costco and Amazon.com are built on this principle—offering consumers the ability to save money by choosing among pricing options.

- **Access.** If cost and quality are equal, customers usually patronize the business that's easiest to access. What matters is whether customers can find your business and patronize it once they locate it; for example, you need good signage, parking, and clear yellow pages listings. Access can also translate into your Web business. How easy is it for customers to find you on the Web? And equally important, does your website describe how to contact or locate your business? See Chapter 18 for more on going online.

Market After the Sale

Some of your best marketing can happen after the sale is made. For example, after customers buy Gunnar Madsen's compact disc of waltz music at CDBaby.com, they receive an email offering free downloads of Gunnar's other music. Later, he writes to customers offering to place them on his mailing list. Author Seth Godin calls this "permission marketing," and he has written a book of the same name. The basic principle: Once the customer responds to your offer, you can get permission to sell more stuff. In other words, the sale is the beginning of the relationship, not the end.

Go Guerrilla

Check out Jay Levinson's *Guerrilla Marketing* (Houghton Mifflin), the first marketing book aimed squarely at small businesses. (Or check out the numerous "guerrilla" books and websites, such as www .gmarketing.com.) Unlike traditional marketing, which requires money, guerrilla marketing usually requires only time, energy, and imagination. Levinson is a proponent of simple marketing devices such as brochures, signs, classified advertising, and low-cost public events—for example, seminars, free samples, consultations, and product demonstrations. His emphasis is on keeping existing customers and getting them to make more transactions. As for your competition, Levinson recommends that you look for ways to cooperate for greater profits—for example, joining together to buy supplies at lower rates or creating a referral system.

Marketing Is a Sensory Experience

Marketing is a lot like dating. You're trying to get somebody interested and then retain that interest while you continue to sell yourself. And much of the attraction is based on sensory experience—how your business looks, how it smells, and the sense of order that it instills. As coffee shops and bakeries know, there's a strong sensory appeal to the smell of their wares. Conversely, consumers can be repulsed by a pet shop that doesn't clean up the cages. Don't underestimate the marketing importance of cleanliness and a sense of order (a clutter-free environment); consumers often equate these qualities with competence and success. Examine every aspect of your business, from the appearance of your staff to your restrooms, and take advantage of this inexpensive marketing fix. Keep in mind that these principles of cleanliness and lack of clutter also apply to the appearance of your signage and website.

Yes, the Customer Is (Almost) Always Right

Did you know that 80% of complaining customers are unhappier after they complain? Since your customers are your best marketing team, it's crazy to lose them through poor service. One of the least expensive, most effective marketing techniques is to adopt customer-friendly policies and to hire and train employees who can carry out these policies. Your customer service program may include response cards, listening without interruption as customers complain, or providing "extras" for customers. Zingerman's, the famed Ann Arbor, Michigan, food emporium, abides by the 10-4 rule: Make eye contact within ten feet of seeing a customer; greet them within four feet. For more on Zingerman's world-famous practices, check out Zingerman's *Guide to Giving Great Service*, by Ari Weinzweig (Hyperion).

The Four Marketing Motivators

In *Direct Mail Copy That Sells* (Prentice Hall), Herschel Gordon Lewis describes what are commonly referred to as the four major marketing motivators: fear, guilt, greed, and exclusivity.

How do they work? Fear is an appeal to whatever the consumer is afraid of—for example, a computer virus, a missed opportunity, auto problems. Gordon thinks that fear, by far, is the greatest motivator, but it works as a marketing motivator only if the customer is provided with a solution to whatever is feared.

Guilt is used to bring back customers who haven't shopped at your store in a while or haven't renewed your newsletter ("we hate losing you ..."). Greed is simple—the customer wants to come out ahead ("Here's a special discount we're making only to existing customers"). And exclusivity is the sense of getting something others can't (American Express Platinum card, anyone?).

These motivators may be popular on Madison Avenue, but for small business owners who do not mount major ad campaigns, this manipulative approach may backfire. Fear, for example, may scare off buyers. Guilt may cause customers to avoid your business. Greed and exclusivity may offend.

Marketing that's based on quality, not manipulation, is always more effective at creating long-lasting customer relations.

Use Words That Sell

Did you know there are 62 ways to say "exciting" and 57 ways to say "reliable?" If you can't afford to hire a professional copywriter for your signs, yellow pages ads, product labels, and so forth, then buy a copy of Richard Bayan's *Words That Sell* (McGraw-Hill). It's functional, helpful, and easy to use. The book has five sections—Grabbers, Descriptions & Benefits, Clinchers, Terms & Offers, and Special Strategies, and is a great way to jump-start your advertising and sign copy.

Don't Rely on Market Research

Market research relies on asking questions of people, observing customer behavior, comparing your customers to those of your competitors, talking to ex-customers who have abandoned you, and examining the demographics of your market. But according to Jim Nelens in *Research to Riches: The Secret Rules of Successful Marketing* (Longstreet Press), you'll always get different conclusions depending on the techniques used. For example, questioning people over the phone often produces different results than questioning the same people in person at the mall; questioning people in the morning produces different results than in the evening. Similarly, you'll get a higher response to a mail survey from older people than from younger ones. Before you conduct research—and particularly if you're thinking of hiring a market research company—check out Nelens' book.

Measure Results

In the marketing world, "accountability" is the term used to describe whether or not a marketing tool is working. Sometimes it's easy to see if a tool is accountable. For example, after Amazon featured Nolo's *Quicken WillMaker* on its home page, online sales of the product doubled. In other cases—particularly with advertising—it's difficult to determine if the effort is working.

The best way to measure results is to provide a special offer tied to the marketing effort. Whether it is television, radio, print, or direct mail, try to provide an offer that's unique to that promotion. That makes it much easier to track effectiveness.

Marketing Your Brand

You may wonder how companies like Harley Davidson, Virgin, or Pepsi became so popular that each has achieved "brand" status—a name that consumers trust and rely upon when making purchasing decisions. Can you create a brand phenomenon like Nike or Ben & Jerry's?

Possibly. But some business owners mistakenly assume that the key to a successful brand is extensive advertising and marketing of a name. Not true. Successful branding results from working diligently to maintain consistently high quality. In short, brand loyalty means that consumers love what you do. Modern advertising theorists say that branding is really an emotional relationship between consumer and company.

If local customers love your business, you've got a brand. For example, the loyal fans of Amoeba Records, a popular chain of used record stores in California, buy thousands of Amoeba T-shirts. "Another example of this," says business consultant Alan Weiss, "is the neighborhood restaurant with an unlisted phone number. Or when you say, 'I'm going to bring this to Paul the Tailor.' That's great branding, too," says Weiss. "Like the bar in the old TV show 'Cheers,' you want to keep coming back."

Without consistent quality, large and small brands will topple. For example, Coca-Cola, by many estimates the most valuable brand name in the world, took a dive in sales and stock value when it tinkered with its quality and consistency and introduced New Coke. Similarly, it took years for the Jack-in-the-Box fast food chain to build back consumer trust (and its brand name) after an outbreak of food poisoning in 1993.

To learn more about branding theories and how you can use their insights to advantage, check out the Branding Blog (www.brandingblog .com) or read the leading book on the subject, *Designing Brand Identity* by Alina Wheeler (Wiley).

INTERNET LINK

You can find links for all the resources in this book at www.nolo .com/wowbusiness.

Your Marketing Toolbox

It's easy to pick the right tool when making a home repair. But it's a little trickier when you open your marketing toolbox. Which marketing tools are you comfortable with? Which will fit your budget? Which reflect positively on your business? Which ones really work for you?

Our suggestion: Look through these common marketing strategies and ruminate on your business for a few weeks. If you have employees or co-owners, talk about what might work to attract and keep customers. Start slowly. Avoid a big budget. Be patient. Measure results. And stick with what works.

Samples and Free Offers

You may hate receiving those free America Online discs—we do—but they're remarkably effective in creating trial users of the AOL service. At one point, the company spent approximately $300 in marketing to reach each new user, yet the results were successful enough to continue the free offers. Similarly, Kiehl's, the high-end skin care retailer is happy to fill each customer's shopping bag with free samples of new products. Can your business afford to offer something for free—for example, a free cookie with every cake or a free cappuccino for every ten purchased? Giving away something you make is usually an inexpensive marketing gesture that will have customers appreciating the value of your products. Customers never seem to tire of these special offers and gifts.

Free offers can function two ways. You may offer existing customers a bonus—for example, Mudpuppy's Tub & Scrub gives a free dog wash after ten purchases. Or you can use free samples to attract new customers—the marketing strategy exploited with much success by cosmetics giant Estee Lauder.

Personal Letters or Cards

Does your insurance agent send you a birthday or Christmas card? Sometimes these efforts seem cheesy; sometimes they're effective. The key to making successful use of personal letters or cards is, well … making them personal. If possible, avoid preprinted labels and form-letter style notes, and if sending out cards, make sure to add something in your handwriting. For example, a musician I know sends out cards announcing upcoming shows. A few years ago, she began writing personal notes on the cards and noticed that attendance increased substantially. Sending a handwritten card to clients—even if it's just to thank them for their continued business—is a small, memorable touch that can go a long way to maintaining customers and clients.

Telephone Marketing

When you pick up the phone to follow up on sales calls or respond to customer inquiries, you're telemarketing, which is just selling your business over the phone. The stigma attached to telemarketing is associated with cold calls—calling strangers whose phone numbers are provided via a subscription list or through an automatic software dialing device. James Stephenson, author of *Entrepreneur Magazine's Ultimate Small Business Marketing Guide* (Entrepreneur), recommends that you make only "warm calls"—calls to people you know or who you know share common interests. For example, if you teach swimming, can you obtain the membership lists of local swimming clubs? Stephenson also suggests avoiding common telemarketing mistakes—for example, sticking to a script and not listening to what the person on the other end is saying. Also, keep in mind that you are prohibited from calling people who have added their names to the federal Do Not Call Registry (www.donotcall.gov) unless you have an existing business relationship.

Postcards, Handouts, and Brochures

For centuries, small business owners have relied on a relatively inexpensive method of conveying marketing information: cards, brochures, and circulars. For example, you can purchase 1,000 color postcards for your business for approximately $100 to $200; you can get 1,000 two-page color brochures for $400 to $500. Unfortunately, the value of these marketing efforts is lost unless your printed material expresses the right message both in form and content, and unless you distribute these materials properly—that is, get them into the hands of targeted customers.

In *Guerrilla Marketing* (Houghton Mifflin), Jay Levinson recommends that you focus on one basic idea that you want to express—for example, "We make the most energy-efficient hot tubs" or "We're the most reliable upholsterers"—and then marry that idea with a suitable image. And always include relevant contact information. Two popular and easy-to-use software programs that can assist in your design are Microsoft *Office Publisher* and Broderbund's *Print Shop Deluxe*. Both provide templates for business publications.

Display and Classified Ads

Did you know 61% of Americans read magazines from the back to the front? According to Jay Levinson, that's one indication that an economical classified ad will have a chance for success. Depending on the size and publication, you may spend $20 to $50 for a first insertion. You'll get a "frequency discount" if you run it three or four times. In addition, many newspapers now run classified ads both in print and online.

Display ads—boxed advertisements that appear in the body of a newspaper or magazine—are more expensive and vary widely in price. To get the rates, ask for the publication's advertising card. There is also a variation, known as a classified display ad—it runs in the classified ad section—which is less expensive than a regular display ad. What size ad should you run? According to studies, one-quarter of readers notice display ads that occupy a quarter or half a page; 40% notice full-page ads.

Because display ads are often lost in a sea of similar display advertisements, you should take a cautious approach when buying ad space. One of the key elements to a successful display ad campaign is placing the ad in the right publication. Ralph Warner recommends trying out one or two different ads as a test and suggests targeting ads—for example, if you are seeking business-to-business customers, advertise in trade publications; if you are seeking tourist business, advertise in local publications aimed at visitors. As with all your advertising, your message must be succinct and convincing. If possible, log responses to the advertisement to measure its effectiveness.

Yellow Pages

Despite the continuing growth of the Internet, a large number of consumers still use the local telephone company's yellow pages. Over 70% of the respondents in one survey had used the directory to contact a local firm, and half of them had made a purchase. If you place a yellow pages ad, emphasize your specialties, put in as much access information as you can, and avoid being cute or too arty—keep in mind that this is an advertisement that will be consulted for at least a year. Compare what your competitors are doing and, as always, track responses, test new ads, and modify when necessary.

Direct Mail

With the advent of the Internet, you might think that direct mail would be dying off, replaced by email advertisements. Not so. According to Seth Godin in *Permission Marketing* (Simon & Schuster), direct mailings have increased in recent years primarily because they are more effective at "interrupting" consumers than advertisements, and their success rate is measurable.

If you're considering direct mail, though, the response statistics are not good. It's often difficult for a small business owner to compete with the big-buck marketers who are content with a response rate as low as five per thousand mailings (0.5%).

To give your direct mailings an edge, Alexander Hiam, author of *Marketing for Dummies* (Wiley), recommends that you always include three elements:

- **bait**—something that captures the reader's attention
- **the argument**—why your product or service can solve a problem for the reader, and
- **a call to action**—an appeal for immediate action.

In direct mail lingo, these three elements are known as the star, the chain, and the hook. Hiam also recommends that considerable effort be devoted to the envelope so that it announces a special offer or benefit or is artistically creative enough to get the recipient to open it.

How do you create your direct mail address list? If you're interested in setting up a database of existing customers, you'll need software such as Microsoft *Access* or *FileMaker*.

Do you want to send your mailings to strangers? Most likely, you will be best served by sending to existing customers. But if you wish to buy a mailing list, contact one of the many companies that sell or rent them to small business owners (the largest of which is www.infousa.com). For more information on creating successful direct mail, read *Direct Mail Copy That Sells*, by Herschel Gordon Lewis (Prentice Hall).

Also, don't forget email. Although you'll likely want to avoid the stigma of unsolicited email—unaffectionately known as spam—you may find that email blasts to existing customers can effectively alert them to special sales or bonus offers.

Radio and Television

Radio (80%) and television (75%) reach more people than newspapers (70%) on a daily basis. Repetitious radio and TV ads can build awareness of your business rapidly. For example, the success of the Mattel toy company was based on the risky (at the time) decision to sponsor "The Mickey Mouse Club" television show.

But for small business owners, using radio and TV can pose so many problems that it's probably not worth pursuing. First, you must target your advertisement so that you're reaching the right listeners or viewers. Second, you must allot quite a bit of your ad marketing budget to produce radio and television advertising. (You'll pay $1,000 to $20,000 per minute for video production, depending on the quality.) Third, more than other forms of advertising discussed in this chapter, radio and TV ads require that you develop a style or angle—for example, humorous, real-life, educational—and that you engage listeners or viewers for 15 to 60 seconds of air time. Finally, the expense and uncertainty of their effectiveness make radio and TV ads an unlikely marketing tool for small business owners.

If you are set on proceeding with radio or TV ads, avoid committing to long contracts until you are satisfied with the initial results. Consider using an ad agency to create or place your radio or TV ads—it may give your business a more professional appearance and can sometimes buy airtime at better rates.

Trade Shows

For many small business owners—especially those in a business-to-business market—trade shows are a key marketing tool. It's at the trade show that you meet the sales people and retailers. There are two important variables in trade show marketing: your choice of show and your booth.

You can find trade show listings for your industry in a trade publication, at industry websites, or by using the search feature at the Ultimate Trade Show Resource (www.tsnn.com). If possible, learn about the previous show. You may be able to do this by questioning participants or checking online. For example, attendees at crafts shows often comment on the shows at the message board on the *Crafts Report Magazine* website. There's no reason to invest in a show if the floors were empty last year.

As for your booth, your initial goal is to get a decent location on the floor and to have a suitable booth size. Get the biggest booth you can afford and invest in a proper display. For information about getting a suitable preassembled booth, type "trade show booth" into a search engine. If cash is really tight, consider sharing a booth with a related business.

Public Relations

How often have you stopped to read a restaurant review posted in a window or a framed article posted in a waiting room? That's public relations at work. The advantages of public relations, as Jay Levinson explains in *Guerrilla Marketing* (Prentice Hall), are that it's free, it provides instant credibility for your business, and it has staying power—you can use reprints as part of a business brochure, for example.

There are two challenges in using this tool: You need to come up with ways to turn your business into news, and you need contacts at local media who will listen to your pitch.

Marketing experts have many suggestions for generating news stories. Jay Levinson recommends connecting your business with something that's in the news right now. Nolo, the publisher of this book, relies heavily on this approach. When news stories appear that relate to the subject of one of its books, a company rep will contact the media to let them know that an expert is available to discuss the matter. The important thing is that you fulfill the reporter's primary requirement: an angle or hook that makes the story interesting to readers. Here are a few suggestions:

- announce survey results
- hold a contest, race, or competitive event and announce the winner
- tie in your business with a holiday
- sponsor nonprofit activities—for example, sponsor a public performance, or
- become a source of expert information.

How do you get the story to the media? Commonly, it's done with a press release that you send to selected media. (To see examples, check out www.prnewswire.com.) Alexander Hiam has some recommendations when drafting press releases. In particular:

- try to include lists of tips, rules, or principles
- offer yourself as an expert on the industry
- keep it short (one page)
- send it to every editor in the area, and
- post your release on the Web.

Here's one other fact to consider: It's possible that if you buy ad space, you're more likely to get editorial space. Though rarely the case in quality media publications, it's not uncommon in less scrupulous local newspapers or magazines.

Online Advertising

Banner ads, keyword buying, and marketing links? These marketing strategies may work for your business just as they have worked for companies such as Netflix and University of Phoenix Online. For more on how to drive customers to your website with these tools, read Chapter 18.

Seminars and Product Demonstrations

In *Marketing Without Advertising*, authors Phillips and Rasberry maintain that seminars and demonstrations add vitality to a business and provide value to customers. This type of presentation may be a class—for example, cooking lessons at a kitchen supply store—or you may want to demonstrate a product or service. For example, if you offer framing services, ask a local photography club to let you demonstrate how to best preserve photographs.

Signs

Don't forget about signs. As Paco Underhill points out in *Why We Buy: The Science of Shopping* (Texere Publishing), if people purchased only the items that triggered their trip to the stores, the retail industry would collapse. What convinces consumers to load the cart and make impulse purchases are signs outside and within a business. It's estimated that new signs inside or outside a business can boost revenue 4% to 8% annually for retailers. Signs work best if they're bold, professionally done, in good condition, consistent with your business, well lit, and tell the viewer your message quickly.

And signs don't just mean words on paper or cardboard. T-shirts, shopping bags, and bumper stickers are also signs and can do a swell job of advertising your goods to the general public.

Outdoor Advertising

What about large outdoor signs like billboards? Considering current traffic statistics, you probably get a decent number of exposures (number of viewers) for outdoor advertising. But the cost is prohibitive—between $3,000 and $5,000 per month to rent a billboard. A less expensive—between $500 and $1,500 per month—way to reach people with outdoor advertising is to purchase transit advertising, such as shelter panels at bus stops or bus posters.

Do You Need a Marketing Plan?

A marketing plan establishes how you're going to spend time and money in promoting your business. Your plan can be professional or informal.

A professional plan usually includes an analysis of your market, the demographics of your customers, your target markets, how you'd like to be positioned within the market, an analysis of your competition, past attempts at marketing and their success rates, and your current strategy and its expenses.

This kind of plan—with its charts and breakdowns of expenditures—is sometimes used as an adjunct for a business plan or as a discrete means of convincing others to invest in your business. If you'd like to create a professional marketing plan, we suggest you invest in *Marketing Plan Pro* from Palo Alto Software (approximately $170), software that enables you to construct a professional marketing plan within a few hours. It includes over 70 sample plans for various small businesses.

More likely, you won't need to prepare a professional marketing plan. Instead, you may want to try an informal plan that will help you organize your ideas on how to maximize your time and budget.

Start by examining your market—what Michael Phillips refers to as the "who" of your marketing plan. Create a list of current customers. You can probably do this by gathering names from checks, credit card statements, emails, and so forth. Those are your initial and direct targets. Next, determine your potential market using the primary and secondary marketing research techniques. Sometimes, in these cases, it helps to also define the total market—how many total customers is it possible to attract, and what size market share do you want (and can handle)? For example, what percentage of a community of 14,000 households is likely to need dry cleaning services? If you coach high school swimmers, how many competitive student swimmers are there within a 20-mile radius of your training center?

The purpose of your plan is to pick and choose among your marketing tools so that your marketing efforts match your budget. Your budget should be enough to reach your market without cutting seriously into your operating revenues. If you can afford it, start by allocating a percentage—say, 10% of your revenue.

Once you know how much you're prepared to spend on marketing, you must choose your tools and estimate the costs over the year. For example, if you create brochures and handouts, take that one-time cost and spread it over the year ($1,200 for four-color brochures = $100 per month).

This is not a simple task, and the resulting budget is not static. Marketing requires monitoring. It's a process of innovation and change; you abandon or modify tools that aren't working and add and test new ones. Consider your marketing plan as a work in progress.

To help you manage your budget, here is a table that lists the common elements in a marketing toolbox.

MARKETING TOOLS	
INEXPENSIVE AND WORTH A TRY	**COST**
Samples and free offers	
Personal letters	
Telephone marketing	
Postcards, handouts, and brochures	
Yellow pages	
Signs	
Seminars, consultations, and demonstrations	
Public relations	
Product demonstrations	
MIGHT BE WORTH IT	**COST**
Classified ads	
Online advertising	
Trade shows	
Direct mail	
Display ads	
WHEN YOU'VE GOT MORE MONEY	**COST**
Radio ads	
Television ads	
Outdoor advertising	

Shipping and Returns

What's the Difference? Drop Shipping vs. Traditional Shipping 208

Shipping and Delays 209

Returns and Refunds 210

I n 2002, Amazon.com lowered its threshold for free shipping from a $99 purchase to one of $49; a year later, it lowered it to $25. Other major retailers, such as Circuit City and Best Buy, soon jumped on the free-shipping bandwagon. The first week Shoes.com offered free shipping, sales jumped 170% and remained high for the rest of the year.

Does this mean that if you ship products, you'd better immediately stop charging for it? Not necessarily. The decrease in profits (from shipping costs) could wreak havoc on your small business's bottom line.

But these examples do demonstrate that your shipping policies can be an important part of your marketing effort. The same is true for return policies. Many companies, such as Land's End and Nolo, the publisher of this book, are willing to accept returns for any product in order to stand behind a true money-back guarantee. These companies believe that if you keep customers happy through these post-sale activities, you'll cement loyalty, and, hopefully, increase sales. In this chapter, we offer some suggestions for your shipping and return policies.

What's the Difference?
Drop Shipping vs. Traditional Shipping

Most businesses that sell products maintain an inventory and ship when orders are received. The advantage of this traditional shipping arrangement is that you have complete control of the order until you hand it off to the USPS, UPS, or FedEx. The disadvantage is that you must keep an inventory, so your sales are limited by your storage space.

Drop shipping is a process in which you sell items you don't keep in stock. Instead, you collect the money and forward the order to a distributor, who ships to the customer using your packaging. Amazon and other online stores perfected this art, and it has since been adopted by thousands of online retailers. The **advantage of drop shipping** is that you can offer a wide variety of merchandise without maintaining an inventory. The **disadvantage** is that you may have to pay setup fees, make a minimum number of orders each month, and deal with refunds if the drop shipper screws up.

Shipping and Delays

For a lot of people, there's a secret thrill when the UPS truck rolls up with a delivery. Conversely, there's a not-so-secret disappointment when a birthday gift doesn't arrive on time. If your products are late getting to customers, not only will it cause you a loss of goodwill, it may also violate federal law. Here are the basics.

When taking orders, whether by phone or online, you must follow the shipping and refund rules of the Federal Trade Commission's Mail or Telephone Order Merchandise Rule, also known as the 30-Day Rule. In a nutshell, the rule mandates that when you advertise merchandise and state the shipping times, you must have a reasonable basis for believing you can meet these shipping deadlines. If you don't say anything about shipment times, you're expected to ship within 30 days from when you received a properly completed order—that is, when you receive the payment and all the information needed to fill the order.

In cases of drop-shipped orders, you (the person taking the order), not the shipper, is responsible for compliance with the rule. The rule does not apply to collect-on-delivery (C.O.D.) orders, sales of seeds and growing plants, or to magazine subscriptions (except for the delivery of the first issue).

If you notify the customer of a delay, you'll need to get the customer's consent. Ditto for online orders (which are complete when the customer clicks it along to you). If you can't get consent to the delay, you must, without being asked, refund the money the customer paid you for the unshipped merchandise. If there's a shipping delay and you don't want to seek the customer's consent, you can simply cancel the order, notify the customer, and refund the payment. Keep a record of how you gave the notice, whether by email, phone, fax, or regular mail, when you gave it, and how the customer responded. Again, if you don't say anything about shipment times at the time of the order, you're expected to ship within 30 days.

If your customer is applying to you to establish a new credit account or increase an existing credit line to pay for the merchandise being ordered, and if you don't give a shipment date, you are allowed 50 (instead of 30) days to ship. The extra 20 days is to give you time to process the credit application. Of course, if you want to use this provision of the FTC rule, you must have a reasonable basis to believe you can ship in 50 days. For more information about FTC rules, visit www.ftc.gov.

Drop shipping. Since you're responsible for the distributor's screw-ups, find out the distributor's return policy and post it at your point of sale or in your catalogue, or, if that's not possible, include it with the order. If the customer complains about the merchandise—for example, it arrives damaged or has a factory defect—the distributor will have to correct the error. But because the customer made the purchase with you, not the distributor, you'll have to stay on top of the transaction—for example, get the RMA (return merchandise authorization) number from the distributor and email it to the customer. The RMA allows you and the distributor to accurately track and process the returned merchandise.

Returns and Refunds

Throughout this book, we have recommended products from two companies, Nolo, the publisher of this book, and Palo Alto Software, the maker of *Business Plan Pro* and *Marketing Plan Pro*. One reason we're comfortable making these recommendations is that both companies have a very simple policy when it comes to refunds. At Nolo, if you're not satisfied with the product for any reason, you can send it back for a refund. Palo Alto software gives you 60 days to return the product for a refund if you're not satisfied.

Our recommendations demonstrate that your return policy can be a marketing tool. What could be better than a money-back guarantee? Millions of consumers confidently patronize certain online businesses—for example, Amazon, Land's End, or REI—because these companies have similar customer-friendly, simple-to-use return policies. On the other hand, every consumer remembers an unpleasant experience trying to return something and probably stopped shopping at that business afterwards.

We're not advocating that every business provide an unlimited return policy, but we do recommend that you establish a customer-friendly policy of some sort and that you communicate it to your customers.

Before you draft that policy, keep in mind the legal rules. You don't have to give a refund unless:

- You broke the sales contract because for example, your goods were defective.
- You have a policy that allows a refund for returns.

What's common? Many businesses let customers return merchandise for a cash refund or at least a credit toward another purchase. For some businesses, this policy may need to be tweaked. For example, a pet store cannot always guarantee satisfaction with a pet, but the store owner can educate the customer about the pet and establish a limited promise—for example, a 48-hour return policy—that may head off disappointment.

If you want to provide refunds and impose conditions on when merchandise can be returned, post your return and refund policy prominently at the point of sale. If you're operating online, that means on your website.

Your state law may require this type of posting, but even if it doesn't, it's a good practice. Typical conditions might require the customer to return the merchandise within 30 days, that the merchandise must be unused, or that the customer must submit a receipt or other proof of purchase. Four states have laws governing refund policies as shown below.

STATE RULES ON REFUNDS	
CALIFORNIA	You must post your refund policy unless you offer a full cash refund or credit refund within seven days of purchase. If you don't post your policy as required, the customer is entitled to return the goods for a full refund within 30 days of purchase.
FLORIDA	If a business does not offer refunds, that fact must be posted. If the statement isn't posted, the customer can return unopened, unused goods within seven days of purchase.
NEW YORK	If a business offers cash refunds, that policy must be posted and the refund must be given within 20 days of purchase.
VIRGINIA	Businesses that don't offer a full cash refund or credit within 20 days of purchase, must post their policy.

Contract Cancellation Laws

Many states have laws regarding cancellation of consumer contracts. For example, in New York and California, a consumer may cancel a contract with a dating service, a health club, or any door-to-door sale within three days. You can find your state's contract cancellation laws by checking your state government website (look for the consumer protection office site), or visiting the Federal Consumer Information Center's website at www.consumeraction.gov.

Working From Home

Best Businesses to Run From Home 215

Self-Assessment: Should I Keep Working at Home? 216

How Much Are You Saving? 217

Do You Have the Right Space? 217

Does Your Home Send the Right Message for Your Business? 217

Will You Have to Contend With Zoning, Lease, or
Homeowners' Association Restrictions? 219

Can People Reach You? 221

Is There Sufficient Parking? 221

Can You Get the Insurance You Need? 221

Are You Too Isolated? 222

How Much Security Do You Need? 223

Can You Separate Your Work From Your Home Life? 223

Tips for Maximum Home Office Efficiency 224

Spend Some Money on a Decent Chair 224

Get the Right Furnishings 225

Get the Right Phone Connections 225

Get the Right Internet Connections 226

Get Organized 227

Hire Experts for One-Time Projects 228

Prioritize Your Work 228

Quick—what do Hewlett-Packard, PowerBar, and Avon have in common, in addition to their stunning success? All of them began as home businesses. Hewlett-Packard took shape in a garage in Palo Alto, California, on property rented by Bill Hewlett and Dave Packard; PowerBar got its start in Brian Maxwell's Berkeley, California, kitchen; and Avon began when author David McConnell began brewing perfume at his New York City home to use as a bonus gift for customers who bought the books he peddled door to door. In this chapter, we'll talk about the issues that arise when you work at home and we'll also help you decide when it's time to move your business out of your home.

Winning the Home Business Battle of the Bulge

When we asked home business owners some of the pitfalls of working from home, more than a few of them mentioned weight gain. It's one of the hazards of sharing a workplace with your refrigerator: Instead of wandering down the hall to talk to a coworker when you need to take a break, some home business owners spend quality time with their leftovers. (One home business owner told us that whenever she got stuck on a project, her first thought was to bake a batch of cookies.) The long hours it often takes to get a new business off the ground can also take a toll—for most of us, healthy eating habits and regular exercise routines fall by the wayside when we spend all of our time working.

Fortunately, working at home also gives business owners the flexibility to squeeze exercise into their day, if they make it a priority. Some people told us that they go for a run or bike ride in the middle of the day when working at home—something they could never do when they worked for someone else. Setting your own hours also allows you to get to a gym during off hours, when you won't have to wait in line for your favorite machines.

Best Businesses to Run From Home

The optimal home business is a service business that won't take up a lot of your living space and doesn't generate a lot of traffic. If you can do your work using only a desk and computer (as a Web designer, freelance writer, or an accountant usually can), or if you can work at your clients' location (like a carpenter, software trainer, or plumber), you may have the perfect home business.

Here are some other types of work that are well suited to a home business:

- home and office cleaning
- traveling sales
- telemarketing
- construction, carpentry, plumbing, and other home repair
- interior design
- financial planning
- desktop publishing
- catering
- Web design and development
- tutoring
- computer programming
- graphic design
- crafts
- accounting or bookkeeping
- consulting (in a variety of fields, from human resources to financial planning)
- writing and editing
- data entry and transcription
- servicing items in a customer's home, from piano tuning to hot tub maintenance to furnace repair, and
- on-site training.

Self-Assessment: Should I Keep Working at Home?

You probably already know the benefits of working at home: Low cost, flexibility, and no commute are at the top of the list for most home entrepreneurs. And you may have encountered some of the disadvantages: Distractions, isolation, and difficulty maintaining an appearance of professionalism can all detract from the home office experience.

To get a realistic idea of whether working at home continues to make sense for your business, however, you need to get to the nitty-gritty: how working at home is affecting your business and your bottom line. Here are some things to consider.

Remodeling Changes the Calculations

Laurie, who plans to start her own business tutoring children in reading, saw her freestanding garage as the perfect home workspace: Clients and their parents wouldn't have to traipse through her home, her own children (and large dog) wouldn't disturb her work, and she would have a separate space to organize her business—away from the curious eyes and hands of her six-year-old son.

When she started doing the math, however, she soon saw that fitting the garage out as a home office would be fairly expensive. The structure was a bit dilapidated and, due to its leaky roof and single window, more than a bit moldy. It would require insulation and some electrical work to handle Laurie's computer equipment. And it would have to be finished on the inside—no more oil-soaked concrete floor, for starters.

In the end, Laurie decided to start seeing clients at their own homes and handle her administrative tasks from a corner of her dining room. In time, her business might make enough money to bring the garage renovations within reach—after all, it's not only a business choice, but also a sound investment in her home's value. For the time being, however, creating a separate home office just didn't make financial sense.

How Much Are You Saving?

It's true that working at home saves money, but how much? Start by looking at the economics of your home office. You won't have to pay any additional rent or mortgage to run your business from home. Compare that to the price of commercial real estate in your area—at a minimum, you would be paying $10 per square foot per month for commercial space. Other costs—equipment, insurance, and services—may be roughly the same whether you work at home or in an outside space. And either way, your business costs are tax deductible. If you will have to build additional space or do extensive remodeling to create a place to work at home, you'll have to figure that extra cost into your calculations.

Do You Have the Right Space?

Sure it's free, but does your home give you enough space—and the right kind of space—for your business? Can you provide a sitting area or a waiting room for clients or customers? If you are selling or making products, do you have space to store your inventory and supplies? If your business requires a lot of equipment, do you have the room to set it up so you can use it efficiently? When you consider space, think about the future, too. If you anticipate having employees, the conventional wisdom is that you'll need at least 150 to 200 square feet per employee. If your business is growing quickly, maybe it's time to consider the home office as a transitional space and start looking beyond your property boundaries.

Does Your Home Send the Right Message for Your Business?

If clients or customers will come to your business, you'll have to consider whether you can make your home business space look professional enough to inspire confidence in visitors. It can be tough to look like an entrepreneur when the entrance to your office is cluttered with children's toys, your desk doubles as your dining room table, or your workspace resides in a spare closet. Can you modify your home to create a businesslike atmosphere? Do you have a separate entrance or a structure (such as a converted garage) that clients can get to without traversing a lot of living areas? Is your work area safe? Do you have aggressive dogs, tripping hazards, or low-hanging beams?

Out of the Closet and Back In Again

James Martel, a professor at San Francisco State University, needed a workspace to write the scholarly papers and books that are so important to an academic career. Although he had an office at the university, he needed to work at home much of the time to care for his two young children.

The problem? James and his partner, Carlos, lived in a two-bedroom Victorian apartment. The high ceilings give the apartment a roomy feeling, but James couldn't take advantage of that vertical space for his home office. The solution he came up with was to turn a small coat closet into an office. The narrow closet was just deep enough to hold a flat surface for his computer on one side; on the other side, his filing cabinet and a couple of mounted shelves store the other tools of his trade, papers, and books.

The irony of a gay man working in a closet wasn't lost on James, but he says it's the perfect solution to his problem. "I would never work in there with the door closed; it's way too claustrophobic. But when I open the door, it feels like an extension of the living room. If the kids are taking a nap or playing, I can keep an eye on them while I work. And when I'm done working, I can just close the door. That keeps the kids out of my workspace—and gives us back our living room. It also means I can leave all of my papers and books spread out, so I can pick up right where I left off when it's time to get back to work."

Will You Have to Contend With Zoning, Lease, or Homeowners' Association Restrictions?

Depending on where you live, zoning laws, lease restrictions, or subdivision rules ("convenants, conditions, and restrictions," or CC&Rs) may affect your ability to run your business from your home. For example, zoning laws may limit or prohibit signs or visible advertising on a residence. These rules may prohibit employees other than domestic help, limit noise levels (typically through imposing "quiet hours" in the evening and early morning), or prohibit any enterprise that would increase traffic or competition for scarce parking spaces. If such a prohibition applies, you might be able to get around it by applying for a variance (an exception to a zoning law), creating more parking, or limiting your work hours, for example.

Six Feet Under? Not In My Backyard

Contrary to what watchers of the HBO series "Six Feet Under" might believe, zoning ordinances often prohibit people from running a mortuary, funeral home, crematorium, or any other type of business relating to dead bodies from their own homes.

Other types of businesses that are frequently prohibited by zoning ordinances include retail stores, vehicle repair shops, manufacturing facilities, animal grooming and boarding operations, and service businesses that tend to attract lots of customers at once, such as nail salons or barber shops.

DON'T

Don't let your home business disturb the neighbors. As a practical matter, the only way you are likely to get caught for violating zoning or other restrictions is if your neighbors turn you in to local authorities. And unless you have particularly mean-spirited neighbors, they are likely to report you to authorities only if your business causes problems for them— for example, if you make noise late at night, your employees park in front of their driveways, or the comings and goings of your clients lead neighbors to think you might be up to something shady.

Here are some examples—from actual lawsuits—of home business activities that caused neighbors to complain:

- A couple in Wyoming began using their property, which was zoned for agricultural use, for some home business ventures, including a company that built log cabins and a ski area (they didn't actually have customers skiing on their property, but did all of the storage, maintenance, design, and administrative work at home). After neighbors repeatedly complained about the dust, noise, use of heavy equipment, and increased traffic, their local government sued the business owners.

- A couple in Waltham, Massachusetts, began operating a photography business in their new home, after receiving approval from a local inspector to do so as long the business complied with applicable zoning restrictions and didn't cause "conditions detrimental to the neighborhood." They found themselves in a lawsuit after neighbors complained that an average of two or three vehicles (and sometimes up to nine) parked at the house; there were excessive package pickups and deliveries; and the neighbors' driveways were often blocked by customers.

- A Maryland man received permission to operate a seniors' assisted living center in his home, but began operating a second center in an adjacent home without permission. He ran into legal trouble when neighbors complained about parking difficulties, increased traffic, the regular presence of emergency vehicles on the street, trash problems, and the way he was disposing of medical waste.

Can People Reach You?

If clients, customers, employees, or others will visit you at home, they'll need to be able to get there—which is easier if you live close to public transit or are otherwise easy to reach. The same is true of vendors and service providers, such as mail and package delivery. Some companies (notably UPS) charge more to make deliveries to a home office than to a commercial address—this may not be a home office deal-breaker, but you should factor any additional charges into your calculations.

Is There Sufficient Parking?

If employees, customers, suppliers, or others will come to your home business, they'll need to be able to park. Do you have space on your property for their cars? If not, does your neighborhood have any restrictions that will make parking difficult, such as a required sticker or permit? If you live in a housing development, there may be restrictions on visitors' parking. And in densely populated cities, it may be tough to find parking under any circumstances. If you can rent a garage or parking spaces from neighbors or create a parking area on your property, that might solve the problem. But don't ask customers or clients to park in your driveway if doing so would block the sidewalk—this will get your customers a hefty ticket in many urban areas and may also provoke the wrath of pedestrians, especially those with disabilities or with baby strollers.

Can You Get the Insurance You Need?

Every small business—even one run from home—should be insured against common hazards and events. Even if you already have home-owner's or renter's insurance, most policies either don't cover home businesses at all, or provide only about $2,500 worth of protection for losses to business property. Because just one uninsured loss could easily put you out of business, you absolutely must protect yourself. If your existing policy doesn't offer enough (or any) protection, you can probably get some basic protection from a home business rider; talk to your insurance agent. (See Chapter 4 for more on insurance.)

If You Need Employees, It Might Be Time to Move

Many small business owners decide to make the move from a home office to commercial space when they hire their first employees. More than 90% of all home businesses have no employees, which isn't surprising. When you operate a business from home, space is usually at a premium, and work areas may overlap with living quarters. It can be hard to bring another person—one who isn't part of your family—into the mix.

Having employees in your home can cause other problems as well. Some zoning ordinances prohibit employees altogether or allow home business to have only one. It might be difficult to attract the right worker to a home office environment, especially if the only amenity you have to offer is space in the fridge for a sack lunch. If you have any family members at home during the day (especially young children), an employee will have to be willing and able to work in that environment. And, if you're unlucky enough to hire someone with sticky fingers or more serious criminal intentions, you could be putting your personal possessions and family at risk.

Are You Too Isolated?

In a commercial workplace, you can share space with folks in similar fields, share resources (such as equipment, office help, and services), and pick up referrals, leads, and tips from those working around you. These are roles that your pets, children, or roommates probably won't be able to fill. What price, if any, will you pay for isolation? Is there any way you can stay in touch with like-minded businesspeople without leasing commercial space? Can you join a group of entrepreneurs, plan to meet a friend or business associate for a regular lunch, get out and see your clients or customers, or take a class in your field? This will help you recharge your batteries, brush up on your work skills, and maybe even drum up some business.

How Much Security Do You Need?

Are you prepared to open your living space to customers or service providers you don't know well? Or does your business need the kinds of safety measures afforded by many commercial workplaces such as security guards, identification badges or other means of limiting access to the facility, and alarm systems? If you have a lot of valuable business equipment and tools, can you safeguard them adequately in your home or driveway?

Can You Separate Your Work From Your Home Life?

To work effectively at home, you need self-discipline and will power. At an outside workplace, the only distractions might be walking to the water cooler or playing solitaire on the computer. At home, however, it's a different story: We all have things we should be doing (folding the laundry or washing the dishes) and things we'd like to be doing (watching television or reading the paper). Unless you can knuckle down and get your work done despite distractions like these—and more compelling distractions, such as spending time with your children or other loved ones—your home business might never get off the ground. Setting up your home workspace in a separate room or outbuilding really helps minimize distractions by keeping you out of household traffic patterns (and giving you a door you can close). If you live with others, consider writing down your work schedule and posting it on the refrigerator or your workplace door—and ask the people you live with not to disturb you during your posted work times.

Never Answer Mommy's Phone

Many parents start home businesses so they can spend more time with their children. But with children at home, it can be a true challenge to carve out uninterrupted time to work—and to maintain a professional business image. Work-at-home parents often come up with a combination of rules for their older children (including a ban on touching the business phone) and flexibility to accommodate the needs of younger ones.

You can find a lot of great information for work-at-home parents on the Web—simply type "home business" and "parents," "mothers," or "fathers" into your favorite search engine to find dozens of sites. A good place to start is The Parent's Home Office, at www.parentshomeoffice .com; it has lots of helpful articles on childproofing your home office, activities to keep kids busy while you work, and much more.

Tips for Maximum Home Office Efficiency

If you've concluded that you want to keep your business at home, you'll want to do all you can to make that business productive and efficient. Taking a few simple steps will help you make the most of your home business.

Spend Some Money on a Decent Chair

Most of us who work at home spend plenty of time sitting down, often in a chair that was previously banished to the attic because it lacked comfort, style, or both. Although this is certainly a cheap seating solution, it's also a sure road to physical problems—and you won't be able to put in the necessary hours if you're not comfortable in your office. For ergonomics and comfort, a good office chair is a must. You should expect to pay several hundred dollars for a decent chair. Among the features to look for are adjustable height and tilt, lumbar support, and padded, adjustable armrests. For an article that explains the various features available and what they do, go to www.office-ergo.com and click "Ergonomic Chairs." You can also find plenty of information on office ergonomics at the website of the UCLA Ergonomics Program, at http://ergonomics.ucla.edu.

Get the Right Furnishings

Many home business owners outfit their offices with whatever unused items they can find in the attic or basement. This is a perfectly sensible plan for furniture to store and hold work supplies (such as bookshelves and filing cabinets), but if clients will see your office, you should spend a little time making these items presentable, perhaps with a fresh coat of paint. (You should also have a comfortable second chair for clients to use.) For your desk or work surface, you'll want something that gives you enough space to work and sits at the right height. Using a work surface that's too small is inefficient—it means you'll have to scatter your equipment and other materials around the room instead of having them all within easy reach.

Saving Money On Office Furniture

You don't have to break the bank to outfit your home office. Look at garage sales, used furniture stores or furniture outlets, and websites such as eBay or Craigslist (www.craigslist.org). You might be able to find a business that has closed and is selling off its equipment on the cheap. For inexpensive new furniture, Office Depot and IKEA are good bets. You can find an extensive list of links to the websites of office furniture companies at www.homefurnish.com; click "Home Office," then "Products."

Get the Right Phone Connections

It used to be that every home business needed more than one phone line: one for talking, another for fax or dial-up Internet connection. That's all changed. High-speed Internet connections don't require an additional phone line, and email has almost done away with fax machines. You can even get rid of the phone lines altogether and run your home business on a cellular phone with a message center and text messaging, which allows you to conduct business everywhere. Whatever phone you get, here's a tip: Get a headset. Not only will it save you from a sore neck, but it also makes communication clearer and allows you to keep your hands free to use your computer or search for paperwork. (P.S. Consider checking out VOIP phones from providers such as Skype.com. They are already saving lots of money for businesses that make international calls.)

Don't Use Your Home Phone Line

Even if you consolidate all of your home business communication needs in one phone number, it shouldn't be the same one you use for personal calls—especially if you share the line with family members. You really don't want customers to get a busy signal while your teenager ties up your only phone line. This will also make it easier to work more efficiently: If you want to turn off or simply not answer your personal line while in the midst of an important project, you won't miss any business calls.

Get the Right Internet Connections

In most parts of the country, even the most stingy business owner should invest in high-speed Internet (also known as "broadband"). Some DSL providers start at $25 to $30 per month (or less). In addition to increasing your business efficiency (ask any high-speed addict), broadband is essential for online sellers or companies that do a lot of website modification. There are, however, many choices, including DSL, cable, satellite, and wireless. Speeds vary depending on the provider and the plan. Cable is considered the fastest medium and may be the ideal choice for online businesses, but a baseline DSL hookup is sufficient for most small business owners. Ideally, you should look for speeds of at least 384Kbps/128Kbps. The first number is the speed at which you download files; the second is your upload speed, when you transfer files or place them at a website. The folks at CNET (www.cnet.com) offer lots of helpful advice for choosing a provider. They also recommend that home business users look for additional features such as free dial-up access (just in case the broadband fails or you're on the road), multiple email inboxes with at least 10MB storage for each, and personal firewall and antivirus software.

Get Organized

Remember the old saying, "A place for everything, and everything in its place"? In a home business, where space is often at a premium, it applies with a vengeance. Keep items you use regularly within easy reach and store the things you use less frequently. Use file folders, desk dividers, bookshelves, and other storage systems to organize your paperwork and project materials. If you're working in a small spot, use vertical space— put shelves, folder racks, or other organizing tools above your workspace.

This Year, Celebrate "Organize Your Home Office" Day

OnlineOrganizing.com has declared the second Tuesday in March to be Organize Your Home Office Day. (Other March organizing holidays include Clutter Awareness Week, Clean Out Your Closet Week, and National Procrastination Week—oh, let's put that one off until April.) Their website (www.onlineorganizing.com) suggests marking the date by, among other things, evaluating your storage system and creating a "paper management center."

Even if your March calendar is already booked, you should make the time to check out this site, intended for professional organizers and the disorganized public. It has lots of helpful articles, links to websites on a variety of topics, a referral service for finding a professional organizer in your area, an online product catalogue, and a long list of tip sheets and checklists that will help you get organized and make the best use of your time. (Our favorite—and a very helpful guide for the home businessperson who faces a lot of unwelcome interruptions—is "20 Ways to Say No.")

Hire Experts for One-Time Projects

Don't reinvent the wheel. If you're facing a one-time task that you don't know how to handle—like designing a website for your business, remodeling a room to serve as a home office, or developing a company logo—it's much more efficient to pay for a few hours of an expert's time and get the job done right than to try to learn how to do it yourself. Used sparingly, expert help can really save time and money. (For information on finding and hiring freelancers, see Chapter 8.)

Prioritize Your Work

Which activities make you money? Those are the ones you should be spending most of your time on. It seems obvious, but many of us procrastinate or simply fail to prioritize our most important work. Some business efficiency experts recommend a triage system for tasks and paperwork—in other words, you sort everything into categories, such as "urgent," "to do soon," "wait," and "forget it," and then prioritize accordingly. Others suggest a grading system: On your to-do list, you give each task a grade, with A tasks having the highest priority. Then, you don't move on to a single B or C task until you've completed your A list.

If you're having trouble figuring out where your time is going, keep a log of your hours for a couple of weeks, recording what you work on and how long you spend on it. You may be surprised at what you find. For lots of good advice on managing your work time, see *Time Management: Proven Techniques for Making the Most of Your Valuable Time*, by Marshall J. Cook (Adams Media). ●

Leasing Space

What's the Difference? Commercial vs. Residential 230

    How Much Rent Can You Pay? 230

    Finding Commercial Space 230

    Dealing With Brokers 231

    Check out Local Restrictions 231

What to Ask When You Look at the Space 232

When You Talk About the Rent 233

    Rent Fluctuations 234

Things to Consider When You Negotiate Your Lease 234

    Your Personal Liability for Rent 234

    How Long Are You Tied to the Property? 235

    What Happens If You Fail to Pay Rent? 235

    What If You Can't Stay? 235

    Resolving Disputes 235

    Can Your Landlord Move You From Space to Space? 236

    Special Lease Restrictions 236

Subleasing 236

Interview with Attorney Janet Portman 237

f you are leasing space for your business for the first time, you're probably wary of the commitment and the potential liability. In this chapter, we'll provide some tips to cut down on the hassle and expense.

What's the Difference? Commercial vs. Residential

You've probably rented a place to live at some point in your life. But your experience as a residential tenant won't be of much help when it comes to leasing business space. Commercial leases usually last five or more years, much longer than the typical residential lease. Commercial leases, unlike residential leases, are usually negotiable. Most important, as a commercial tenant you don't have the consumer protections—for example, strict laws regarding the return of security deposits—that you get when you rent a house or apartment. Finally, commercial leases are usually harder and more expensive to break than residential leases.

How Much Rent Can You Pay?

Before you start shopping for a space, you need a budget. How much can you spend on rent? If you don't know, you'll need to do some financial forecasting (we explain how in Chapter 2). Keep in mind that monthly lease payments aren't always a fixed payment based on square footage. Often, additional hidden payments can surface. In "When You Talk About the Rent," below, we present the myriad ways that rent is calculated for commercial leases.

Finding Commercial Space

Start with local newspaper listings and Craigslist (www.craigslist.com), the popular Internet advertising database (under "Housing," click on "Office/Commercial"). Craigslist usually posts the square footage, rent, available amenities, location, and photos of the space.

Beyond Craigslist, there are two companies that dominate commercial leasing: LoopNet (www.loopnet.com) and CoStar Group (www.costar com). Both sites have extensive national listings and both can refer you to a broker in your area who can assist you in the process.

Dealing With Brokers

Most commercially leased space is handled by a broker who is paid by a landlord. You can hire your own broker or agent to find properties for you and represent only your interests, but it's not common for small businesses. Usually, the same broker represents both parties (known as "dual representation").

Dual representation can, of course, create a conflict of interest, especially if the broker wants to please the landlord, not you. But professional brokers make an effort to please both sides. "On a dual representation," says Eric Schafer, a broker with the Hawthorn Group in San Francisco, "I tell both sides it's not going to be one-sided and that the deal is going to be somewhere in the middle. If they're not happy with that, don't do the deal."

Despite a broker's assurances, you're probably correct to wonder about allegiances. Brokers may not be willing to push for a better deal for you either because they believe they've reached the lowest price or because they expect to negotiate other deals with the landlord. Don't be shy about pushing your broker for a better deal.

One way to measure a broker's credibility is to ask questions: Who pays the broker? How much? Does the broker have any other financial arrangements with the landlord? "The more [the broker] won't disclose to you, the more I would find another broker," says James Chaconas, a commercial broker in Ann Arbor, Michigan.

Check out Local Restrictions

You want to be sure that any space you're considering is okay for your business in terms of local land use rules. If you're in doubt about zoning, learn about applicable rules from your local planning department (check your local government website). In addition to zoning, your local government may impose other limitations; it may limit the number of certain types of business in a neighborhood or require that businesses provide off-street parking, close early on weeknights, or keep advertising signs to a minimum. You can usually find these rules at the planning department or, if your town has one, your local business development office.

What to Ask When You Look at the Space

When you visit, bring your tape measure and camera to verify or record information you'll need later. A photo can also document the condition in which you rented the space should an issue arise when you move out. Here are some questions to take with you:

What about modifications? Will you need to add cubicles, raise a loading dock, or rewire for better communications? Make sure that you will be allowed to make the necessary changes. Will you have to pay the full cost for improvements that will be permanent and increase the building's value, or will the owner chip in?

What about restrooms? When Steve Jobs unveiled his design of the building that would house his company, Pixar, it had only one restroom for all 700 employees. Employees objected, and the design was changed. On your walk-through, check the restrooms and make sure they match your needs.

Is there enough parking? Ask about guaranteed parking spaces and street parking.

Can you open the windows? Fresh air is not an option in many newer buildings.

Who controls heating and cooling? You may want one or more thermostats in your workspace, versus a central control, especially if you're going to be working hours when the central control cuts the heating or cooling way back.

Is there soundproofing? If you want quiet or you're making noise, soundproofing between walls and floors should be a priority.

Is there storage space? Find out if the building has extra storage space in a basement or other out-of-the-way area.

Who are the other tenants? What do they do? Will you have competitors? Are they noisy?

How's the security? Check the locks, lights, alarm system, doors, and windows. How safe is the neighborhood?

When You Talk About the Rent

If you're not familiar with the difference between a gross lease and net lease, here's how it works. In a gross lease, you pay a basic rent, usually based on square footage. The landlord pays for all property expenses such as utilities, taxes, and maintenance. With a net lease you pay a fixed rental charge plus a portion of the building's property taxes, insurance, and maintenance costs.

Security deposit. Many commercial landlords require tenants to pay one or two months' rent up front as a security deposit. The landlord will dip into this deposit if you fail to pay the rent or other sums required by the lease such as insurance or maintenance costs.

Alterations. Unless you are fortunate enough to find space that was previously owned by an identical business, you'll need to modify the space to fit your needs and tastes. These modifications are known as improvements or "build-outs." In some markets, the landlord will pay for them; in others you'll probably have to pay or compromise.

Property tax increases. Under a net lease, you may have to pay a pro rata portion of increases in the building's property taxes—for example, if you rent one-fifth of the total space in the building, you may be obligated to pay one-fifth of any increase.

Common area maintenance costs. In a net lease, you pay for common area maintenance (CAM)—a percentage of the costs to maintain the lobbies, hallways, garages, and elevators. Sometimes you have to pay for maintenance of the heating, ventilation, and air conditioning system (referred to as HVAC). If you can, get an estimate of these annual costs based on the previous tenant's use.

Insurance. A net lease tenant usually contributes to the cost of insurance for the building. This gets tricky if another tenant—for example, a bail bond business—causes the building's insurance to go up. In addition, the lease will require that you carry a renter's commercial liability policy. (You'd probably want it, anyway.) You may also want to obtain a business interruption policy that covers lost income and expenses resulting from property damage or loss—for example, if a train derails and collides with your 6,000-square-foot commercial space (which happened to a business in Fort Worth, Texas, in 2004). There's more on insurance in Chapter 4.

Rent Fluctuations

Your final consideration is whether your rent will fluctuate. Many gross leases include an "escalation clause" that sets a fixed monthly rate with periodic increases. The increases may be a flat percentage—for example, 3% a year—or $0.10 per square foot per year. Or the increase may be variable and tied to increases in a national indicator, commonly the Consumer Price Index (CPI). In this case, if you're paying $5,000 a month and the CPI jumps 5% in one year, your payments will jump to $5,250. In some markets, tenants have more clout; if you're in that situation, you can probably negotiate a cap on the increases.

INTERNET LINK
You can find links for all the resources in this book at www.nolo .com/wowbusiness.

Things to Consider When You Negotiate Your Lease

If you're concerned about personal liability, legal disputes, or your business going under, below are some things you should consider when negotiating your lease. For more help, read *Negotiating the Best Lease for Your Business*, by Fred Steingold and Janet Portman (Nolo).

Your Personal Liability for Rent

You'll be personally liable for any amounts due if you are a sole proprietor or a general partner. If you are a corporation or an LLC, the landlord can reach only the assets of your business. Your personal assets are not at risk unless you signed a personal guarantee.

A personal guarantee is a promise that you will pay any debts arising from a breach of the lease. It's possible that in certain real estate markets, the landlord may waive the guarantee, limit it to the first year or two of the lease, or ask for a larger security deposit instead. If you're uncomfortable with a personal guarantee, keep the lease short, perhaps limited to a one-year term.

How Long Are You Tied to the Property?

If things go bad and you can't continue to pay rent, you may be sued for the remaining value of the lease. For that reason, some start-ups, uncertain of their future, prefer leases of one year or less or a month-to-month tenancy.

What Happens If You Fail to Pay Rent?

Most leases give you 30 days to "cure" your first failure to pay rent, which means you have 30 days to pay before the landlord can terminate the lease and begin eviction proceedings. The landlord also may take some "self-help" measures, such as deducting the money from your security deposit (which you will then have to refill). Although the landlord is legally entitled to all of your rent through the end of the lease term even if you vacate the premises, in most states, the landlord must take reasonable steps to re-rent the space and credit the new rent money against your debt (called "mitigation of damages").

What If You Can't Stay?

You can either try to sublet the property (see "Subleasing," below) or offer to buy out the lease. With a buyout, you negotiate a lump sum payment—usually an amount that's considerably less than the remaining rent payment. That will end fears of a lawsuit (and large judgment) against you and will help the landlord cover vacancy costs when looking for a new tenant.

Resolving Disputes

Some leases have a provision requiring arbitration or payment of attorney fees in the event of a dispute. Arbitration and mediation are ways you can iron out problems without going to court. An attorney fee provision awards attorney fees and court costs to the winner of any dispute, which could be very expensive if the landlord sues you to recover rent. These provisions, common to many agreements, are discussed in Chapter 10.

Can Your Landlord Move You From Space to Space?

Believe it or not, some leases give the landlord the right to substitute other space—in the building or elsewhere—for the space described in the lease. Even if the lease requires the landlord to pay for the cost of a move, it's usually a poor idea to agree to such a deal.

Special Lease Restrictions

Some landlords prohibit you from doing certain things—for example, using kilns or cooking food. Review the lease for forbidden uses.

SEE AN EXPERT

Call a lawyer once you have agreed upon all of the lease terms, but before you sign it. It's usually not worth bringing in a lawyer before that point, since the deal may never get finished.

Subleasing

Sometimes, the ideal space for a business is one that someone else is renting. If you rent from a tenant, you're the subtenant and must abide by the terms that the landlord set up with the tenant. If you are subleasing, get a copy of the prime lease (the one between the landlord and tenant) and check for the following:

- **Is the landlord's consent needed for subletting?** If it is, make sure you have written consent before proceeding.
- **Must the landlord consent to improvements?** If so, don't sign unless the landlord gives the needed approvals in writing.

- **What charges will pass through the prime lease to you?** In addition to rent, will you (as subtenant) be responsible for common area maintenance, taxes, and insurance?
- **Is the tenant in good standing?** Speak with the landlord to determine whether there's a dispute brewing between the landlord and tenant. You (as subtenant) definitely don't want to be in the middle.

Incubators: An Alternative To Commercial Leasing?

Incubators are facilities that generally offer low rent and a variety of services, such as management advice and assistance; telephone answering, fax, secretarial, bookkeeping, and copying; and possibly reduced-cost professional services. According to studies, your chances of success—for example, lasting to your fifth anniversary—increase dramatically if you use incubator services. Many incubators can help you to get angel financing. Another innovative option offered by some incubators is group health insurance—a valuable option for the small business owner. To find out more about incubators in your area, check the National Business Incubation Association (www.nbia.org) or type "business incubators" into your search engine.

Interview with Attorney Janet Portman

The following is an interview with attorney Janet Portman, who is the author or co-author of several books about renting, leasing, and purchasing real property including *Negotiate the Best Lease for Your Business* (Nolo).

QUESTION: Janet, let's say you're new to leasing commercial space. Is there a number one or number two concern that a businessperson should be aware of?

JANET PORTMAN: Of course, the first thing you think about is "Can you afford the rent?" That's an obvious one. But a not-so-obvious one, and one you're not likely to think about when you are planning to stay in the place where you're renting, is the need to have an exit strategy which you can build into the lease, and it need not even be an exit strategy, it can be a "flexibility strategy."

You need to think about what would happen if you want to expand or if you want to contract if you want to stay in the same place when the lease term expires, and you want some assurance that you'll be able to do that. If you want to bring in a subtenant because you don't need some of your space, or perhaps you want somebody to take over for a period of time during the season where you don't need as much space—those are all flexibility rights that you might not be thinking about when you enter into the lease, but they are very important, especially the final one, which is how do you get out early if you need to. And if you build in that kind of flexibility from the beginning, then you've given yourself the ability to change as conditions and as your business grows and changes.

QUESTION: Is it better to form an LLC or a corporation before leasing property in order to limit your personal liability?

JANET PORTMAN: Well, there are two kinds of protection you want as a businessperson. The first is from lawsuits from the public in general—your customers, your vendors and so on. The second one is protection from the landlord should you be unable to pay the rent, or perform any other legal obligations or monetary obligations under the lease.

Now, if you have a business in which it's likely that you can be sued for big money—such as running a restaurant, running a gymnasium—then your risk and your exposure is rather high and you would want to form an LLC to protect yourself from lawsuits of that nature. Will that do you any good with respect to your landlord? Probably not, because the landlord is going to ask you to forego your corporate or LLC shield by giving either a personal guarantee or offering someone who is financially viable, such as a friend or another business.

QUESTION: Let's talk about the length of the lease. Are there any general rules for when shorter is better?

JANET PORTMAN: The moving pieces in that equation are the market as best you can guess. What's going to be happening with this particular property within the next few years—and in particular, at the end of your lease term—and the other important piece, of course, is what's likely to be happening with your business. If you can conclude that the value of the property will be going up and the value of properties in general are going to be going up, and that your business is likely to flourish—of course, everyone hopes that it will—then you might opt for a longer lease term so that you don't face the hassle of having to re-rent.

On the other hand, if you're not quite sure of the viability of the neighborhood, or if you're frankly not quite sure about the viability of your own business, you might want a shorter term because you might jump at the ability to get out of the lease sooner.

QUESTION: Janet, as you explain in your book, most landlords are represented by their own broker known as the "listing broker," and for a lot of business owners it's not possible for them to have their own broker, who is a "tenant's broker." Since this is a reality for so many businesspeople, do you really have to worry if you're only dealing with a listing broker?

JANET PORTMAN: Yes, you do have to worry because you need to realize that the broker who's working for your landlord has a legal duty to advance the best interest of the landlord, not you. So you're up against a stacked deck to begin with. And if you can't afford your own broker, the thing you should do certainly is to, at some point in the lease negotiation, show the lease to a reputable attorney who's familiar with tenant issues and who will be representing your interest. The amount of money you're going to spend on that lawyer for a lease review and suggestions will pale next to the monetary consequences of signing the lease that's stacked in the favor of the landlord.

QUESTION: What do you estimate is the amount of money that you'll pay for that type of legal representation?

JANET PORTMAN: You know, large metropolitan area, you're looking at $200 to $250 dollar an hour fees. You could easily spend a thousand dollars asking for a review and having a meeting with the attorney, getting some suggestions as to where you should push, where you can afford to give up, and what's really critical.

And, in particular, understanding the consequences of what you're about to sign, even if you don't get your way. A thousand dollars in the long run is not that much, especially if you think about what you'd have to pay as a retainer if you end up going to a lawyer, fighting over a lease clause, litigating a lease clause that you could have mitigated, that you could have avoided, possibly, if you'd reviewed that clause with a lawyer before you signed it.

QUESTION: In your book, you provide a lot of great advice about what to look out for, and how to negotiate a commercial lease. But what do you say to a landlord, who says, "take it or leave it?"

JANET PORTMAN: Landlords aren't stupid and they're going to say "take it or leave it," if it's a landlord's market. If space is tight, if their property is highly desirable, if there are 17 stellar businesses lined up behind you who are willing to sign on the dotted line without reading the lease, then the landlord can afford to say "take it or leave it." The only thing you can say at that point is "Okay," or "See you later."

A landlord who says "take it or leave it," who doesn't have the advantage of the marketplace, however, is being foolish. And you'll find out very quickly whether that person is bluffing and can be dealt with or whether, in fact, the market is behind him and he has every ability to hand the lease to the next guy in line and get a tenant.

If you have a landlord who says "Take it or leave it," and you know darn well that the property isn't all that advantageous, that anybody looking at it is going to be asking for the same things you are, and you point that out to the landlord and you still come up against a stone wall, I think you're dealing with somebody who's unreasonable, who's unrealistic and you probably don't want to do business with that person anyway. So, look elsewhere.

QUESTION: What if you're offered an opportunity to sublease property? Is there a primary concern you should keep in mind?

JANET PORTMAN: Yes, if you are the tenant and you're about to sublease to someone or you would like to be the subtenant and get space from your friend down the street, the first thing that both of you need to check out is whether the person with the lease has a right, under the lease, to sublease. Most smart landlords will put a clause in their leases which says that the tenant may not sublease or assign the space without the landlord's consent.

And reasonable landlords will add in the lease clause that the consent of the landlord will not be unreasonably withheld. Which means simply that the landlord won't arbitrarily say "No," that the Landlord will apply reason and good sense and objective business criteria to evaluating the subtenant. But the first thing is to check the lease and see what the procedure is for subleasing.

If you don't do that and you bring somebody in on your own, then the landlord will have every right to not only kick that person out, but that would constitute a breach of the lease, and it might constitute grounds for the landlord to terminate your lease.

QUESTION: In light of the disasters that happen to so many businesses from earthquakes, hurricanes, and other natural disasters, what type of concerns would that raise when negotiating a lease? Will the landlord's insurance cover your business?

JANET PORTMAN: The landlord insures the building. But your business property, your inventory, your tools, everything that you bring into the space to operate your business is not covered by the landlord's insurance policy. And in order to cover it, you have to take out your own policy on your equipment. Incidentally, most leases will require you to do that, because the last thing the landlord wants is to have you facing a huge loss, unable to recover, unable to pay the rent and there goes his tenant. So it's very important to make sure that you get that coverage even if it's not required, but don't be surprised to see it in your lease.

Another issue to look for in the lease is a clause that describes what will happen if the property is damaged through fire, flood, anything actually short of the ultimate cataclysms such as a hurricane or a tornado or an earthquake. I mean, you could have damage from a simple kitchen fire or equipment fire. It's a good idea to have a clause in your lease that sets this out. Landlords, of course, will want the ability to declare either that the lease is over, you have no more right to stay there, and they're going to go ahead and fix it—and they also want the right to decide instead that the lease will simply be suspended while they make repairs.

You, on the other hand, of course, want the ability to make the decision whether you stay or go. It's a common negotiating point. Who gets to declare what will happen? Will the lease simply be suspended while repairs are being made or will the lease be declared over? Now, if the building is utterly destroyed, then there's really no question—the lease is over.

But, often times, the problems are less all encompassing and the question for the tenant is, "Do I want to just get out of here and start anew, or am I willing to wait a period of weeks, or even months while repairs are being made and then move back in?"

QUESTION: Speaking of disasters, if you're leasing property, what happens if the landlord goes bankrupt or someone forecloses against the building?

JANET PORTMAN: This is an area that very few people understand—landlords and tenants. And it's actually very important because it happens quite commonly. The general rule is that if you have signed your lease, after the landlord put up the building as collateral for a loan or after the landlord bought the building, and of course, the building is more or less collateral for his mortgage payment, then if he fails to pay out on the loan and it's foreclosed, or doesn't keep up with his mortgage payments, then a foreclosure will terminate your lease, unless you have some protection in the lease itself saying that whoever takes over at that point will honor your lease.

The flipside of that is that if your lease pre-dates either of those two events, then legally you would survive the foreclosure. In other words, if the building is put up as collateral for a loan after you've moved in, and the landlord doesn't make his loan payments, and the lender forecloses, you would survive.

And what you want, in any situation, is you want to sort of short-circuit those two rules. And simply provide in the lease itself that if there is a foreclosure of the building, that not only will you have the right to stay where you are, regardless of the dates involved, but the new owner will be required to let you stay.

That's a very complicated clause. It's called a "Subordination Attornment and Non-Disclosure Clause." It probably takes the cake for the most complicated and mouthful clause in the lease, but it's very important so that you don't find yourself out on the street because a new owner has taken over. ●

Taking Your Business Online

How to Get a Site Up Tomorrow 244

    Information-Only Websites..244

    Selling Products and Taking Orders Online 246

    If You Can't Handle Site Creation 248

Driving Traffic to Your Site 249

    Great Content and Links 249

    Search Engines and Keywords...249

    Banner Ads 250

    Affiliate Programs...251

    Building a Community...252

    Legal Rules 252

Let's begin with the most basic fact: You don't have to have a website. If you're happy with the way your business is marketed and you already have more orders than you can handle, you probably don't need to establish a presence in cyberspace.

But if you're looking to set up an online store, or you just want to place a signpost on the Internet directing customers to your business, here are some quick solutions and some pointers that will eliminate some of the mystery surrounding the creation of websites.

Websites perform two basic business functions: First, they're marketing tools—think of them as flashy cyberspace billboards. Second, they are revenue generators—you can use them to sell most products and some services.

How to Get a Site Up Tomorrow

Yes, you can launch a website in just a few hours; we'll explain the basics, below. If you're interested in providing an information-only website—the equivalent of an online billboard—you can do so quite easily and inexpensively (sometimes for free). If you're interested in selling products, the fastest and least expensive way to start taking online orders is to create a community store—for example, an eBay, Yahoo! or Amazon store, as described below. If you're interested in doing more—for example, setting up a store that's not affiliated with a community or creating a chat room or offering downloads or webcasts, we'll provide some suggestions, but you will probably need outside help from a website developer.

Information-Only Websites

Do you plan to use your site primarily to provide information about your business? For example, if you're a service provider or a professional, you may want to create a site that lists some basic contact information, a biography, a synopsis of your services, and perhaps some useful material for customers. Or, if you're an accountant, you may want to periodically post tax tips. You can design and launch a site like this pretty easily. Here are a couple of routes you can take:

Create a blog. A blog, short for Web log, is the fastest way to acquire Internet real estate. Initially, blogs were used as journals. Nowadays, they've come to mean any easily updated Web page. Blogs provide an inexpensive means (many are free) for people to learn about your business. Check out Blogger (www.blogger.com), Typepad (www.typepad.com), or WordPress (www.wordpress.com). All you do is start an account, pick a template and the background colors for your blog, and then upload text. If you can manage the photo-uploading details, you can use photos as well. Check it out; it really is very simple. You can list contact information, provide a bio, and post regular updated information about your business. For example, check out the Crixa Cakes blog-styled site, www.crixa.net (hmmm!). Daily postings include specials of the day as well as job postings and other information. The advantage of a blog is that you can establish one in less than an hour. The disadvantage is that in order to maintain interest, you'll need to regularly refresh it with new information.

Use a small business site template. Sites such as Microsoft's OfficeLive (http://smallbusiness.officelive.com) and Yahoo! Small Business (http://smallbusiness.att.yahoo.com) offer website-in-a-box options that provide small business websites at low cost (and sometimes for free). These sites make site construction easy and fast by providing templates.

Build a site from scratch. Millions of people have done it and you can, too. Once you master the website software, you can create a basic website of five to ten separate Web pages in a few hours. To create these basic sites, you'll need three elements:

- **A domain name.** You can get your domain name (your address on the Web—for example, www.nolo.com) at a domain name registrar or through a hosting company (see below). Expect to pay between $10 and $35 a year.

- **Website development software.** You use this to create your website. You create it on your own computer and then transfer it to your hosting company. There is a learning curve for website software, and the three leading products are Macromedia *Dreamweaver*, Adobe's *Go Live*, and Microsoft *Expressions*. Expect to spend a day or two learning how to master the software. All of these products offer tutorial programs that will help you create your own site. One of the best ways to master website creation is to take a one-day introductory course. Check your local adult education providers.

- **A hosting company.** A hosting company, sometimes referred to as an Internet Service Provider or ISP, rents you space on its equipment. You give the host your domain name information (or they'll get the domain name for you) and your website design and imagery, and they broadcast your website for the world to see. Expect to pay $5 to $50 a month for Web hosting, depending on the bells and whistles. To get an idea of your options, type "web hosting" into an Internet search engine.

Selling Products and Taking Orders Online

If you're interested in selling products online, you'll need to do more than if you're setting up an information-only site. Like a jukebox, your sales site will have to look good on the outside but also house some complex inner mechanics. Buyers need to examine images of items, fill shopping carts, pay with credit cards, and process orders. You can set up a sales site fairly quickly using one of the community store systems described below. It's also possible to set up your own online store from scratch, but doing so requires some programming skills and savvy. Unless you're familiar with Web maneuvering, you are best leaving that to a website developer.

Community stores. If sales sites can be divided into two categories, they would be community businesses (based on the eBay business model) and everyone else. The emphasis at eBay—and what initially distinguished it from everything else on the Web—is community. Buyers rate sellers, communicate with each other, follow prescribed community rules, and to some extent, make the rules. (They even voted on the company name.) The eBay-style business model has since spread to other online services—for example, Amazon Marketplace and Yahoo! Stores. Like eBay, these stores operate within a community and share similarities in appearance because they are based on similar templates.

Community stores offer a complete turnkey solution—that is, they'll help you quickly set up your site and make it possible for you to accept credit card payments. All you'll need to do is pay the fees and provide photos and copy for your products. For a good example of a successful community store, check out the Yahoo! Store for the Vermont Teddy Bear Company at http://store.yahoo.com/vtbear.

Building a store from scratch. There are some things to be said for running a store outside of a community like Yahoo!, eBay, Amazon, and MSN. You are not obligated to follow community rules or to pay a percentage of sales to the community landlord. And you have greater autonomy, more creative freedom in site design, and the potential for greater revenue.

But building a store from scratch is not as simple as creating an information site from scratch, as described above. You have to go through the same basic steps—get a domain name, design your site, and locate an ISP—with one twist: You need to incorporate a shopping cart and credit card payment system.

And that's one reason why community stores are so popular; they handle both of these procedures for you. Few business owners can handle these tasks themselves—are you familiar with CGI scripting?—and the great majority outsource the tasks to companies (including website hosting companies) that provide shopping cart solutions. For example, PayPal, discussed below, offers a shopping cart program as part of its merchant tools. For more information on shopping cart providers, type "shopping cart services" into a search engine. These companies will handle all of your back-end details and deposit payments into your account.

PayPal (www.paypal.com), an online payment system owned by eBay, is an intermediary for credit card payments as well for bank transfers. If you're selling only a few items, you may be able to avoid the shopping cart system with a simple order form and a link to PayPal. Or, if you wish, PayPal can provide a more advanced shopping cart solution.

If You Can't Handle Site Creation

If you can't or don't want to deal with website creation, get a developer to do it for you. Expect to pay between $500 to $2,000 for a basic site (five to ten pages). Developers may also assist you on a regular basis by offering Web hosting and regular maintenance. If you plan on including streaming video, animation, or other sophisticated online features, you'll likely need the help of a developer. You can find developers online or in your local yellow pages.

Keep in mind that websites are not static; they need to change as your business changes. So unless you set up a system to update the site yourself, you'll have to keep returning to a developer for every fix. The best solution: Have the developer set up the site and then teach you how to update it.

There's an added benefit of using developers: They are often savvy in methods of popularizing sites (using some of the methods described below) and you may benefit from their online marketing knowledge.

Where's The Banana?

Many books have been written about the art and science of creating websites. One of the most popular (and shortest) is Seth Godin's *The Big Red Fez: How to Make Any Website Better* (Free Press). According to Godin, Internet users are like the performing monkey with the red fez: They'll do tricks for you as long as they can see the reward—the banana. On a Web page, unless the "banana" is obvious—the user recognizes it within three seconds—you've probably lost business. In other words, don't provide too many choices and don't obscure your banana with too many drop-down menus or flashy but slow-to-load graphics. Focus on what's working the best at your site and make it prominent and easy to find—for example, at Amazon, you'll have no trouble recognizing and clicking on the blue box marked "Ready to Buy?"

Driving Traffic to Your Site

How do you get people to come to your website? Here are some common approaches.

Great Content and Links

The most effective and low-cost method of driving traffic to your site is to create great content that encourages other sites to link to you. For example, Nolo, the publisher of this book, provides extensive free legal information at its website (www.nolo.com), making it one of the most linked-to legal sites on the Web. By the way, if you are interested in seeing who is linked to your website, type "link:" followed by the address of your website into the Google search engine; for example, type "link:www.nolo.com."

Search Engines and Keywords

Most people find their Web destinations via search engines, which have two types of listings: relevant and sponsored. Relevant listings are the primary search results that appear on the search page. Relevance (the order in which they are listed) is determined by the search engine algorithm, a mathematical formula that uses factors such as the content in a site, its domain name, material in its header (the headline that appears in the bar on top of your browser), information in its metatags (information buried in the website code), and the number of sites that are linked to it.

There are many ways to increase your relevance at a website; if you want to, check out one of the many books or websites devoted to that purpose. Type "increase traffic website" into a search engine.

Sponsored links usually appear at the top and in the right margin of the page. You can become a sponsored link by purchasing (or bidding on) keywords at a search company. For example, at Google.com, you can click on the "Advertising Programs" link and buy keywords (Google calls them "Adwords") for a small setup fee (approximately $5). Keywords are the terms that people type into the search engine. For example, if you had purchased the words "crochet" and "baby," then your ad would pop up when a user searched for crocheted baby hats.

In reality, keyword buying is a lot more complex. Your choice of keywords is crucial, because if you use terms that are not specific or appropriate, you will have wasted your money. Often, you must bid for keywords against competitors, and if you have the top bid, you will pay that amount every time someone clicks on your link when it appears in the search engine results.

There's strong sentiment for and against keyword buying. Some marketing people believe that it's useless trying to outbid competitors all the time and that the only one who profits is the search engine. In addition, keyword prices have escalated in the past few years, making them a more expensive form of marketing.

Others, in crowded fields, believe that keyword buying is an effective way to rise to the top of the heap. In any case, everyone agrees that if you do buy keywords, you must closely monitor their effectiveness. If you are not getting any results from the purchase of certain keywords, ditch those terms—fast. And, of course, if keywords in general are not generating sufficient returns, stop paying for them. For more information, type "Buy keywords" into your search engine. Finally, some search engines, such as Overture, merge relevance and sponsorship. The more you bid, the more relevant your search results.

Banner Ads

Banner ads, as you're probably aware, are short advertising messages that appear at websites. Like billboards, you can buy this advertising space and place your ads strategically across the Web. Like any form of advertising, you have a challenge: to get the viewer's attention and to motivate the viewer to click though to your site. It's a big challenge for a small ad. You can get some help on the Web at sites such as www.wowbanners.com.

Your other challenge with a banner ad is to buy space at sites that are likely to be visited by your target audience. There are a lot of ways to buy banner ads on other websites. You can click on a site that has a sign seeking advertising ("Advertise on our site"), buy ad space from a third-party agent—for example, www.bannerspace.com, or type "buy banner ad" in your search engine—or you can do a banner ad exchange (check one of the many free banner ad exchange sites). When someone clicks on the banner ad, they're directed to your site. Unless you're using a free banner ad exchange, you pay for these ads either by impression (every time your banner appears), by click-through (every time someone clicks on your banner ad), or by sale (every time someone clicks on your ad and then buys your product). Expect to pay a rate of $2 to $3 per every thousand people who see your banner ad.

As with keywords, banner ads must be closely monitored for effectiveness. If you're not getting responses, promptly modify or pull the ad.

Affiliate Programs

An affiliate program is any kind of program where one website pays another for delivering sales or traffic. For example, Amazon pays its affiliates for driving sales of a specific book. For many businesses, it may be too difficult or cumbersome to set up an affiliate system. (In fact, you may find it easier and more profitable to participate in someone else's affiliate program.)

But if you sell one-of-a-kind or niche products at your site, you can offer commissions (or other rewards) to other sites that drive customers to click through and buy those products. For example, a maker of high-end custom audio equipment may wish to establish an affiliate system with audiophile websites; the maker of safety helmets for young baseball players may wish to affiliate with local Little League sites.

Building a Community

If your customers have something in common, you have an opportunity to unite them in a community at your site. For example, if your business sells soccer supplies, you may want to set aside a portion of your site for a chat room or other community exchange for soccer players in your area, create links for soccer enthusiasts, offer a method of buying discounted tickets to soccer matches, or perhaps even offer an interactive prediction game in which players pick World Cup winners. The key is to take a hint from eBay and unite your customers in a community atmosphere.

Legal Rules

Many sites post "terms and conditions" somewhere on the site. Do you need them, too? Maybe.

If your site sells products, you may need notices regarding credit card use, refunds, and returns (known as "transaction conditions"). For example, you might want to announce that your business will accept returns up to 30 days after purchase. You may also want to include disclaimers—statements that inform customers that you won't be liable for certain kinds of losses they might incur. For example, you may disclaim responsibility for losses that result if pottery breaks when a customer ships it back for return. For more information on establishing refund policies, see Chapter 15.

If you are gathering information from your customers, including credit card information, you should post a privacy policy detailing how this information will be used or not used. Yahoo!'s privacy policy (http://privacy.yahoo.com) is a good example of a broad, easy-to-understand policy. You can check out other policies by typing "privacy policy" in a search engine. Pick and choose the elements that apply to your site. Whatever policy you adopt, be consistent, and if you are going to change it, make an effort to notify your customers of the change.

If your site provides space for chats or postings from the Web-surfing public, you'll want to limit your liability from offensive or libelous postings or similar chat room comments. There are three things you can do. First, regularly monitor all postings and promptly take down those you think are offensive or libelous. Second, if asked to remove a posting by a third party, remove it while you investigate. If you determine—after speaking with an attorney—that you are entitled to keep the post, then you can put it back up. Third, include a disclaimer at your site that explains you don't endorse and aren't responsible for the accuracy or reliability of statements made by third parties. This won't shield you from claims but it may minimize your financial damages if you're involved in a lawsuit over the posting.

Regardless of what your site does, you should include notices regarding copyright and trademark—for example "Copyright © 2008 RichandAndrea.com" or "Cyzuki is a trademark of Cynthia Lloyd."

If you are catering to an audience under 13 years old, special rules apply. You should learn more about dealing with children at the Federal Trade Commission's website, www.ftc.gov/kidzprivacy. ●

Should You Quit Your Day Job?

Go Part-Time, Flextime, or Telecommute 256

    Flextime..256

    Telecommuting..256

    Part-Time/Job Sharing 257

    Get Organized 257

    Get Help 258

    Get the Right Day Job..258

Three Reasons to Keep Your Day Job..259

How Do You Know When to Quit Your Day Job? 259

    What's the Psychological Effect?..260

Has does Superman do it? He's busy saving the world and yet he still has time for his job at the *Daily Planet*. If you're one of the millions of small business owners who also hold down a day job, you probably wish you had super powers, too. How else are you supposed to maintain your dual identity, grow your business, and still succeed at your 9 to 5? Here are some suggestions.

Go Part-Time, Flextime, or Telecommute

Is there any way for you to tweak your work schedule, reduce your hours, or telecommute? Many companies offer these options, but don't be dismayed if your employer is not one of them—yet. You may be able to convince your boss to change course. There are books, career counselors, and websites that are devoted to helping you achieve that goal. One site, Work Options (www.workoptions.com), helps you write a proposal for your boss and even provides scripted responses to typical objections such as, "We've never done this here before" or "If you telecommute, everyone will want to." Here's how these arrangements can work for you.

Flextime

Flextime lets an employee work a nontraditional schedule—for example, working a full-time job in less than five days. At least one study has found that flextime improves productivity, lowers costs, and decreases absenteeism.

Telecommuting

It's no surprise that more employers are providing some telecommuting (working at home) option. It cuts operating costs (especially costs associated with real estate), it brings some workers (especially salespeople) closer to customers, and like flextime, it's great for keeping employees loyal and happy by eliminating grinding commutes and allowing workers to spend more time with their families.

Part-Time/Job Sharing

Going part-time (assuming you can afford it) allows you to keep work benefits and a regular paycheck. Some employers create part-time positions by job sharing—when two workers share the duties of one full-time job. Although job sharing may not sound workable, it is effective. For example, after the furniture chain Ikea began providing benefits such as job sharing (as well as telecommuting and condensed work weeks) sales staff turnover dropped from 76% to 36%.

Get Organized

If keeping a job and running your business is making you feel scattered, take some time to improve your organizational skills. It may be the easiest, least expensive way to improve your business and reduce some of your stress.

Two of the most popular organizational gurus are David Allen, author of *Getting Things Done* (Penguin) (www.davidco.com), and Julie Morgenstern, author of *Organizing From the Inside Out* (Holt) (www.juliemorgenstern.com).

David Allen's methodology combines discipline, action, and office supplies. (Yes! Here's to any system that encourages a trip to Office Depot.) With Allen, every task triggers an action—you either do it, delegate it, or defer it. One tip from David that works for everyone is to get rid of things that don't require action. It's surprising how many nonaction items clutter up your life and work—for example, emails and letters for which responses aren't required, articles to be read, and activities for which someone else should be providing action. These things can be trashed or incubated (held in a tickler file for review). This system alone can clear about one-quarter of your daily paperwork.

Julie Morgenstern concentrates on organizing your mind first and your tasks second. Unless you get your mind in order, she says, you'll continue to create unrealistic schedules that increase frustration. Once you see your day like a map, you can chart your course. One tip from Julie that worked for me was to time my activities in my audio business with a stopwatch. I learned that my estimates were way off and that I was spending twice as much time audio editing as I had calculated.

Get Help

Sometimes the best way to juggle the day-job/business lifestyle is to bring in someone else to help with your business. That doesn't mean you give up control. You can hire a contractor or employee and pay them based upon sales or other revenue. The point is to find someone to help with the heavy lifting. In Chapter 8, we provide more information on hiring contractors and employees.

Get the Right Day Job

Some people are lucky enough to have a day job they enjoy and a business they love. That's the approach taken by Tom Kuhn, a San Francisco dentist who, for the past 30 years, has led a secret life as "Dr. Yo," the mastermind credited with creating the high-end, collectible yo-yo market. Despite his success in the yo-yo business, Tom never wanted to quit his day job. He enjoys being a dentist, and his yo-yo business often benefits from the advice of patients—for example, a lawyer patient recommended he obtain a patent for his famous 3-in-1 No Jive yo-yo and another patient recommended that he consult with NASA about using space age materials for yo-yo axles. "It's difficult to split your energies, but I always thought of myself as a dentist first," says Tom. His successful company remains a leader and an innovator despite 30 years of (pardon the pun) industry ups and downs.

If you're not satisfied with your day job, maybe you should consider an alternative. Okay, okay, it's not an easy thing to do—but sometimes the change can help your business by bringing you in contact with new people or a new industry.

As you can imagine, there are many books, videos, and websites offering advice on changing your job. In the book department, you can't go wrong with the classic *What Color Is Your Parachute?* by Richard Nelson Bolles (Ten Speed Press). As for websites, the leader is Monster.com (www.monster.com).

Three Reasons to Keep Your Day Job

Before you quit your day job, consider that besides losing your regular paycheck—which many entrepreneurs use to pull in the financial slack from their business—quitting can also affect the following:

- **your credit rating.** Having a day job makes it easier to borrow money and get credit cards and loans.

- **your tax deductions.** At tax time, your dual identity lets you deduct your business losses from your day job income.

- **your benefits.** Health insurance, dental insurance, stock options, vacation days, pension plans, and discounts at Six Flags are some of the hard-to-replace benefits provided by day jobs. (And no, purloined office supplies are not a job benefit. See below.)

How Do You Know When to Quit Your Day Job?

If you are not obligated to support anyone, you're indifferent to your current day job, flush with cash, and in love with your new business, you're an ideal candidate for quitting your day job. Unfortunately, few of us match this description. Before we take the big step, we want to be sure there's firm footing where we land. You'll need to consider the following:

What's the financial effect? If you haven't made a business plan, now's the time. If that seems too difficult, at least do basic financial forecasting. (See Chapter 6 for more on business plans and forecasting.) Estimate living expenses for a year by making a budget based on the past year (or past two years, if possible). Will you have enough income from your business to live and pay your expenses (including health insurance)? Do you have a financial cushion like a savings account that will pay all expenses for six months? How close are you to retirement age, and how will leaving your job affect your retirement? There are no bright lines for determining the right financial mix, but when you weigh these factors you should feel comfortable that you could weather a worst-case scenario.

If you do decide to quit, here are two tips:

- **Don't burn bridges.** You may want the job back.
- **Get your teeth cleaned.** Before you leave your job, get in any last doctor and dental appointments

What's the Psychological Effect?

How much of your identity is embedded in your current day job? What are you going to miss about it? Many departing employees are surprised how much they miss the social life provided by a regular job. How does your family feel? Will they support your decision? Are people counting on you to take care of them? Again, there are no simple yes or no answers. You need to examine all of these personal factors before making your decision. Experts use self-actualization techniques to help you make these decisions. You can see how these techniques work in Barbara Sher's book, *I Could Do Anything If I Only Knew What It Was* (Dell).

DON'T

Unfortunately, your employer may not share your enthusiasm for your small business, particularly if it's perceived as competing. Here are some "Don'ts" for moonlighting employees and how to avoid them.

Don't steal office supplies. If you want to avoid problems with your employer, don't stock your new business with supplies from your day job. In *The Scorecard at Work* (Holt), author Greg Gutfeld says stealing office supplies is one of the five fastest ways to get fired. Historically, employees rationalize this theft, saying "the company can afford it." Since office supplies account for a fairly large chunk of the $67 billion lost to employee theft each year, employers apparently don't think they can afford it—and are now more than ever on the lookout for disappearing staplers.

Don't use customer lists and trade secrets. Don't start a competing business using your employer's trade secrets. Almost every employer has valuable confidential information that it wants to keep under wraps. It could be a sales plan, a list of customers, a manufacturing process, or a formula for a soft drink. In legal terms, these are your employer's trade secrets. You have an obligation to preserve these secrets whether or not you ever sign a nondisclosure agreement. Not all customer lists or business information amount to trade secrets. But, unless you can hire an attorney to sort out the legalities, stay away from your employer's confidential information. There's more on trade secrets in Chapter 11.

Don't assume you own what you create for an employer. Even without a written employment agreement, an employer often ends up acquiring ownership of an employee's innovations. Always tread carefully if you're starting a company based on a product developed during your employment. You may not own the work you're creating. This issue often arises in tech businesses, particularly software and Internet ventures.

Don't violate noncompete and nonsolicitation agreements. A noncompetition agreement (also known as a "noncompete" or "covenant not to compete") is a contract in which you agree not to compete with your former employer for a period of time. A nonsolicitation agreement restricts your ability to solicit your former employer's clients or employees. These two agreements are often folded into an employment agreement or become part of a termination agreement that an employee must sign to get a severance package. If your moonlighting business is competitive, you'll likely be in violation of the noncompete and your employer will be able to shut you down.

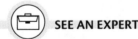 **SEE AN EXPERT**

Call a lawyer when...

- you receive a request from another business or its attorney asking you to stop using a trademark
- you're in doubt about rights to innovations or other products created during employment
- you're unsure whether your new business will compete with your employer, or
- you're using information or customer lists gleaned from a previous employer.

Hobby or Business:
How It Affects Taxes

What's the Difference? Hobby vs. Business...264

How the IRS Judges Your Business 264

Use Depreciation to Show a Profit..265

Proving a Profit Motive...266

If You're Audited 268

Classic Hobby Loss Abuse...269

When we ask whether you have a hobby or business, we're only concerned about one thing—taxes. If Uncle Sam looks at your return and concludes that you have a hobby, not a business as you claimed, you'll have to provide evidence that you're serious about making money. If you cannot convince the tax authorities that you've got a serious and documented desire to profit, you may have to pay back taxes and penalties.

What's the Difference? Hobby vs. Business

If you have a business, you can deduct your losses from other income, such as salary, your spouse's income, or interest and investment income. This is a big benefit for the one-quarter of individually owned businesses reporting a deductible loss each year. A business can also carry over deductions from year to year even if it doesn't expect to earn any money for a long time.

If you have a hobby, you can deduct your expenses from your hobby income only. So if you lose $5,000 on your venture, you can't deduct it from other income. This is the "hobby loss rule." And a hobbyist can't carry over deductions to use them in future years when income starts rolling in; they're lost forever.

How the IRS Judges Your Business

If you want to succeed in an IRS audit over the hobby loss rule, you must demonstrate that your primary motive is to earn a profit and that you continuously and regularly engage in your business over a substantial period.

Here are the rules:

• If you earned a profit from your business in any three of the last five years, the IRS presumes it is a business and is unlikely to question you about it.

• If you didn't earn a profit in any three of the last five years, you will have to show that you behave as if you want to earn a profit (explained below).

When Do You Have a Profit?

You have a profit when the taxable income from an activity is more than the deductions for it—that is, you are not claiming a loss. There is no set amount or percentage of profit you need to earn to satisfy the IRS.

Use Depreciation to Show a Profit

Sometimes you have a choice about whether or not your business will show a profit on paper. For example, in my first year of my audiobook business, I had approximately $14,000 in expenses—almost all of it for equipment. If I deducted all of these expenses from income, as I was entitled to do, I would show a loss of about $3,000 that year. But I had a choice, as do many small businesses that buy depreciable equipment. Instead of deducting the full amount of that equipment in one year, I could depreciate some or all of it over three or five years (depending on the equipment), which would let me show a profit in the first year. This tactic would also give me deductions for the next year, when I knew my expenses would be low. Learn more about tax strategies in Chapters 21 and 22 or from your accountant or tax preparation expert.

Form 5213: Wait One Year

If the IRS challenges your deductions during your early years, you can ask it to wait a year by filing IRS Form 5213, *Election To Postpone Determination as To Whether the Presumption Applies That an Activity Is Engaged in for Profit.*

Proving a Profit Motive

Was Amazon.com a hobby? It took the company seven years to turn a profit. Ditto for the search engine Ask.com. Both ESPN and OfficeMax did it in six years. *Sports Illustrated* took 11 years to show black ink; Turner Broadcasting took 12. That was nothing compared to the robotics firm Uninmation, which took 19 years. Did the fact that these companies failed to show a profit in three out of their first five (or ten) years cause the IRS to categorize them as hobbies?

No. If you are audited and you can't show a profit, the IRS will still consider your enterprise a business if you can prove you are guided by profit motive. The IRS measures your profit motive by looking at five "business behavior" factors. Studies show that taxpayers who satisfy the first three factors—you act like you're in business, you demonstrate expertise, and you show time and effort expended—are routinely classified as businesses even if they don't expect to profit for years.

- **Act like you're in business.** Keeping good books and other records goes a long way to show that you carry on activities in a businesslike manner. For example, husband and wife sculptors were able to claim business losses by providing records of exhibits at museums and galleries and testimonials to their skill and sales potential from art experts. (*Rood v. U.S.*, 184 F. Supp. 791 (D. Minn. 1960).) Read more about recordkeeping in Chapter 2.

- **Acquire expertise within your industry.** Having expertise in the industry shows you're serious about your business. To demonstrate this, it helps to show that you're savvy within your field. For example, an inventor developed a miles-per-gallon indicator but gave up on it after learning that General Motors was developing something similar. The tax court found a profit motive in the inventor's decision to drop the project; it showed he was savvy enough to realize he couldn't compete against GM. (*Maximoff v. Commissioner*, T.C. Memo 1987-155.)

- **Work regularly.** The IRS is looking for proof that you work regularly and continuously, not sporadically, on your business. What's "regularly and continuously"? One court accepted 20 to 30 hours per week (*Maximoff v. Commissioner*, T.C. Memo 1987-155); another accepted 25 hours per week for three years, then five to ten hours per week for two years (*Luow v. Commissioner*, T.C. Memo 1971-326). When a taxpayer couldn't establish the time spent, a court called it a hobby (*Everson v. Commissioner*, 2001 TNT 115-8).

- **Establish a record.** Having a record of success in other businesses in the past—whether or not they are related to your current business— creates the likelihood that your activities are a business.

- **Earn some profits.** Even if you can't satisfy the three-out-of-five-years profit test, earning a profit one year after years of losses helps show you are in a business.

The IRS is skeptical of taxpayers who claim large business losses but who have substantial income from other sources. Unfairly or not, if you have a modest income, you'll fly lower on the IRS radar screen. The IRS also may be doubtful of your motives if you're having lots of fun. Deductions for a snowboarding business will raise more red flags than deductions for a coffee shop.

Whether you race bicycles or gamble on dogs, the IRS is primarily concerned with whether you operate like a business. Here are two examples:

- **Here comes speedy.** Robert worked for 20 years in sales and market research when his position was terminated. After that, Robert's life went to the dogs ... or at least to the dog track. He decided to make gambling his job. When the IRS questioned him about it, he was able to show that he had spent 60 to 80 hours each week for 48 weeks either at dog tracks or at home studying racing forms, programs, and other materials. Even though his efforts generated a net gambling loss of $2,032, the U.S. Supreme Court ruled that Robert was engaged in a business. (*Commissioner of Internal Revenue v. Groetzinger*, 480 U.S. 23 (1987).)

- **Deducting her derailleur.** Donna, a customer service manager for a sporting goods company, hoped to make money as a cycling champ. When the IRS questioned her, she demonstrated her expertise and documented her diligence in pursuing her goal; she raced 30 times a year, trained daily, and had sponsors who provided bicycles, clothing, and, occasionally, entry fees. Even though she incurred expenses that exceeded her racing income, the court ruled that bicycle racing was her business. (*In re Fletcher*, 248 B.R. 48 (Bankr. D. Vt., 2000).)

DON'T

Don't be inconsistent. Don't tell the IRS something that's inconsistent with what you're telling everybody else. Here's an example of what can go wrong:

A couple bred dogs and claimed breeding expenses as a business deduction. When they sought a zoning exemption to keep more dogs at their home, they assured the town that dog breeding was a hobby, not a commercial venture. Whoops! You can't have it both ways, said the tax court. It ruled against the deductions and imposed a penalty. (*Glenn v. Commissioner*, 97-1 U.S. Tax Cas. (CCH) P50,101 (6th Cir. 1996).)

If You're Audited

These days, most people who disobey tax rules have a good chance of escaping the IRS's clutches; in 2007, only one in 100 individual taxpayers were audited. Most of these audits were triggered by a computer analysis known as the discriminate function system (or DIF), which looks for red flags in a tax return. One of the red flags is "losses from an activity that could be viewed as a hobby, rather than a business." Several factors arouse suspicion:

- the individual filing has substantial assets
- the deduction is very high, perhaps tens of thousands of dollars, and
- the business is one that could be considered a leisure experience—such as horse breeding or yacht charters.

When suspicious factors light up, the odds of being selected by the DIF system increase. However, be aware that every once in a while, the IRS breaks from this pattern and selects an otherwise unlikely candidate for audit.

That's what happened to Don, a university librarian, who has a side business writing songs. He rarely profited from his venture and has claimed losses of a few hundred dollars for several years. When Don was called in for an audit, he was most concerned about verifying expenses from three or four years earlier; he hadn't kept all his receipts.

Don's lawyer told him not to worry about receipts because if the IRS ruled against Don on the hobby/business issue, all of his deductions would vanish. Instead, the lawyer suggested that Don focus on proving that he operated a business.

Business records and other documents create a convincing factual trail. When Don met with the IRS auditor, he provided statements from performing rights societies (organizations that collect money for songwriters), small checks for foreign radio play, reviews of his records, and correspondence to and from music publishers and record companies. When the IRS agent saw the recordings, he asked Don to sing. The auditor ruled in Don's favor. "When I was leaving," said Don, "he gave me advice: 'Next time, make some money—it looks better.'"

Classic Hobby Loss Abuse

To give you an idea of some of the extreme abuse the IRS is looking to stop, here are two classics:

- **The 27-year search for the perfect steak.** When Maurice wasn't in the Canary Islands living off a family trust, he traveled the world sampling food and wines. For 20 years, he gathered material for his book, My 27-Year Search for the Perfect Steak—Still Looking. Two publishers rejected the book, and he abandoned plans for publication. Maurice claimed that the book was part of his bid to create a business around his "multimedia personality." He claimed losses of approximately $22,000 and $28,000 for two years. The IRS disallowed the deductions since Maurice couldn't show any evidence he was working towards his multimedia personality goal or that he had an expectation of profit. (*Dreicer v. Commissioner*, 78 T.C. 642, 1982 U.S. Tax Ct. LEXIS 109, 78 T.C. No. 44 (1982).)

- **How to heat a palm tree.** Martin, a wealthy inventor and manufacturer of farm implements, decided to build a luxury house with swimming pool and tennis courts. The house had some creative features—there was no wood used in the construction, only glass, plastic, and aluminum; there were motorized drapes, an automatic watering system for the lawn, and even a palm tree with a warming coil in the planter. In a deft creative accounting effort he deducted the cost of his new home from his income, calling it experimentation for his inventing business and claiming that he planned to exploit the home's innovations. The tax court wasn't persuaded. Apparently, Martin had not done any research before commencing the costly construction to determine if a market existed for the types of innovations he had in mind, and he didn't keep any records during the construction process so that he could later commercially apply these innovations. He had moved his family into the house immediately upon completion and apparently forgot about taking any further steps towards profiting on his "housing experiments" until three years later—at about the same time that the Internal Revenue Service was auditing his income tax returns. (*Mayrath v. Commissioner*, 357 F.2d 209 (5th Cir. 1966).)

For more assistance, the Internal Revenue Service website (www.irs.gov) is the best source of tax information and provides a special section for small business owners and the self-employed at www.irs.gov/businesses/small/index.html.

Paying Your Taxes

Audit Flags: Who's More Likely to Get Audited?..272

How Businesses Are Taxed..273

What Taxes Your Business Will Have to Pay 275

Paying Estimated Taxes...276

Preparing Your Taxes 279

Keeping Records for the IRS..282

When you work for yourself, preparing and paying your taxes is more complicated than it is when you work as someone else's employee. You'll have plenty of new tax forms to complete, new rules to follow, and strategic decisions to make. The good news is that most small business owners can tackle their new paperwork using a Web-based or software tax preparation program, once you know your obligations.

The basic formula for paying tax on a business is the same as paying tax on a salary or other sources of income. You must pay tax on your net income—the money you earn from your business less your deductions. As a business owner, however, you have some additional tax obligations. For example, you have to pay self-employment taxes, which fund your Social Security and Medicare contributions. If you have employees, you'll have to pay part of their Social Security and Medicare payments, pay federal unemployment tax, and withhold (and periodically send to the government) income tax from your employees. And you'll probably have to pay your income taxes in four installments throughout the year, rather than all at once on April 15.

Audit Flags: Who's More Likely to Get Audited?

The odds of being audited are slim—generally between 1% and 1.2% of taxpayers are audited each year. Usually, the decision of who gets audited is based on a computer analysis known as the discriminate function system (or DIF), which looks for red flags in a tax return.

Be aware that every once in a while, the IRS breaks from this DIF pattern and randomly selects an otherwise unlikely candidate for audit.

For more assistance, the Internal Revenue Service website (www.irs .gov) provides a special section for small business owners at www.irs.gov/ businesses/small/index.html.

INTERNET LINK

You can find links for all the resources in this book at www.nolo
.com/wowbusiness.

How Businesses Are Taxed

How you pay taxes on your business profits will depend on how you
have structured your business. As explained in Chapter 3, there are four
basic business forms: sole proprietorship, partnership, limited liability
company (LLC), and corporation. For tax purposes, however, there are
only two types: those whose owners pay tax on business income on their
individual tax returns (called pass-through entities, because income and
expenses pass through the business to the owner) and those that must
pay their own taxes.

The vast majority of all small business owners are running a pass-through
entity. Sole proprietorships, partnerships, LLCs, and S corporations (corporations that elect to be taxed like a partnership—see Chapter 3 for more
information) are all pass-through entities. A pass-through entity does not
pay its own taxes. Instead, its profits or losses pass through to the owners,
who must report those amounts on their personal tax returns.

Here are the basic rules:

- **Sole proprietors** report business income and expenses on IRS
  Schedule C, *Profit or Loss From Business*, which they have to file
  along with their personal tax returns (IRS Form 1040).

- **Partners** report their share of partnership income and expenses on
  IRS Schedule E, *Supplemental Income and Loss*, which they must file
  along with their 1040s. In addition, the partnership itself must file
  an informational return (IRS Form 1065, *U.S. Return of Partnership
  Income*) and provide each partner with an IRS Schedule K-1,
  Partner's Share of Income, Credits, Deductions, etc., which lists each
  partner's share of income and expenses.

- **Shareholders in S corporations** report income and expenses on their personal tax returns (IRS Schedule C, *Profit or Loss From Business*, and IRS Form 1040). In addition, the S corporation must file IRS Form 1120S, *U.S. Income Tax Return for an S Corporation*. This return gives the IRS information, but you don't use it to figure tax owed.

- **LLC members** report their income and expenses just like sole proprietors if they have one-member LLCs. In a multimember LLC, members report their income and expenses just like partners. A multimember LLC also has to file IRS Form 1065, *U.S. Return of Partnership Income* and issue an IRS Schedule K-1 to each member. (LLCs may, however, choose to be taxed as C corporations by filing IRS Form 8832, *Entity Classification Election*.)

- **Shareholders in C corporations** differ from their business brethren because the C corporation is the only business form that is not a pass-through entity. A C corporation must file its own tax return and pay its own taxes on corporate income. (It does so by filing IRS Form 1120, *U.S. Corporation Income Tax Return*.) Corporate shareholders have to pay personal income tax (on the 1040) only on any business income paid out to them as compensation or dividends. This is where the potential tax-saving benefits of incorporating come from: Because shareholders can decide how much corporate income to distribute and how much to retain in the corporation, they can allocate most of the money to the taxpayer with the lowest rates—usually, the corporation.

HOW BUSINESSES REPORT INCOME			
TYPE OF BUSINESS	OWNER PAYS TAX ON PERSONAL TAX RETURN	BUSINESS PAYS TAX ITSELF	BUSINESS MUST FILE ITS OWN TAX RETURN
Sole proprietor	x		
Partnership	x		x
One-member LLC	x		
Multimember LLC	x		x
S corporation	x		x
C corporation		x	x

What Taxes Your Business Will Have to Pay

There are three basic types of taxes a typical self-employed businessperson might have to pay: income taxes, self-employment taxes, and employment taxes. In addition, if you sell goods or services on which your state imposes a sales tax, you will have to collect this money and periodically hand it over to your state taxing authority.

Income taxes. You will have to pay income taxes on the net profit your business earns. The federal government imposes an income tax, as do the governments of most states. Some local governments also get into the act by taxing businesses within their jurisdictions; a few use an income tax, while others use some other method (an inventory, payroll, or business equipment tax, for example).

States That Don't Impose Income Taxes
Alaska, Florida, Nevada, South Dakota, Texas, Washington, and Wyoming.

Self-employment taxes. You are responsible for paying your own Social Security and Medicare taxes. Unlike employees, whose employers are legally required to chip in for half of these amounts, you will have to pay the entire bill—currently, a 12.4% Social Security tax and a 2.9% Medicare tax on all of your taxable income from self-employment. However, you are entitled to deduct half of these taxes from your gross income for purposes of calculating your income tax, so the total effective self-employment tax rate is about 12%. To report and pay self-employment taxes, you must file IRS Form SE, *Self-Employment Tax*, along with your annual tax return.

Employment taxes. If you have employees, you will have to pay half of their Social Security and Medicare taxes, as well as unemployment tax and perhaps temporary disability tax (to your state taxing authority). You'll also have to withhold taxes from your employees' paychecks and deposit them with the IRS. To report and pay unemployment tax, you file IRS Form 940, *Employer's Annual Federal Unemployment Tax (FUTA)*

Tax Return. To report all withholdings and pay your share of Social Security and Medicare, you must file IRS Form 941, *Employer's Quarterly Federal Tax Return.* The rules for employment taxes can get pretty tricky, and many employers are required to make quarterly filings with the IRS. For more information, check out IRS Publication 15 (Circular E), *Employer's Tax Guide* (you can get it at www.irs.gov).

Sales tax. Almost every state has a sales tax. You're undoubtedly used to paying sales tax as a consumer, but now that you're in business, you'll be on the other end of the transaction: You'll be responsible for collecting sales tax from your customers and paying that money to the state. State sales tax rules vary considerably: Some states tax only sales of goods, while others also tax services; in every state, certain sales are exempt from tax (that is, you don't have to collect or pay tax on the sale), but every state's list of exempt transactions is different, and states have different rules about when and how you must submit the tax you collect to the state taxing authority. To find the rules in your state, your best bet is to go straight to your state tax agency for help (you can find a list of links at www.irs.gov). You can also get a lot of good basic information, as well as details about every state's sales tax scheme, at www.toolkit.cch.com (look under "Controlling Your Taxes" in the Small Business Guide).

Paying Estimated Taxes

When you own your own business, clients and customers don't withhold taxes from what they pay you. This is a financial advantage for you; you not only receive the full amount you are owed, but also have greater freedom to plan your finances. The IRS is not so enthusiastic, however; it wants to get your tax dollars right away, rather than waiting for you to pay the whole tab on April 15.

That's why self-employed people have to pay estimated taxes—taxes on their estimated annual incomes, paid in four installments over the course of each year. These payments must include both estimated income tax and estimated self-employment taxes.

ESTIMATED TAX PAYMENT SCHEDULE	
INCOME RECEIVED	**ESTIMATED TAX DUE**
January 1 through March 31	April 15
April 1 through May 31	June 15
June 1 through August 31	September 15
September 1 through December 31	January 15 of the following year

You don't have to pay estimated taxes until you earn some income. For example, if your business doesn't bring in any income by March 31, you don't have to make an estimated tax payment on April 15.

Not everyone has to pay estimated taxes. You don't if:

- you expect to owe less than $1,000 in federal tax for the year

- you paid no taxes last year, if you were a U.S. citizen and your tax return covered the full 12-month period, or

- your business is a C corporation and you receive dividends or distributions of profits from your corporation on which you will owe less than $500 in tax for the year. (You don't have to pay estimated taxes on salary you receive from your corporation; instead, you report that income and pay tax on it annually, on your personal tax return.)

But even if you don't have to pay estimated taxes, you might want to do it anyway. Paying estimated taxes spreads your tax bill over the entire year, so you won't have to come up with all of the money at once. On the other hand, as long as you really have enough socked away to cover your bill, paying it all at once will give you the benefit of that money—and its interest-earning power—for a longer period of time.

No Tax Last Year = No Estimated Tax This Year

No matter how much money you earn or how much you expect to owe in federal income and self-employment tax, you have no obligation to pay estimated taxes if you had no tax liability in the previous year. This is true regardless of the discrepancy between this year's and last year's earnings. However, you must have filed a tax return for the previous year in order to take advantage of this rule.

For example, after Eddie Lee Williams was convicted of cocaine distribution and money laundering, the IRS went after him for failing to report—and pay estimated taxes on—his drug-related income. (Yes, the government expects people to report income from illegal activities.) Based on Williams's bank records and purchases (including three cars in a single year), the IRS estimated that he earned more than $100,000 in unreported income in 1989, a year for which he never filed a tax return. The tax court found that Williams was liable for failing to file a return and report this income, and that he owed a substantial amount in unpaid income taxes. However, the court refused to find Williams guilty of failing to pay estimated taxes on the income. The reason? Williams and his wife filed a return in 1988, in which they reported only $2,000 in income and for which they owed no tax. Because Williams owed no tax for the previous year, he was not required to make estimated tax payments in 1989, even though his earnings skyrocketed. (*Williams v. Commissioner*, TC Memo 2003-216.)

There are three ways to figure out how much estimated tax to pay. The easiest method is to simply pay exactly what you owed in federal tax the previous year (or a bit more, if you earned more than $150,000). However, if you don't expect to owe as much this year, you may want to look into the second and third methods listed below; although they are more complicated, they could result in a lower tax bill.

1. **Pay what you paid last year.** To use this method, simply divide your total federal tax payments for the previous year by four, then pay that amount when estimated taxes are due. (If you earn more than

$150,000 annually—$75,000 for married people filing separately—you'll have to pay 110% of your previous year's tax bill.) As long as you pay this amount, you won't owe the IRS any penalties, even if your current year's income is higher and you end up owing more tax at the end of the year.

2. **Make payments based on your estimated income.** If you expect to earn less this year than you did last year, you might save money by making tax payments based on this year's estimated taxable income. The catch, of course, is that it can be very tough to estimate income and expenses ahead of time. The IRS knows this, and won't charge you any penalties as long as your estimated payments cover at least 90% of the current year's tax bill (of course, you will have to pay the additional tax). To use this method, estimate your total taxable income for the year, calculate the tax you will owe (don't forget self-employment taxes), and pay one quarter of that amount when each estimated payment falls due.

3. **Make payments based on your estimated quarterly income.** Under this method, you calculate your taxable income (including prorated deductions) at the end of each payment period, then pay that amount on the due date. This is probably the toughest method to use, but may be worthwhile if your income fluctuates a lot throughout the year (for example, if your business is intensely seasonal). It allows you to pay little or no estimated tax during your "dry" periods, and save your tax bills for more profitable days.

Preparing Your Taxes

Before you sit down to fill in your tax forms, we advise following a two- (okay, sometimes three-) step process. First, do as much research as you need to understand the decisions you'll have to make. For example, as explained in Chapter 22, you often have a choice of either depreciating a major purchase or deducting its entire cost in the year you buy it. Only you can decide which makes more sense for your business, and you'll probably need to learn more about each option to make the right choice.

The information in this book will give you a jump on your research; for more help, start with Nolo's tax deduction books: *Deduct It!* and *Home Business Tax Deductions*, both by Stephen Fishman.

There are also plenty of great websites that offer free tax information. The best place to start is the IRS website, www.irs.gov. You can find a lot of useful articles and links on its home page for small businesses and the self-employed, and its free publications are loaded with information. You can download your tax forms here, too. A few other tax sites we like:

- **www.taxmama.com.** This site features a long list of free articles on topics like ten things taxpayers forget to tell their accountants, why you shouldn't rely on advice you get from the IRS over the phone, whether you should buy or lease a car you plan to use for business, and much more.

- **www.turbotax.com.** Along with Intuit's *TurboTax* tax preparation products, this site offers lots of free information on business tax issues. Select "Tax Calculators & Tips" to see the list.

- **www.hrblock.com.** Tax preparation giant H&R Block offers many free tips for taxpayers. Select "Tax Tips" to begin.

Once you are ready to actually prepare your returns, you have a number of options, ranging from filling in the forms yourself to hiring a certified public accountant to do your taxes. Often, the best choice falls in the middle of this range: using a Web-based or software program to complete your tax forms. These programs are cost-effective, can save you a lot of time and stress, and will help you not only complete the forms properly, but also figure out when you need more information to make the right decision.

Even With Separate Accounts, You Might Have Some Explaining To Do

Although many taxpayers fear an audit of their claimed deductions, the IRS is actually much more interested in income than expenses. Unreported income is often the first thing auditors look for, and they will be very suspicious if you have significant deposits beyond the income you claimed on your return, even if those deposits are to your personal account. If you have significant nontaxable income, make sure to keep the records you'll need to prove where it came from.

And don't expect the IRS to take your word for it, especially if you claim that the money belongs to someone else and just happened to find its way into your bank account. Judging from cases decided by the U.S. Tax Court, this is a fairly popular argument that is extremely likely to fail, unless you can show written proof of your claim and it looks like something other than a tax evasion ploy.

For example, a couple named the Armstrongs dutifully reported Mr. Armstrong's meager salary as a bus driver, but failed to report almost $40,000 in additional money that showed up in one of their bank accounts (opened under a false name). Because the Armstrongs had previously been in trouble for selling amphetamines and other drugs, the IRS had a pretty good idea of where this extra money came from. But the Armstrongs insisted that they had received the money from "Mr. Bell," a man who used to live in their apartment building. The very generous Mr. Bell had given them this money for safekeeping, never asking for a receipt or for access to the accounts, and told them they could use the money whenever they were in difficulty. Alas, Mr. Bell had died by the time the Armstrongs faced criminal charges for tax evasion; the jury convicted the couple. (*Armstrong v. U.S.*, 327 F.2d 129 (9th Cir. 1964).)

Both of us use—and are huge fans of—*TurboTax*. It is compatible with *Quicken* bookkeeping products, so you can import data from your records to your tax return. The program uses a question-and-answer interview format, so you can simply provide the requested information and count on the program to use it to fill in the appropriate forms. And you can always go back to a previous year's tax return to make instant comparisons and see how your business looks to the IRS over time. If you get stuck on a question or realize that you need to talk to a tax professional before deciding how to respond, you can simply exit the program and pick up where you left off once you have the information you need.

Keeping Records for the IRS

If you face an audit, the IRS is not going to take your word for anything. You'll have to come up with receipts, cancelled checks, bank statements, and other records to support both the amount of income you claimed and any business deductions you took. You really can throw it all in a shoebox if you want, but most business owners find it easier to use a set of file folders or an accordion file (you can buy one that's already labeled with common business expense categories at an office supply store).

Here's a brief rundown on what you need to keep as proof of income and expenses:

- **To document income,** you'll need copies of your bank statements, copies of checks you've deposited, copies of any 1099s you received, and, if you have nontaxable income, copies of documents showing the source of that income (for example, from an inheritance). Remember, the IRS is less interested in the business income you reported than in the income it thinks you failed to report. This means your job is not really to prove the amount of income your business earned, but to prove that any income you didn't report came from a nontaxable source.

- **To document most business expenses,** you must keep records showing what you bought, who you bought it from, how much you paid, and the date of the purchase. In most cases, you can prove this with your receipt and a cancelled check or credit card statement (which proves that the receipt is really yours).

- **To document vehicle expenses,** you must keep records of the dates of all business trips, your destination, the business purpose of your trip (for example, to meet with a client or scout a retail location), and your mileage.

- **To document meals and entertainment,** you must keep records of what you paid for, who you bought it from, how much you paid, the date of purchase, who you were with, and the business purpose of your meeting. The first four facts are often included on a receipt; the remaining two you can record in a date book or calendar.

- **To document your use of property,** you must keep records of how much time you spent using it for business and using it for other purposes. This rule applies to "listed property," items that the IRS believes people often use for personal purposes, including computers and cameras. (There really is a list of listed property, and you can find it in IRS Publication 946, *How to Depreciate Property*.) You might also want to keep track of the time you spend in your home office, to prove that you used it regularly. You can keep these records in a log or journal.

DON'T

Don't expect the IRS to allow your tax deductions if you don't keep records to back them up. If you have no records at all, your deductions will be disallowed in an audit, and you might face penalties as well. If you can prove that you had some business-related expenses of a type that makes sense for your line of work, the IRS may still allow a deduction, but it will be much smaller than what you claimed. Under the Cohan rule (named for a tax suit against entertainer George Cohan), if you can show some proof that you incurred deductible expenses, the IRS can estimate those expenses and allow a deduction for that amount. But, as you might expect, the IRS's estimates will be low. And this rule doesn't apply to expenses for travel, vehicles, gifts, and meals and entertainment. The IRS requires more detailed records for these types of deductions.

Donald Teschner, who played guitar, violin, and mandolin in Rod Stewart's band, found himself on the losing end of the Cohan rule. He claimed an employee deduction for stage clothing, including silk boxers and leather pants, but couldn't provide sufficient documentation to back up his claim that these items were required for his work. The court found that he could deduct only clothing so "flashy and loud" that it was not suitable for everyday wear, and further found that his receipts weren't sufficiently detailed to prove what he spent for flashy items as opposed to regular clothes. However, the court, apparently willing to believe that a musician backing up the man who sings "Do Ya Think I'm Sexy?" has to make some effort to stand out on stage, allowed him $200 of his claimed $695 deduction. (*Teschner v. Commissioner of Internal Revenue*, TC Memo 1997-498.)

How Long Should You Keep Records?

In most situations, the IRS has up to three years to audit you after you file a tax return (or after the date when your tax return was due, if you filed early). However, if the IRS claims that you have unreported income exceeding 25% of the income you did report, it has six years to audit you. And if you didn't file a return or the IRS claims that your return was fraudulent, there is no audit deadline; you're always fair game.

Based on these rules, some experts advise that you simply give up and keep all of your tax records forever. We certainly think there's no harm in keeping all of your actual tax returns forever; they don't take up much space and can help you track the financial life of your business over time. The supporting documents are another story. Unless you filed a fraudulent return (and this is something only you can decide), you can generally get rid of supporting documents six years after you file your tax returns.

Tax Deductions

What's a Tax Deduction Worth? 286

Tax Deduction Basics...290

Deducting Home Office Expenses 292

Qualifying for the Home Office Deduction 292

What You Can Deduct...295

Deducting Long-Term Assets 297

    Special Rules for Computers, Cell Phones, and Other
        Potential Toys...298

Section 179..298

Depreciation..299

Deducting Vehicle Expenses..300

Deducting Travel Expenses..301

Deducting Meals and Entertainment...303

An Interview with Attorney Stephen Fishman..304

As a businessperson, you probably already know one of the cardinal rules of business: You have to spend money to make money. The good news is that the government is prepared to give you some of that money back by allowing you to deduct most of what you spend on your business.

When you consider what a great deal the government is offering, you'll realize how important it is to understand tax deductions. By letting you deduct your expenses, the government is essentially offering to pick up part of the tab for your venture. After you factor in federal income taxes, state income taxes, and self-employment taxes, every dollar you spend on deductible business expenses could save you more than 40 cents on your tax bill. The offer is on the table; it's up to you to take advantage of it by claiming every tax deduction to which you're entitled.

This chapter explains some of the most common deductions. However, once you start racking up deductible expenses, you'll need more information. Nolo offers two great books on the subject: *Deduct It!* and *Home Business Tax Deductions*, both by Stephen Fishman. You can also find a lot of helpful guidance, including publications that explain various types of deductions, at the IRS website, www.irs.gov.

What's a Tax Deduction Worth?

A deduction is the cost or value of something that you can subtract from your gross income (all the money you earn) to determine your taxable income (the amount on which you have to pay tax). It's not a dollar-for-dollar proposition: You don't save the entire amount you paid for deductible goods and services. But because you don't have to pay tax on this amount, a deduction can save you almost half of what you spend.

The exact amount you'll save by taking a deduction depends on your tax bracket—the tax rate that applies to your income. The higher your bracket, the more every deduction is worth. Here's an example to show you how it works:

EXAMPLE: Simon spends $2,000 on a computer for his business. He's in the 25% federal income tax bracket. By deducting the cost of the computer, he doesn't have to pay tax on $2,000 of his income. That saves him 25% of $2,000, or $500. But that's not all. The state where Simon does business imposes a 6% income tax, so Simon saves an additional $120 there. And Simon doesn't have to pay self-employment taxes—the amount self-employed people have to chip in to fund their Social Security and Medicare—on this money, either. The self-employment tax rate works out to about 12%, for an additional $240 savings. Simon ends up saving $860, almost half of what he paid for his computer.

DON'T

Don't overlook deductions. Many entrepreneurs miss out on valuable business deductions simply because they don't know which expenses they can deduct. Many of us itemize our deductions on our personal tax returns, but once you start a business, a whole new range of deductions becomes available—and it sure pays to spend some time learning what they are.

Dan Hoffman, CPA and director of the San Francisco-based accounting firm Lautze & Lautze (www.lautze.com), says that new business owners often forget to deduct:

Bad debts. If someone owes your business money and it's starting to look like you're never going to get paid back, you might be able to deduct the amount of the bad debt. However, you won't be able to deduct a debt for services you performed unless you already reported the money you're owed as income—that is, unless your business pays tax on an accrual basis. (See Chapter 2 for more information.)

Casualty losses. If your business property is damaged or destroyed by fire, vandalism, flood, or some other sudden, unexpected, or unusual event, you can claim the amount of the loss as a deduction—but only to the extent that the loss isn't covered by insurance.

Dues, subscriptions, and fees. Dues or fees you pay to professional organizations—such as a trade association or membership group—are deductible business expenses. So are charges for subscriptions to professional, technical, or trade journals in your field.

Education expenses. If you buy books, take a college course, or attend a convention to keep up with the latest trends in your field, you can deduct your costs. As long as the expenditure either improves your business-related skills or is required to maintain your professional status (like continuing legal education for lawyers), it's deductible.

Phone bills. If you have a separate business line in your home office, you should deduct not only the costs associated with that phone, but also the cost of occasional business calls you make from your cell phone or personal phone line.

Retirement plans. You can deduct the money you contribute to most types of retirement plans that you set up for yourself or your employees. And if you qualify, you can deduct some of the start-up and administrative costs of a pension plan you establish for your employees. (See IRS Form 8881, *Credit for Small Employer Pension Plan Startup Costs*, for more information.)

Federal and state tax credits. Tax credits may be available to businesses that help further particular civic goals—for example, by hiring employees through a welfare-to-work program, doing business in designated "empowerment" or "renewal" zones (communities that are struggling economically), or using solar energy. You can find information on federal credits in IRS Publication 334, *Tax Guide for Small Business*; for information on state credits, contact your state taxing authority.

INTERNET LINK

You can find links for all the resources in this book at www.nolo .com/wowbusiness.

Postponing Start-up Costs

If you've already incurred start-up costs, you'll have to follow the rules laid out above. And, if you won't spend more than $5,000 on start-up expenses, you can simply deduct them all at once. However, if you're looking at more than $5,000 in future start-up costs, it's worth taking a couple of steps to avoid having to spread out part of your deduction over the next 15 years.

The key is to start your business before you lay out significant amounts of money; that way, your expenses are usually immediately deductible. If you will offer services, your business starts when you first make your services available to the public, whether or not you actually have any customers. If you'll be making products, you're in business once you start the process, even if you have not yet solicited any sales or completed any products.

Here are two ways to convert what would be start-up costs into immediately deductible business expenses:

- **Postpone major purchases until you're up and running.** Once you hang out your shingle, you can buy that fancy computer system and office furniture, or shell out thousands of dollars for advertising.

- **Postpone paying for purchases.** If you absolutely have to pay for some expensive items or services before you open your doors, buy them on credit (or ask to be billed later). As long as you're a cash-basis taxpayer (see Chapter 2 for more on this), you haven't actually incurred an expense until the money leaves your wallet. And as long as you pay the bill after you start up, you'll probably have an immediately deductible expense.

Tax Deduction Basics

How much you can deduct and when you can take the deduction depend on the type of expense. There are four basic categories of deductions, and the rules for each are a bit different.

Start-up expenses. Money that you spend before your business is up and running—such as the cost of researching what kind of business to start or advertising your grand opening—are start-up expenses. When it comes to dealing with these expenses, you can either:

- **Treat them as part of your basis in the business.** This means that you cannot deduct them, but you can add them in when you calculate the value of your business for purposes of figuring out your capital gain (or loss) when you sell or shut down.

- **Deduct them over time.** You may deduct up to $5,000 of them right away; you must deduct the remainder over the first 180 months you are in business. (A different rule applies to start-up costs incurred before October 24, 2004: You may not deduct any right away; instead, you deduct them in equal amounts over the first 60 months you are in business.)

Operating expenses. Once you are in business, your day-to-day costs are operating expenses. These might include money you spend on office rent, employee salaries, travel, professional services, office supplies, advertising, interest on business loans or purchases, and so on. As long as you aren't paying for something that you will use for more than a year (such as a vehicle or computer—see below), you can deduct these expenses in the year when you spend the money. The IRS has created special rules for operating expenses that it believes are often overstated or abused: travel, vehicle, and entertainment expenses. (These are covered in more detail below.)

My Three Deductions

If you hire your own children, spouse, parents, or anyone else who might have a legitimate personal claim to your financial support, then you'll have to be ready to prove that they really performed work for you and that it was worth what you paid them.

Don't follow the example of Gary Bybee, who claimed to be working with a team of professionals in his toxic waste disposal business. In fact, his only employees were his three sons, whom he said he hired to do research and read periodicals at their respective universities. He also claimed that, rather than paying them a salary, he found it more convenient to pay for their college tuition and living expenses. Needless to say, the court disallowed his claimed deductions for their travel and home office expenses—in fact, the court found that Bybee wasn't running a business at all. (*Bybee v. Commissioner of Internal Revenue*, 29 F.3d 630 (9th Cir. 1994).)

Capital expenses. If you buy things for your business that have a useful life of more than one year—like a car, furniture, or machinery—then you have purchased a long-term asset. You usually have the choice of either depreciating these assets (deducting a portion of the cost for each year of the item's useful life, as determined by the IRS) or deducting them all at once. (See "Deducting Long-Term Assets," below, for more information.)

Inventory. Special rules apply to inventory, the products you make or buy to sell to customers. You must wait until you sell inventory to deduct the cost of making or buying it. This is why so many businesses are desperate to get rid of their inventory at the end of the year: They want to take a larger deduction, and they want to minimize their burden when it comes time to count inventory for tax purposes.

Deducting Home Office Expenses

If you run your business from your home, you may be able to deduct expenses relating to your home workspace. Although commonly referred to as the "home office" deduction, this deduction actually applies to any home space you use for your business, including a studio, workshop, or laboratory.

Whether or not you qualify for a home office deduction, you can always deduct the direct costs of running your business—for example, if you buy a computer to use in your business, pay for high-speed Internet access to do your work, or use your personal phone for business calls, you may deduct those costs whether or not you claim the home office deduction. But using the home office deduction allows you to claim a portion of the costs of your home—rent, utility bills, cleaning services, homeowner fees, and so on—as a business expense.

Qualifying for the Home Office Deduction

To qualify for the home office deduction, you must first satisfy the IRS's threshold test:

- You must use your home workspace regularly and exclusively for business (unless you store inventory or run a day care center at home—see below).

- You use your home workspace **exclusively** for business, not for personal or other purposes. You don't have to devote an entire room to your business to qualify; you can use a portion of a room as a home office, as long as you use it exclusively for business. If you mix business with pleasure—for example, you use your workspace to correspond with clients and handle business bookkeeping, but also to play online poker and pay household bills—then you won't qualify for the home office deduction.

- You must also use your home office **regularly**—that is, on a continuing basis, not just for occasional work. The IRS has never clearly explained exactly what it considers regular use. One court found 12 hours a week sufficiently regular, but no one really knows how low you can go.

If you use your home office exclusively and regularly for business, you will qualify for the home office deduction if you meet one of these five additional tests:

- **Your home office is your principal place of business.** If you do all or almost all of your work in your home office, you meet this test. If you work in more than one location, however, you'll have to show that you do your most important business activities at home or that you do your administrative or management tasks at home. For example, if you are an interior decorator who works in clients' homes, you will qualify for the home office deduction if you do your planning, scheduling, billing, and so forth at home.

- **You meet clients or customers at home on a regular basis.** For example, if you are a masseuse who treats clients in your home or a couples counselor who conducts therapy sessions at your home, you may take the home office deduction.

- **You use a separate freestanding structure on your property exclusively for business.** Some examples might be a detached garage, cottage, or workshop.

- **You store inventory or product samples at home.** However, you cannot have an outside office or other workplace outside your home. For example, if you are a traveling salesperson who goes to potential customers' homes to peddle your wares, you will qualify—unless you have an outside office for your business. You don't have to use your storage space exclusively for business to qualify—regular use is enough.

- **You run a day care center at home to care for children, people who are at least 65 years old, or those who are unable to care for themselves.** You don't have to use your day care space exclusively for business, but you must use it regularly. For example, if you use your living room for day care during the day and for entertaining and relaxing in the evening, you can still claim the deduction.

Your Home Office Might Be a Vehicle

You don't have to live and work in a house to take the home office deduction: Apartments, condominiums, or even motor homes, houseboats, and other vehicles that double as your home and workspace can qualify, but you must meet the tests set out above. The combined facts that you own a vehicle that you use as a residence and you run a business are not enough, in themselves, to prove your entitlement to the deduction.

Carlton Perry found this out the hard way, when the tax court disallowed all of his deductions for business use of his motor home. Perry claimed that he ran a real estate rental business from the vehicle, but couldn't show regular or exclusive use. The tax court was unmoved by the records he produced at trial: A 61-page handwritten account of the trips he and his wife took in the vehicle, which included entries on the flowers and trees they saw, the food they ate, the sunsets they watched, and the places they hiked together, but failed to make any mention of business use of the vehicle. (*Perry v. Commissioner of Internal Revenue,* TC Memo 1996-194.)

DON'T

Don't expect the IRS to believe that you use most of a small home exclusively for your business, especially if you don't live alone. IRS auditors have homes, too, and they understand that it's very difficult to devote your only bedroom or all of your shared living space exclusively to your business.

For example, one taxpayer claimed that he used the "great room"—a combination living and dining room—of his rented house exclusively for his real estate business. The tax court didn't buy it, primarily because his home had only one bedroom and a kitchenette in addition to that great room, and his girlfriend lived with him. Although the court didn't doubt that he did some work at home, it refused to accept his argument that he and his girlfriend did all of their living, dining, and entertaining in the bedroom (or that the sofa and dining room table were used exclusively for work). (*Szasz v. Commissioner of Internal Revenue*, TC Summary Opinion 2004-169.)

On the other hand, if you can prove that you really do use a lot of your living space for work, you might have a good claim. For example, a professional concert violinist successfully claimed the home office deduction for her entire living room, even though she shared a one-bedroom apartment with her husband and young daughter. The court noted that her living room contained no typical furnishings, only shelves for sheet music, recording equipment, a small table, and a chair for her practice sessions (and her daughter was not allowed to play there). (*Popov v. Commissioner of Internal Revenue*, 246 F.3d 1190 (9th Cir. 2001).)

What You Can Deduct

Using the home office deduction, you can deduct a portion of your household expenses, including:

- rent
- mortgage interest and property taxes (the advantage of taking a portion of these costs as a business deduction rather than a personal deduction—as you are entitled to do on IRS Schedule A, *Itemized Deductions*—is that it reduces your business income and so your self-employment taxes)
- condominium or homeowners' association fees
- depreciation on a home you own
- utilities
- insurance
- maintenance and cleaning
- security costs, and
- casualty losses.

The exact amount you can deduct depends on how much of your home you use for work. There are two ways to measure this:

Home Office Deduction Tips

Plenty of taxpayers don't take a home office deduction because they believe it is likely to trigger an audit. The IRS says such beliefs are misguided, but it never hurts to cover your bases. Follow these tips to maximize your benefits—and minimize your chances of losing an audit.

- **Devote a separate room exclusively to your business.** While you can take a home office deduction even if you use only a portion of a room for work, it's much easier to designate an entire room: The math is easier, you won't have to worry about physically separating your work from your personal space, and you'll have an easier time satisfying the IRS that you use your office exclusively for work.

- **Do the math to figure out which method yields the highest deduction.** Of course it's easier just to count rooms, but take the time to measure your square footage as well. Depending on your home's layout, it may give you a bigger deduction.

- **Create visual aids.** Take a picture of your home office and draw up a simple diagram of your home layout showing the space you use for business. This can help you prove, if it's ever necessary, that you claimed the correct percentage.

- **Keep a record of home office activities.** If clients or customers visit, ask them to sign a log book. Note the time you spend on business in your date book or calendar.

- **Use your home office as your business address.** It will be easier to prove that your home is your principal place of business if you designate it as such. Have business mail delivered there and put your address on business correspondence, cards, and your letterhead.

- **Save those receipts (and other records).** When you take the home office deduction, you can claim expenses that you might not think of as business related, such as a portion of your rent, utility payments, or house-cleaning fees. This means that you'll have to save bills and receipts for these expenses along with your other business records.

- **Using the room method,** you divide the number of rooms you use for business by the total number of rooms in your home (not including bathrooms, closets, and other storage areas). For example, if you use the spare bedroom of your four-room home for business, you can deduct 25% of your household expenses.

- **Under the square footage method,** you divide the square footage of the area you use for work by the total square footage of your home (you don't have to include stairways, hallways, landings, entries, attics, or garages in your calculations). For example, if you use a 10' × 20' room as an office in your 1,000-square-foot home, your home office deduction percentage is 20%.

In addition to deducting a portion of overall household expenses, you may deduct 100% of any expense that is solely for your home office. For example, if you pay someone to paint the entire interior of your home (including your work area), you may deduct only the home office portion of the cost. But if you hire a painter just to paint your home office, you can deduct the entire amount.

Deducting Long-Term Assets

Long-term assets are things that have a useful life of more than one year, as determined by the IRS. Examples include computers, equipment, machinery, and furniture. There are two ways to deduct long-term assets. You can:

- deduct them immediately under Section 179 of the Internal Revenue Code if they meet the requirements, or

- depreciate them (deduct a portion of the value each year of the item's useful life).

Special Rules for Computers, Cell Phones, and Other Potential Toys

The IRS has created special rules for things that can easily be used for personal purposes, including computers, vehicles, cell phones, stereo equipment, and cameras. For these types of property (called "listed" property), you are required to keep a log proving that you use the item for business, even if you use it only for business and never for fun. The only exception is computers: If you use your computer exclusively for business, you don't have to keep a log. The moral of the story, for many small business owners, is that it makes more sense to buy a separate computer solely for business use than to go through the hassle of making a note every time you (or a family member) log on.

Section 179

Using Section 179 allows you to deduct long-term assets in the year when you buy them. You can't deduct more than you earn for the year, but you may carry over a Section 179 deduction to a future year, when your business is doing better. If you're fortunate enough to have skyrocketing profits, you can deduct up to a current limit of $128,000 (for tax year 2008).

Section 179 is only for tangible personal property—in other words, you can't use it to deduct the cost of land or buildings, or intellectual property, such as patents and copyrights. To take the deduction, you must use the item more than half of the time for business in the year in which you buy it. This means that if you buy an item for personal use (such as a computer or desk) and then start using it in your business more than one year later, you can't use Section 179. It also means that if you use an item at least half of the time for personal (nonbusiness) purposes, you can't take the deduction. If you use the item more than half of the time for business, you may deduct only a percentage of what you paid—for example, if you paid $2,000 for a computer that you use 75% of the time for business, you can deduct $1,500.

Does Depreciation Ever Make Sense?

Unless you buy more than $128,000 worth of business property in a single year, you'll probably be able to deduct long-term assets right away under Section 179. So why would anyone ever depreciate these assets instead?

Generally, they wouldn't (unless they use the item less than half of the time for business, in which case they cannot use Section 179). In a couple of situations, however, spreading out your deductions makes sense:

- **You need to show a profit.** If you're pushing up against the IRS's hobby loss rule (see Chapter 20), you may need to show a profit in order to prove that you're really running a business. Depreciation gives you a smaller deduction, which might mean the difference between a profit and a loss.

- **You expect to earn more in the future.** If you expect to be in a higher tax bracket later, you might want to depreciate. Because the value of a tax deduction depends on your tax rate, a deduction will save you more in taxes if your earnings are higher.

Depreciation

Depreciation spreads your deduction out over the useful life of a long-term asset—three to seven years for most business equipment and electronics. Rather than deducting the entire cost at once, you take the deduction in installments, according to one of several formulas accepted by the IRS. Depreciation is pretty complicated; the IRS guide to the subject (Publication 946, *How to Depreciate Property*) is more than 100 pages long. There are exceptions, limits, and traps for unwary deduction claimers. If you're planning to use depreciation, get some accounting assistance.

Deducting Vehicle Expenses

Most small business owners do some driving for business—to pick up supplies, visit clients, go to the post office, and more. If you're one of them, you have the choice of two different ways to calculate your vehicle deduction: the standard mileage rate or the actual expense method.

If you use the standard mileage rate, you can claim a set deduction (50.5 cents per mile for 2008; you can always find the current rate at www.irs.gov) for every mile you drive for business. You can claim a few additional expenses—including parking fees and tolls—on top of the mileage rate. You can't deduct the cost of repairs, maintenance, gas, insurance, or other costs of operating your car, because these costs are figured into the standard rate. You can use the standard rate only for a car that you own. If you don't use the standard rate in the first year when you drive your car for business, you won't be able to use it for that car, ever.

To use the actual expense method, you can deduct all of your car-related costs—including interest payments, insurance, license fees, oil and gas, repairs and so on—for business use of your car. You can also depreciate the car, which means you take a set deduction each year to reflect the car's declining value over time. If you also use the car for personal reasons, you can deduct only a portion of your expenses. Using the actual expense method is much more time-consuming than using the standard mileage rate, but it might be worth the extra work if you have an expensive car and so can take a fairly hefty depreciation deduction.

Whichever method you use, you'll have to keep careful records. Because the IRS believes that taxpayers often overstate how much they use their cars for business, it has some special rules for vehicle deductions. You'll have to keep track of your business and personal mileage; the easiest way to do this is to keep a log in your car and record the odometer reading at the beginning and end of every business-related drive. If you use the actual expense method, you'll also need to keep records of all of your vehicle expenses.

Avoid the Commute by Working at Home

Ordinarily, you aren't allowed to deduct mileage for commuting—driving between your home and your workplace. However, if you qualify for the home office deduction, your home is your workplace. This means that you're logging deductible miles whenever you leave home for business.

Deducting Travel Expenses

If you travel overnight for business, you can deduct your airfare, accommodations, and more. And the IRS doesn't require you to travel steerage; you can deduct your costs even if you stay at four-star hotels and enjoy the comforts of the first-class cabin.

However, the IRS also knows that most of us aren't going to travel to a distant city and spend our every waking moment working—we also want to see the sights. So it has created a set of rules delineating exactly which costs you can deduct and how much of your trip has to be business related in order to take a deduction. These rules depend on where you travel and how long you stay.

If you travel within the United States, your transportation costs (air and cab fare, for example) are deductible as long as you spend at least half of your trip on business. On days when you're doing business, you can also deduct your "destination" expenses, such as hotel costs, 50% of your meal expenses (see below for more on this 50% rule), local transportation (including car rental), telephone bills, and so on. On days when you're just having fun, you can't deduct these costs. And you can't deduct the cost of a spouse or other companion who comes along for the ride unless that person is your employee and has a genuine business reason for tagging along.

State Your Business

It isn't enough to keep records of what you paid for airfare, car rental, meals, and so on; you must also have some proof that you actually did business on your trip, in case you're audited. Take notes in your date book or calendar indicating whom you met with, sales calls, and other business activities. Keep copies of the business cards of people you spoke to, contracts you entered into, or other written records of the work you did.

If you don't, you could end up like Rick Richards, a screenplay writer and creator of country and gospel music, who tried to claim travel expenses for a number of trips he and his wife took together. He claimed to have gone to Las Vegas and Branson, Missouri, to meet with performers and work on his screenplays. He also tried to deduct trips to Alaska and Mexico, including airfare, fare for a cruise ship, and the cost of escorted side tours, which he claimed to have taken to gather "on-site data and photos" for screenplay projects. (He also claimed all of his wife's expenses, because she went along as his photographer.) The court disallowed the expenses, finding that Richards couldn't prove that they were for business rather than pleasure; although he kept records of what he paid for everything, none of those records indicated that the trips had a business purpose. (*Richards v. Commissioner of Internal Revenue,* TC Memo 1999-163.)

If you travel outside the United States, the rules depend on the length of your trip. If you're gone for fewer than seven days, you can deduct your transportation costs and your destination expenses for days you spend working. If your trip lasts more than seven days and you spend more than 75% of your time on business, the same rules apply. However, if you spend between 50% and 75% of your time on business, you may deduct only the business percentage of your transportation costs (you can still deduct destination costs for the days you spend working). And if you spend less than 50% of your time working, none of your costs are deductible.

Although these rules may already seem complicated, there are many more that are too detailed to explain here. The IRS has really gone to town in imposing requirements for travel deductions because this is an area where there has been a lot of abuse. As a result, there are special rules for cruises, conventions, side trips, and more. For all the details, read IRS Publication 463, *Travel, Entertainment, Gift, and Car Expenses.*

Deducting Meals and Entertainment

If you entertain customers, advisers, suppliers, or other business associates, you may be able to deduct 50% of your costs. However, because lots of people have cheated on this deduction, there are many rules about what you can deduct and how you can prove that you really had a business purpose.

To claim a deduction, you must be with someone who can benefit your business in some way; you can't deduct the cost of entertaining family friends, for example, unless they also do business with you. In addition, you must actually discuss business before, during, or after the event. If you plan to claim that you discussed business during the event, you won't be able to deduct much more than meals, because the IRS believes that most types of entertainment—going to the theater, a ball game, or a cocktail lounge, for example—are not conducive to serious business discussions.

The IRS won't accept certain expenses as entertainment costs, including the cost of renting or buying an entertainment facility (such as a fishing lodge or tennis court), club dues, membership fees, or the cost of nonbusiness guests. This is another area where the rules can get pretty complicated. For more information, see IRS Publication 463, *Travel, Entertainment, Gift, and Car Expenses.*

My Big Fat Business Meeting Deduction

Discussing business at an event doesn't automatically make it a deductible entertainment expense. The IRS will look closely at the nature of the event—that is, whether it looks more like a business setting or a purely pleasurable one.

For example, one New Yorker tried to deduct part of the cost of his daughter's wedding reception as business entertainment. He claimed that 90 of the 242 guests were business associates or their spouses, that he spent exactly three-eighths of his total time speaking to them (including time in the receiving line), and that the conversations involved only business topics.

The court didn't buy this argument. Although it conceded that the taxpayer may have been seeking to improve business by inviting these guests to the wedding, it found that the reception was "a personal and family celebration"—not a business meeting. (*Leubert v. Commissioner of Internal Revenue*, TC Memo 1983-457.)

An Interview with Attorney Stephen Fishman

The following is an interview with attorney Stephen Fishman, who's the author of several of Nolo's books on tax deductions including *Deduct It! Lower Your Small Business Taxes, Home Business Tax Deductions, Every Landlord's Tax Deduction Guide,* and *Tax Deductions for Professionals.*

QUESTION: Steve, what's one tax deduction that a lot of people overlook?

STEVE FISHMAN: One deduction many people don't take, even if they're entitled to it, is the home office deduction. Many people are afraid it will result in IRS audit, or they don't understand that they are entitled to it, and it is one of the best deductions for self-employed people—if you use a home office exclusively for your business, you would be entitled to it, and it's especially a good deduction if you're a renter because it will enable you to deduct a portion of your rent, an expense that is ordinarily not deductible.

QUESTION: If you're making the home office deduction, which do you recommend using, the square footage method or the room method?

STEVE FISHMAN: I recommend trying both and using the one that gives you the greatest deduction. Generally, the room method will give you a larger deduction, but it won't always. It depends on how many rooms you have in your house obviously. If you have one room, you'll be better off with the square footage. It depends on the size of the room and the number of square footage in your house. I would try both and use the one that gets the largest deduction.

QUESTION: You say in your books that you can't deduct commuting to your job, but that you can deduct traveling from your home office to a client. Why is that so?

STEVE FISHMAN: Commuting from home to the office or another workplace is considered a personal expense. Commuting from one business place to another is considered a business expense. When you have a home office, your home is now a place of business. So, you're going from one place of business to another. And that is now a business expense, not a personal expense.

QUESTION: Here's a similar question for travel deductions. Which makes more sense, using the standard mileage method or the actual expense method?

STEVE FISHMAN: The standard mileage method would generally not totally recompense you for your actual expenses, but it's much easier to use because there's far less recordkeeping involved. That's why most people use the standard mileage rate. If you like to get every cent you possibly can and you don't mind keeping track of every penny you spend on your car, you can use the actual expense method, and you will probably get a somewhat larger deduction. Of course, it depends how many business miles you drive.

QUESTION: The rules for deducting entertainment seem so tricky as to make it not worth the effort.

STEVE FISHMAN: It's not very hard at all. You just have to keep track of how much you spend and note the business reason for the expense, and keep your receipts. If they're more than $75, you get the deduction. For many people, it's an extremely valuable deduction—if you have a lot of business entertainment, you can deduct 50% of your business meals, which can be a very substantial deduction for some people. You have to have a business purpose—you have to eat with a client or a customer and you have to discuss business either before, during, or after the meal.

QUESTION: Steve, let's talk about the 179 deduction for a second. Since Congress has extended the amount that you can deduct under 179, does it ever make sense to claim depreciation?

STEVE FISHMAN: There are some things you can't use Section 179 for—for example, when you convert personal property to business property, and you can't use [Section 179] for real property either. So there are times you have to use depreciation. If you spend over $500,000 in one year, your deduction is also limited under Section 179.

Also, if your income is quite low this year, you might prefer to depreciate the expense if you expect your income to go up substantially in future years. You take the depreciation deduction on those future years when your income is higher and you pay a higher tax rate.

QUESTION: What's a tax credit and how can you find out if your business is entitled to one?

STEVE FISHMAN: A tax credit is an amount you're allowed to deduct from your income tax. For example, if you get a $1,000 tax credit, you can deduct $1,000 from your income tax, which makes it much better than a tax deduction, which only reduces your taxable income. An example of a tax credit is when people refurbish their property to make it accessible for the disabled. You can have up to a $5,000 tax credit every year.

QUESTION: What kind of deductions can you make if your business is the victim of some natural catastrophe, such as an earthquake, flood, or a hurricane?

STEVE FISHMAN: You may deduct the uninsured loss from your tax as a loss, a business loss.

QUESTION: What if the insurance hasn't paid? How do you know what you can deduct?

STEVE FISHMAN: You have to estimate how much you're likely to recover from your insurer and just deduct the amount that you don't expect to recover.

QUESTION: What kinds of deductions can a small businessowner make for retirement plans?

STEVE FISHMAN: Well, there are a vast array of deductions when you're self-employed. You have, of course, the traditional IRA, which anyone can have. You have special IRAs for self-employed people, called SEP IRAs.

QUESTION: When you say self-employed, do you mean you have your own business?

STEVE FISHMAN: That's right. You have your own business.

QUESTION: Since such a small percentage of people are audited, does a taxpayer really need to be that concerned about dotting their i's crossing their t's when it comes to deductions?

STEVE FISHMAN: Well, it's really true that only a small percentage are audited; only about 2% of self-employed people are audited. So the odds are that you will not be audited. However, if you have a lot of odd-looking things on your tax return, that will definitely increase the odds you will be audited. And there's always the chance you'll be audited. About 200,000 self-employed people were audited last year. And there's always a chance you could be one of them. Depends if you want to play what they call "the audit lottery." You can do that and you may win. You may not. It's up to you.

Index

A

Access to your goods and services, 191
Accountability of marketing tools, 194–195
Accounting, 13, 19–22
Accounting methods, 14–16
Accounts payable, 17, 21
Accounts receivable, 97–106
  checks for, 100
  collections, 102–106
  credit card payments, 100–101
  credit extension, 102
  invoiced accounts, 98–99
  overview, 16, 21, 98
Accrual method for accounting, 15–16
Acid-test ratio, 26
Act of God provision in contracts, 147
Actual expense method for vehicle tax
  deduction, 300, 305
Administration for Children and Families, 122
Administrative activities, delegating, 6, 258. *See
  also* Employees
ADR (alternative dispute resolution), 148,
  235–236
Advertising
  avoiding, 190
  direct mail, 199–200, 209
  discriminatory terms in, 117
  display and classified ads, 198–199
  marketing vs., 190
  online, 203, 249–251
  outdoor, 204
  with printed matter, 197–200, 203
  on radio or television, 200–201
  samples and free offers, 196
  seminars and product demonstrations, 203
  signs, 203
  in yellow pages, 199
  See also Marketing
Affiliate programs, online, 251
After-sale marketing, 191–192, 208
Alpert, Herb, 166
Alterations to leased space, 232, 233

Alternative dispute resolution (ADR), 148,
  235–236
American Society of Industrial Security, 161
Amortization, 68
A&M Records, 166
Angel brokers, 77
Angel investors, 76–78
Arbitration provision in contracts, 148, 235–236
Armstrong, Edwin H., 162
Assets, 19, 265, 279, 297–299
Assignment of rights, 163
Attorney fee provision in contracts, 147, 236
Attorneys
  for incorporation paperwork, 39
  for infringement lawsuits, 162, 163, 164
  for intellectual property disputes, 164
  for lease agreement reviews, 239–240
  for reviewing contracts, 141, 152, 236
  for start-up practices, 261
  for trademark questions, 177
  Volunteer Lawyers for the Arts, 164
Audit provision in contracts, 144
Audits. *See* IRS audits
Automatic renewal of contracts, 144

B

Bad debt tax deductions, 287
Balance sheets, 20
Bank loans, 37, 69–73
Bankruptcy of customers, 105
Bank's motivation for lending, 71–73
Banner ads, online, 250–251
BDCs (business development centers), 74
Berberich, Chad, 54, 62
Bias in form agreements, 139
Big Red Fez, The (Godin), 248
Bike racing as business, 267–268
Billboards, 204
Blogs, 245
Boilerplate provisions in contracts, 145–147
Bookkeeping. *See* Recordkeeping and
  bookkeeping
BOP (business owner's policy), 54

Borrowing money. *See* Financing your business

Brand marketing, 195

Break-even analysis, 23–24

Briarpatch Network (San Francisco, Calif.), 5

Bridge loans, 70

Brochures for marketing, 197–198

Brokers for commercially leased space, 231, 239

Burn Your Business Plan (Gumpert), 84

Business approach, modifying your, 6

Business development centers (BDCs), 74

Business directories, 9

Business entities

  cash flow problems related to, 17–18

  expert interview on, 41–46

  and financial forecasting, 23

  formalities for forming, 31, 32–33, 35

  and pass-through taxation, 31, 32, 34, 38, 40, 273

  sole proprietorships, 30–31, 38–39, 55, 184, 273

  See also Corporations; Limited liability companies; Partnerships

Business ideas, 153–166

  categorizing your ideas, 154–155, 156–158

  disputes over ownership, 163–164

  employees' or contractors' ideas, 165, 261

  enforcing your rights, 155, 162–163

  ensuring your rights, 155, 158–161

  ideas that worked, 166

  licensing or selling your rights, 163

  overview, 154

  proprietary ideas or information, 154, 155, 158, 163

Business interruption insurance coverage, 51–52, 233–234

Business loss tax deductions, 306–307

Business names

  choosing, 168–169

  domain name for website, 245

  fictitious, 183–184

  generic names, 173

  overview, 157

  trademark vs., 168

  See also Choosing your business

Business owner's policy (BOP), 54

Business plan, 83–96

  company summary, 87–88, 93–94

  competition, 88–89

  executive summary, 86, 93

  financial projections, 90–92, 95–96

  management team, 86–87, 95

  market growth analysis, 89–90

  market strategies summary, 88, 94–95

  overview, 84–85

Business Plan Pro software, 84, 85, 96

Business types. *See* Business entities

C

California LLC fees, 36

CAM (common area maintenance), 233

Capacity to repay loans, 71

Capital, 71

Capital expenses, 291

Capital gain or loss, 290

Capitalization, 17. *See* also Financing your business

Car insurance, 51

Cash flow, 16–18, 70–71, 114

Cash flow forecasts, 24–25, 86, 90, 92

Cash flow statements, 22

Cash method for accounting, 15–16

Cash value insurance policies, 50

Casualty loss tax deductions, 287

C corporations, 33, 274

Cell phone tax deductions, 298–299

Chaconas, James, 231

Checks, accepting for accounts receivable, 100

Children, 130–131, 224, 291

Choice of law provision in contracts, 146

Choosing your business, 3–10

  employment outside your business, 255–263

  experience and skills related to, 7–8

  home-based, 215

  loving what you do, 4–6

  overview, 4

  See also Business names

Claim, 48

Clients, insurance supplied by, 59
CNET, 227
Cohan rule, 283–284
Collateral, 71, 72
Collection agencies, 105
Collections, 102–106
Collections Made Easy (Frischer), 98, 103
Commercial Collection Agency Association, 103
Commercial leases. *See* Leasing space
Commercial space, leasing, 230–231, 232
Commission, 48
Common area maintenance (CAM), 233
Communities, online, 251–252
Community property states, 31, 129–130, 132
Community stores, online, 244, 246–247
Company summary, 87–88, 93–94
Competitors
  collection databases for, 106
  and naming your business, 169, 174
  summarizing in business plan, 88–89
Computer tax deductions, 297–299, 298–299
Conditions of a loan, 71
Confidentiality provision in contracts, 142
Consumer Price Index (CPI), 234
Contracts, 135–152
  attorney fee provision, 147, 236
  bias in, 139
  boilerplate provisions, 145–147
  cancellation laws, 212
  common provisions, 142–145
  dispute resolution, 147–148, 235–236
  drafting and formatting, 140–141
  electronic agreements, 140
  escalation clause in rent agreements, 234
  form agreements, 138–139
  negotiating, 151–152
  noncompete and nonsolicitation agreements, 261
  oral agreements, 138
  recordkeeping for, 150–151
  release for use of name or image, 165
  research prior to signing, 137

  reviewing, 141, 149–150, 152, 236
  signers, 142
  See also Leasing space
Copyright protection, 158
Corporations
  C corporations, 33, 274
  contract signers in, 142
  conversion to, 38–39
  dissolution of, 42–43
  expert interview on, 41–46
  income splitting, 34, 43, 132
  insurance coverage for, 50
  and landlords, 234–235, 238
  overview, 33–34, 35
  S corporations, 33, 40, 274
  taxation of, 34–37, 43–44, 274
Cost of goods sold, 21
Costs. *See* Expenses
Covenants in contracts, 143
CPI (Consumer Price Index), 234
Crafts Report Magazine (website), 201
Credit card debt, 68–69
Credit card payments, accepting, 100–101
Creditors, 103–105
Credit reference form, 99
Credit risk modeling (CRM), 71
Crocker, James H., 157
Current debt to net worth ratio, 26–27
Current ratio, 25–26
Customer diversity, 17
Customer feedback, 8
Customer lists, 157–158
Customers
  brand loyalty of, 195
  creating, 8–10
  and home-based businesses, 217–218, 221, 223
  liability waivers signed by, 63
  motivation of, 191, 193–194, 249–252
  and naming your business, 174
  See also Marketing
Customer service, 193, 209–210

D

Databases, protecting, 157–158
Databases for collections, 106
Databases for direct mail campaign, 200
Day care centers, 293
Debt
  bad debt tax deductions, 287
  equity vs., 66–68
  funding options for paying, 18
  loans, 37, 66–74
  overview, 19, 20
  See also Financing your business
Debt-to-equity ratio, 26–27
Deductibles, 48, 61
Demand letters, 104
Depreciation, 265, 279, 299
Design patents, 160
Diener, Ed, 7
DIF (discriminate function system), 268, 273
Direct Mail Copy That Sells (Lewis), 193
Direct mail marketing, 199–200, 209
Disability insurance, 56
Discount for accounts receivable, 104
Discriminate function system (DIF), 268, 273
Dispute resolution, 147–148, 163–164, 235–236
Divorce and the family business, 129–130
Dog track gambler position, 267
Dolby, Ray, 166
Domain name for website, 245
Drop shipping, 208, 210
Dual representation by brokers, 231, 239
Dues, tax deductions for, 288

E

E-commerce, 101, 176, 244, 246–247,
  252–253. *See* also Website for your business
E-contracts, 140
Education expense tax deductions, 288
Electronic agreements, 140
Employees, 107–124
  finding the right person, 116–119
  fringe benefits for, 34, 49
  and home-based businesses, 222, 258

ICs vs., 109–115
  insurance benefits for, 49
  internship programs vs. hiring, 118
  legal and paperwork requirements, 120–124
  ownership of ideas from, 165, 261
  See also Payroll taxes
Employer identification number (EIN), 123,
  180–181
Employment and Training Administration, 55
Employment eligibility verification, 122
Employment outside your home-based
  business, 255–263
  avoiding problems, 260–261
  getting organized, 257–258
  hiring help, 258
  loving your job, 258
  quitting, 259–260
  reasons for, 259
  work hours, 256–257
Employment practices liability (EPLI), 54
Employment taxes, 275–276
Endorsements, 48, 61
Entertainment expenses, 283, 303–304, 305–306
Entire agreement provision in contracts, 145
Entrepreneur Magazine's Ultimate Small
  Business Marketing Guide (Stephenson), 197
Entrepreneurs, 6, 7–8, 10, 86–87, 95. *See* also
  Choosing your business
EPLI (employment practices liability), 54
Equity, 20, 26–27, 66–68
Equity financing, 66, 67
Escalation clause in rent agreements, 234
Estimated income, 279
Estimated taxes, 276–279
Event insurance, 52
Exclusions, 48
Exclusively for business use, 292, 296
Executive summary for business plan, 86, 93
Exit strategy for leases, 237–238
Expenses
  documenting, 282–284, 296, 306
  forming an LLC or corporation, 30
  overview, 17

See also Leasing space; Tax forms and payments; specific items that cost money
Experience of entrepreneur, 7–8, 86–87, 95
Expert interviews, 41–46, 237–242, 304–307
Experts for one-time projects, 228. *See also* Independent contractors
Extended period of indemnity, 52

F

Fair use rights, 164
Family businesses, 126–130, 132
Family Business (magazine), 131
Family limited partnerships (FLPs), 133
Family members
  borrowing money from, 75
  children, 130–131, 224, 291
  hiring, 108, 127–131, 291
  See also Married couples
Federal Consumer Information Center, 212
Federal tax credits, 288, 306
Federal taxes as personal debt, 37
Federal Trade Commission (FTC), 209
Fees, tax deductions for, 288
FICA taxes, 131, 275–276
Financial projections, 22–25, 90–92, 95–96. *See also* Cash flow
Financing your business, 65–82
  angel investors, 76–78
  cash flow funding options, 18, 70
  with credit cards, 68–69
  equity vs. debt financing, 66–68
  information required by lenders, 80–81
  with loans, 37, 68, 69–75
  overview, 68, 79
  smart money vs. dumb money, 79
  social lending networks, 75
  state or local lending assistance, 74
  with stock, 82
  venture capitalists, 82
  See also Personal guarantees
Fishman, Stephen, 304–307
504 loan program, 74
Fixed costs, 23
Flexibility strategy for leases, 237–238

Flextime, 256
FLPs (family limited partnerships), 133
Force majeure provision in contracts, 147
Forecasting, 22–25, 86, 90–92, 95–96. *See also* Cash flow
Form agreements, 138–139
Formalities for forming a business, 31, 32, 35
Forum-selection clauses in contracts, 146–147
Fraud, 78, 101–102, 284
Friends, 75, 108
Funding options for managing cash flow, 18, 70. *See also* Financing your business
Furnishings for home-based businesses, 224–225
FUTA taxes, 131, 275–276

G

Generic names, 173
Getting Things Done (Allen), 257
Getting to Yes (Fisher and Ury), 151
Google advertising programs, 249–250
Governing law provision in contracts, 146
Government websites, 9
Gross lease, 233
Gross profit percentage, 23
Guarantors, 72–73
Guerrilla Marketing (Levinson), 192, 198, 201–202
Guide to Giving Great Service (Weinzweig), 193

H

Handouts for marketing, 197–198
Harassment of creditors, 103
Health and Human Services Department, 122
Hiring the right person, 116–119. *See also* Employees
Hobby loss rule, 264, 269–270
Hobby vs. business, 264, 269–270
Hold harmless agreements, 63
Home-based businesses, 213–228
  client or customer considerations, 217–218, 221, 223
  home life separate from, 223–224
  insurance coverage for, 56, 221–222
  overview, 214–216

savings from, 217

social isolation issues, 222

space considerations, 217, 218

tax deductions for, 292–297, 304–305

tips for, 224–228

and vehicle expenses, 51, 283, 301

zoning issues, 183, 219–220, 222

Homeowners' association restrictions, 219–220

Homeowners' insurance, 56

How to Run a Thriving Business (Warner), 191

How to Write a Business Plan (McKeever), 85, 96

I

ICs. *See* Independent contractors

Ideas. *See* Business ideas

Income

documenting, 282

operating income, 22

relying on one customer or product for, 17, 18

reporting to IRS, 15, 273–274, 281

before taxes, 22

Income splitting, 34, 43, 132

Income statements, 21–22

Income taxes, 275

Incorporation, 30, 132. *See* also Corporations

Incorporation services, 38

Incubator services, 237

Indemnification agreements, 52, 63, 143

Independent contractors (ICs)

for coverage when you're away, 258

employees compared to, 109–112

employees vs., 113–115

finding the right person, 116–119

legal and paperwork requirements, 119–120

for one-time projects, 228

ownership of ideas from, 165, 261

website developers, 248

for writing a business plan, 85

Information-only websites, 244–246

Infringers, 155, 162, 172

Initial public offering (IPO), 82

Insurance, 47–63

basic coverage, 49–53

business interruption coverage, 51–52, 233–234

employees and need for, 54–56

group plans, 56–57

for home-based businesses, 221–222

liability insurance, 45–46, 50

moneysaving tips, 58–63

overview, 48

package deals, 54

renter's commercial liability, 233, 241

Insurance agents or brokers, 58–59, 61

Insurance companies, money owed by, 17–18

Insurance Information Institute, 54

Integration provision in contracts, 145

Intellectual property (IP), 156, 159–161, 164, 166. *See* also Business ideas; Trademarks

International sales, 106

Internet connections, 226–227

Internet Service Provider (ISP), 246

Internship programs, 118

Invalidity provision in contracts, 146

Inventory and cash flow, 16

Inventory and taxes, 291

IP (intellectual property), 156, 159–161, 164, 166. *See* also Business ideas; Trademarks

IPO (initial public offering), 82

IRS

determinations of business vs. hobby, 264–269

IC vs. employee determination, 110–111

and profit motive, 5, 10, 266–268

Section 179 deductions, 298–299, 306

tax laws for businesses, 273–274

See also Taxation; Tax forms and payments

IRS audits

and business vs. hobby issues, 264, 269–270

discriminate function system, 268, 273

likelihood of, 272, 281, 307

overview, 268–269

proving profit motive, 266–268

recordkeeping in case of, 282–284

separating personal and business transactions for, 27–28, 281

IRS Form 940, Employer's Annual Federal Unemployment Tax (FUTA) Tax Return, 275–276

IRS Form 941, Employer's Quarterly Federal Tax Return, 276

IRS Form 1065, U.S. Return of Partnership Income, 273, 274

IRS Form 1096, Annual Summary and Transmission of U.S. Information Returns, 119

IRS Form 1099-MISC, Miscellaneous Income, 119

IRS Form 1120, U.S. Corporation Income Tax Return, 274

IRS Form 1120S, U.S. Income Tax Return for an S Corporation, 274

IRS Form 5213, Election to Postpone Determination as To Whether the Presumption Applies That an Activity Is Engaged in for Profit, 265

IRS Form 8832, Entity Classification Election, 274

IRS Form SE, Self-Employment Tax, 275

IRS Form SS-4, Application for Employer Identification Number, 180–181

IRS Form W-4, Employee's Withholding Allowance Certificate, 120–121

IRS Publication 15 (Circular E), Employer's Tax Guide, 276

IRS Publication 463, Travel, Entertainment, Gift, and Car Expenses, 303

IRS Publication 929, Tax Rules for Children and Dependents, 131

IRS Publication 946, How to Depreciate Property, 299

IRS Schedule C, Profit or Loss from Business, 273, 274

IRS Schedule E, Supplemental Income and Loss, 273

IRS Schedule K-1, Partner's Share of Income, Credits, Deductions, etc., 31, 32, 273, 274

ISP (Internet Service Provider), 246

J

Jobs, Steve, 38

Job sharing, 257

Jurisdiction provision in contracts, 146–147

K

Key person insurance, 53

Keywords and search engines, 249–250

Knockout searches, 170

Kuhn, Tom, 258

L

Labor Department, 55, 123, 124

Lake, Christopher, 114

Landlords
bankruptcy of or foreclosure against, 242
and LLCs or corporations, 238
negotiating with, 238–240, 241–242
and their brokers, 231, 236–237

Lawsuits, 105, 161, 162–163, 174

Lawyers. See Attorneys

Lease restrictions, 236

Leasing space, 229–242
commercial vs. residential process, 230–232
dual representation by brokers, 231, 239
exit or flexibility strategy, 237–238
expert interview on, 237–242
incubators vs., 237
maintenance costs for, 233
negotiating leases, 238–240
overview, 232
personal liability for, 37, 234–235
rent calculations, 230, 233–234
resolving disputes, 235–236
security deposits for, 230, 233, 235
subleasing, 236–237, 240–241
subordination attornment and non-disclosure clause, 242
See also Contracts

Legal names. See Business names

Legal self-help material, 138–139

Lenders, 80–81

Levinson, Jay, 192

Liabilities, 19. See also Debt

Liability (legal)
insurance for, 45–46, 50
of LLCs and corporations, 35, 37
for partners in general partnerships, 32

and personal guarantees, 37, 68, 72, 234–235
professional liability insurance, 54, 57
renter's commercial liability, 233, 241
for sole proprietorships, 31
Liability waivers, 63
Licenses and permits, 186
Licensing business ideas, 163
Life satisfaction and money, 10
Limited liability companies (LLCs)
contract signers in, 142
conversion to, 38–39
dissolution of, 42–43
expert interview on, 41–46
insurance coverage for, 50
and landlords, 234–235, 238
overview, 30, 33–34, 35
state fees, 36
taxation of, 34–36, 274
Limited partnerships, 40, 42, 133, 180, 273
Lines of credit, 70
Listing broker vs. tenant broker, 239
LLC or Corporation? (Manusco), 45
LLCs. *See* Limited liability companies
Loan guarantees, 37, 68, 72
Loan guarantors, 72–73
Loans, 37, 66–74. *See* also Financing your business
Local business licenses, 182
Local development funds, 74
Local zoning laws, 183, 219–220, 222, 231
Logos, 157
Long-term assets, 265, 279, 297–299
Losses, forecasting, 24, 90, 91

M

Madsen, Gunnar, 191
Mail or Telephone Order Merchandise Rule (FTC), 209
Maintenance costs for leased space, 233
Malpractice insurance, 54, 57
Mancuso, Anthony, 41–46
Mansel, Mike, 51, 52, 63

Marketing
advertising vs., 190
after sale, 191–192, 208
brands, 195
customer service as, 193
demand analysis, 8–10
market growth analysis, 89–90
and name choice, 169
overview, 189, 196, 206
plan and budget for, 204–206
public relations as, 201–202
sensory experiences related to, 192
strategy summary, 88, 94–95
telemarketing, 197
tips for, 190–195
in trade shows, 201
See also Advertising; Website for your business
Marketing for Dummies (Hiam), 199–200
Marketing plan, 204–206
Marketing Plan Pro (software), 204
Marketing Without Advertising (Phillips and Rasberry), 190, 203
Market research, 194
Market Research Toolbox (McQuarrie), 8–9
Married couples
in community property states, 31, 129–130, 132
hiring your spouse, 127–130, 291
and loan guarantees, 72
as one sole proprietor, 31
and tax deductions for travel, 301
Martel, James, 218
McAllen, Mike and Carrie, 59
Meal expenses, 283, 303–304, 305–306
Mediation provision in contracts, 148, 235–236
Medicare taxes, 131, 275–276
Microloans, 73–74
Microsoft, 110
Mileage rate for vehicle tax deduction, 300, 305
Mission statement, 93
Modifications to leased space, 232, 233
Money management, 11–28
accounting methods, 14–16
basic accounting, 13, 19–22

cash flow, 16–18, 22, 70–71, 114
  forecasting, 22–25, 86, 90–92, 95–96
  and insurance premiums, 61, 62
  overview, 12–13
  ratios, 25–27
  separating business and personal transactions, 27–28, 281
Moss, Jerry, 166
Motivation of customers, 191, 193–194, 249–252

N

Named peril insurance policies, 49
Names. *See* Business names
National Association for the Self-Employed, 56
National Venture Capital Association, 82
Need, customer's, 191
Negligence, liability for, 37
Negotiating contracts, 151–152
Negotiating leases, 238–240, 241–242
Net income, 22
Net lease, 233
Noncompete and nonsolicitation agreements, 261
Nondisclosure agreements (NDAs), 161

O

Oakland, Calif., 183
Office furniture, 225
Official Gazette (USPTO), 172
One-time event insurance, 52
One-time projects, 228
Online advertising, 203, 250–251
Online communities, 251–252
Online community stores, 244, 246–247
Online job listings, 116
OnlineOrganizing.com (website), 227
Online selling, 101, 244, 246–247, 252–253. *See also* Website for your business
Operating expenses, 21–22, 290–291
Operating income, 22
Oral agreements, 138
Organize Your Home Office Day, 227
Organizing From the Inside Out (Morgenstern), 257–258
Organizing your business, 227, 257–258
Outdoor advertising, 204

P

Parents, hiring, 132
Parent's Home Office (website), 224
Parking for home-based businesses, 221
Partnership agreements, 33
Partnerships
  contract signer for, 142
  converting to corporation or LLC, 38–39
  limited partnerships, 40, 42, 133, 180, 273
  overview, 30, 32–33
  taxation of, 32, 273
Pass-through taxation, 31, 32, 34, 38, 40, 273
Patents, 159–160
Payroll systems, 114, 121
Payroll taxes
  calculating, 114, 121
  for disability insurance, 56
  for employees of LLCs, 39
  federal or state collection options, 37
  for unemployment insurance, 55
  for your children as your employees, 130–131
PepsiCo, 169
Permission Marketing (Godin), 199
Permits and licenses, 186
Personal finances, 27–28, 259–260
Personal guarantees
  for leases, 37, 234–235
  for loans, 37, 68, 72
Phillips, Michael, 5
Phone bill tax deductions, 288
Phones for home-based businesses, 225–226
Policy, 48
Portman, Janet, 237–242
Postcards for marketing, 197–198
Post-sale marketing, 191–192, 208
Predatory lenders, 81
Premium, 48
Prepayment penalty, 68
Price of goods and services, 191
Primary market research, 8–9
Prioritizing potential risks, 60–61
Prioritizing work, 228
Product demonstrations and seminars, 203

Product diversification, 18
Product sales online, 244, 246–247, 252
Professional liability insurance, 54, 57
Professional organizations, 139
Professional patent searches, 159–160
Professions requiring permits and licenses, 186
Profit
  forecasting, 24, 90, 91
  gross profit percentage, 23
  and IRS, 265, 266–268
  as motive for business, 5, 10, 266–268, 299
  using depreciation for showing a profit, 265,
    299
Profit margin ratio, 27
Profit motive, 5, 10, 266–268, 299
Promissory notes for creditors, 103
Property, documenting use of, 283, 296
Property insurance, 49–50
Property taxes for leased space, 233
Proprietary ideas or information, 154, 155,
  158, 163
Provisional patent applications, 159
Public relations, 201–202
Purpose for business, 6

Q
QuickBooks, 13, 14, 19, 21, 24, 25, 121
Quick ratio, 26

R
Radio advertising, 200–201
Ratios, 25–27
ReadyMade (magazine), 79
Recordkeeping and bookkeeping
  for contracts, 150–151
  documenting expenses, 282–284, 296, 306
  for employees, 120–124
  of home office activities, 283, 296
  for independent contractors, 119–120
  for IRS, 266, 282–284
  overview, 12–14
  preparing financials, 72
Refunds and returns, 210–212
Registration

of fictitious business name, 183–184
with government agencies, 180–183
of ideas, 155
of trademarks, 170–173
Regular business use, 292–295
Release for use of name or image, 165
Renewal provision in contracts, 144
Rent calculations, 230, 233–234
Repackaging pitches, 78
Replacement cost insurance policies, 50
Representations in contracts, 143
Research to Riches (Nelen), 8, 9, 194
Retirement plan tax deductions, 131, 288, 307
Return merchandise authorization (RMA), 210
Returns and refunds, 210–212
Riders, 48, 61
Risk management, 53, 60–61, 99
Risk Management Associates (RMA), 25
RMA (return merchandise authorization), 210

S
Safety precautions and insurance premium, 61
Sales tax, 276
SBA loans, 73–74
Schafer, Eric, 231
S corporations, 33, 40, 274
Search engines and keywords, 249–250
Seasonal businesses, 17
Secondary market research, 9–10
Section 8 Declaration of Continued Use, 172
Section 179 deductions, 298–299, 306
Secured loans, 68
Security deposits, 230, 233, 235
Self-actualization techniques, 260
Self-employment taxes, 275, 276–279
Seller's permit, 184–186
Selling business ideas, 163
Seminars and product demonstrations, 203
Sensory experiences related to marketing, 192
Service marks, 168. *See also* Trademarks
7(a) loan program, 74
7(m) microloan program, 73–74
Severability provision in contracts, 146
Shipping, 208–210

SIC (Standard Industrial Classification), 25
Signature loans, 69–70
Signs outside and within the business, 203
Social lending networks, 75
Social Security income, 132
Social Security taxes, 131, 275–276
Software
  for business plans, 84
  for databases, 200
  for graphic design, 198
  for marketing plan development, 204
  for tax preparation, 280, 281–282
  for website development, 245–246
  See also QuickBooks
Sole proprietorships, 30–31, 38–39, 55, 184, 273
Special form insurance policies, 49
Spouse. *See* Married couples
Standard Industrial Classification (SIC), 25
Start-up costs, 216, 289, 290
Start-up funding. *See* Financing your business
State business licenses, 181–182
State fees for LLCs or corporations, 36
State laws
  on business names, 168, 184
  on contract cancellations, 212
  on ICs vs. employees, 109
  on LLC formation, 42
  on new hire reporting, 122
  on partnerships, 33
  on payment of taxes, 37
  on professional permits and licenses, 186
  on refunds, 211
  on seller's permit, 184–186
  on unemployment taxes, 123
State loans or lending assistance, 74
State sales tax, 184–185, 276
State tax credits, 288, 306
Statute of limitations for IRS audit, 284
Stock, 37, 82, 132
Subleasing, 236–237, 240–241
Subordination attornment and non-disclosure
  clause, 242
Swing loans, 70

T
Taxation
  corporate rates, 34, 36, 43–44
  FICA taxes, 131, 275–276
  FUTA taxes, 131, 275–276
  hiring family members, 130–132
  of hobbies vs. businesses, 264, 269–270
  of LLCs and corporations, 34–37, 43
  of pass-through entities, 31, 32, 34, 38, 40, 273
  tax brackets, 286–287
  unemployment taxes, 123, 275–276
  See also Payroll taxes
Tax deductions, 285–307
  basic deductions, 290–291
  depreciation, 265, 279, 299
  expert interview on, 304–307
  for home-based businesses, 292–297, 304–305
  for long-term assets, 265, 279, 297–299
  overview, 286
  retirement plans, 131, 288, 307
  for start-up costs, 289, 290
  for travel expenses, 301–303
  value of, 286–288
  for vehicle expenses, 300–301, 305
Tax forms and payments
  employment taxes, 275–276
  estimated taxes, 276–279
  overview, 272
  prepaying, 279–281
  reporting income to IRS, 15, 273–274, 281
  sales tax, 276
  self-employment taxes, 275, 276–279
  tax laws for businesses, 273–274
  See also entries beginning with "IRS Form"
TaxMama.com (website), 280
Taxpayer identification number (TIN), 120
Telecommuting, 256
Telemarketing, 197, 209
Telephone bill tax deductions, 288
Telephones for home-based businesses, 225–226
Television advertising, 200–201
Temp agencies, 117
Temporary disability taxes, 275–276

Termination provision in contracts, 144–145

Term loans, 70

Term provision in contracts, 144

Teschner, Donald, 283–284

"Those Magic Phrases—How to Negotiate Like a Pro" (Glatzer), 151–152

TIN (taxpayer identification number), 120

Toys R Us, 18

Trade associations, 9, 117, 139

Trademark Applications and Registrations Retrieval database (TARR), 170, 173

Trademark Electronic Application System (TEAS and TEAS Plus), 171

Trademark Electronic Search System (TESS), 170

Trademark parodies, 177

Trademarks, 157, 168, 170–177. *See also* Business names

Trademark symbols, 173

Trade organizations, 139

Trade publications, 9, 117, 119

Trade secrets, 142, 160–161, 260–261

Trade shows, 201

Transit advertising, 204

Travel expense tax deductions, 301–303

Triangles in a family business, 130

Turbo Tax software, 280, 281–282

U

Ultimate Trade Show Resource, 201

Underwriter, 48

Unemployment compensation, 109, 123

Unemployment insurance (UI), 54–55, 109

Unemployment taxes, 123, 275–276

U.S. Citizenship and Immigration Services (USCIS), 122

U.S. Copyright Office, 158

U.S. Patent and Trademark Office (USPTO), 159–160, 169, 170–173

USCIS Form I-9, Employment Eligibility Verification, 122

USCIS (U.S. Citizenship and Immigration Services), 122

USPTO (U.S. Patent and Trademark Office), 159–160, 169, 170–173

Utility patents, 159–160

V

Vehicle expenses, 51, 283, 300–301, 305

Venture capital, 82

Virgin Money, 75

Volunteer Lawyers for the Arts, 164

W

Waiver of liability, 63

Waiver provision in contracts, 146

Wall Street Journal, 77

Warranties, 143

Warranty provision in contracts, 143

Weak trademarks, 173

Web insurance, 53

Website for your business, 243–253

attracting customers, 191, 249–252

e-commerce, 101, 244, 246–247, 252–253

getting site up, 244–248

hiring a developer, 248

legal rules for, 252–253

Weight gain from working at home, 214

Weiss, Alan, 195

Why We Buy: The Science of Shopping (Underhill), 203

Williams, Jeff, 6

WIN Innovation Institute, 159

Words that sell, 194

Words That Sell (Bayan), 194

Workers' compensation insurance, 55, 123

Work Options (website), 256

Wozniak, Steve, 38

Writing down ideas, 155

Y

Yellow pages, 199

Z

Zoning requirements or restrictions, 183, 219–220, 222, 231

Get the Latest in the Law

Nolo's Legal Updater
We'll send you an email whenever a new edition of your book is published!
Sign up at **www.nolo.com/legalupdater**.

Updates at Nolo.com
Check **www.nolo.com/update** to find recent changes in the law that
affect the current edition of your book.

Nolo Customer Service
To make sure that this edition of the book is the most recent one, call us at
800-728-3555 and ask one of our friendly customer service representatives
(7:00 am to 6:00 pm PST, weekdays only). Or find out at **www.nolo.com**.

Complete the Registration & Comment Card ...
... and we'll do the work for you! Just indicate your preferences below:

Registration & Comment Card

NAME _____ DATE _____

ADDRESS _____

CITY _____ STATE _____ ZIP _____

PHONE _____ EMAIL _____

COMMENTS _____

WAS THIS BOOK EASY TO USE?   (VERY EASY)   5   4   3   2   1   (VERY DIFFICULT)

☐ Yes, you can quote me in future Nolo promotional materials. *Please include phone number above.*

☐ Yes, send me **Nolo's Legal Updater** via email when a new edition of this book is available.

Yes, I want to sign up for the following email newsletters:

  ☐ **NoloBriefs** (monthly)
  ☐ **Nolo's Special Offer** (monthly)
  ☐ **Nolo's BizBriefs** (monthly)
  ☐ **Every Landlord's Quarterly** (four times a year)

☐ Yes, you can give my contact info to carefully selected
  partners whose products may be of interest to me.

Send to: **Nolo** 950 Parker Street Berkeley, CA 94710-9867, Fax: (800) 645-0895, or include all of
the above information in an email to regcard@nolo.com with the subject line "WHOO2."

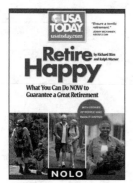